A WILD FLIGHT
OF GORDONS

A WILD FLIGHT OF GORDONS

Archie Gordon
5th Marquess of Aberdeen

WEIDENFELD AND NICOLSON
LONDON

Typeset by Deltatype, Ellesmere Port
Printed in Great Britain by
Butler & Tanner Ltd
Frome and London

Contents

Illustrations

Gight Castle in 1851
Mrs Byron by Thomas Stewardson *(John Murray Publishers Ltd)*
General Patrick Gordon of Auchleuchries *(George D. S. Gordon)*
Admiral Thomas Gordon *(A. Yakovlest)*
Tsar Peter the Great
William, 2nd Earl of Aberdeen *(National Galleries of Scotland)*
George, 3rd Earl of Aberdeen *(National Galleries of Scotland)*
Haddo House *(National Trust for Scotland)*
George, Lord Haddo *(National Galleries of Scotland)*
General William Gordon of Fyvie *(National Galleries of Scotland)*
William Gordon of Fyvie by Beechey
Fyvie Castle with the Gordon Tower
Adam Lindsay Gordon by Sir Frank Madden
Lord George Gordon *(British Library)*
The young George Gordon with his rifle *(Marquess of Aberdeen)*
George H. Osborne *(Marquess of Aberdeen)*
Richmond, Maine *(courtesy Richmond Historical Society)*
The 7th Earl of Aberdeen *(Marquess of Aberdeen)*
The Marquess of Aberdeen with the Marquess of Huntly *(Marquess of Aberdeen)*
Archie Gordon with Queen Mary *(Marquess of Aberdeen)*

Acknowledgements

Acknowledgements are due to the past Chairman of the Haddo House Estate Trust, now disbanded, for the indefinite loan of a number of papers belonging to the Haddo House Muniment Room, and to their present owner Alexander Gordon; Rosa Dickie; the Parliamentary Record Office; the Royal Commission on the Ancient and Historical Monuments of Scotland; the Scottish Record Office (Register House and West Register House); Dr Dorothy Johnston of Aberdeen University Library; Gordon Struble of Bath, Maine; William Toner of Portland, Maine; Mrs Polly Roberts of Richmond, Maine; Mrs Pauline (Earl) Cronk of Richmond, Maine; Mrs Melvin Othelar Randall of Dresden, Maine; the Earl of Moray; Robin Gibson of the National Portrait Gallery, London; Dr Rosalind Marshall of the Scottish National Portrait Gallery; Dr Iain Brown, National Library of Scotland; James Miller of Sotheby and Co.; the Hon. Patrick Lindsay of Christies Ltd; the Librarian of the Isaac Umberhine Library Association, Richmond, Maine; the Scottish National Portrait Gallery; Mary Chubb, who not only typed the entire work but also contributed valuable editorial comments and corrected the proofs; my editor Alex MacCormick for encouragement and timely criticism.

Introduction

At first the idea was to write a book about the Scottish aristocracy in history, and to examine whether it has survived. The thesis, if it may be so called, was to be exemplified by the discernible facts about a selection of men throughout the history of Scotland whom I was capable of exposing, or about whom I already had sufficient knowledge on which to base the necessary research. The question 'What is an aristocracy?' was to be answered by making an assumption that our understanding of the term today refers it to a ruling élite, principally – but not entirely – self-selected by some kind of hereditary succession or connexion. It then became necessary to define and work upon criteria that would distinguish an aristocracy characteristically, if not uniquely, Scotch.

At once clouds filled a mind never too clear about definitions. First of all, what was Scotland? When did it effectively become one nation? There was an awareness of two systems at least, if not three, working side by side through history until recent times – in historians' terms. There was the highland, Celtic culture whose system of land tenure and of the inheritance of chief – and chieftainship – was different from that of the Anglo-Normans, whose feudal law obtained in lowland Scotland (except for parts of the Borders and much of Galloway) from an early period after the Normans had spread throughout England. There was then also the Viking strain, whose detritus in place names in eastern, lowland Scotland indicates a considerable presence, but whose social organization was of more noticeable consequence in the Celtic west and in Ireland. The Celtic cultures did not believe in towns; they did not care for so close an assembly of so many individuals. Those Danish Vikings did, as the origin of the principal cities of Ireland demonstrates. In the highlands and islands of Scotland there was not so much scope for the founding of cities, by Vikings or anybody else. Geography saw to that. Geography and the migrations of people saw to other curious movements. Leaving aside Charlemagne's encouragement of Scotch scholars to attend his Court, mostly from Northumbria (which extended to Edinburgh), there were Saxon fugitives from the Norman Conquest who settled in Scotland as far north as the Tay and, in addition, there were the founders of families – Bruce, Fraser – who have a good claim to Norman or post-Norman origin. For the Stewarts an emigration to Scotland of Bretons before the Conquest is claimed. None of these immigrants from the soft south can have cared deeply for the rough, hard climate and soil. Another movement of peoples, sudden, warlike and improbable, was the incursion into Ireland of a small horde of Celts, Picts and Saxons under Eochaidh Buidhe, king of Alba or Dalriada. In AD 637 the Irish response was savage and determinant. At the Battle of Moira in that year there was great slaughter (aided no doubt by those vast Irishwomen who could never keep away from a battle) over seven days' fighting, at the end of which the Scotch invader was totally defeated; an Irish counterpart of Charles Martel's defeat of the Moors at Poitiers in 732. Intrusion into Ireland from Great Britain did not begin with Henry II's Strongbow taking the Pale of Dublin, nor finish with the Calvinist plantation men of the seventeenth century. Imagine: if the king of Dalriada had succeeded, half Ireland might have been a Scotch colony for centuries. As it happens, warriors from Scotland often assisted the Irish in their struggles against English domination.

In those early times there was no clear demarcation between the ways of the Celtic highlandmen and the feudal lowlanders. No boundary existed, neither geographically nor in social organization. As Professor T. C. Smout observes in *A History of the Scottish People*: 'Highland society was based on kinship modified by feudalism, Lowland society on feudalism tempered by kinship. Both systems were aristocratic, unconscious of class, designed for war.' I quote the second sentence because it hangs from the first, which is to me more important, but I am not clear what he means by 'aristocratic', though I am aware of the force of the phrase 'unconscious of class' as regards Scottish society in those early mediaeval times, and of its persistence into our own otherwise class-ridden society. Even the ancient Celtic earls or mormaors were brought within a feudal relationship to the sovereign, and so were their lowland contemporaries, notable amongst them being the earldom of Huntly, created for the Seton son of a Gordon heiress in 1445.

2

The Gordons had first moved from the border county of Berwick upon being granted the lands of Strathbogie in Aberdeenshire by King Robert the Bruce early in the fourteenth century. There was a brief scuffle when Sir Adam de Gordon was ousted in favour of Edward I's nominee, but Strathbogie was restored to the Gordons only a few years after the interlopers had been pushed out and they have been there, and everywhere else in north-east Scotland, ever since. By the middle of the fifteenth century there were so many persons of the name of Gordon holding charters of land, however small, in counties Aberdeen and Banff that one must assume that the principle of kinship held sway. However prolix with legitimate and bastard offspring, one man cannot have been the ancestor of so many men of property of one name in so short a time. Small neighbours of this powerful and aggressive race, 'designed for war', may have found protection a convenience as well as an obligation and thus recognized an overlordship by adopting the overlord's name. This was characteristic of the Highland clan system, and the Gordons occupied country where highland and lowland meet, merge, overlap and conflict. (There is an example in another family which emerged later in history but swiftly achieved even greater success long after the days of borrowing surnames from overlords. The Duff family, of clear lowland origin, helped their rise to fortune first by marrying a Gordon and, two or three generations later, one of them grew rich by acting as factor or tacksman to a Marquess of Huntly, and was thus able to buy large properties at a time when many lairds had become impoverished. The Duffs have held immense estates in the Gaelic-speaking areas of Upper Deeside gained from the forfeiture suffered by the Earl of Mar after 1715, including the lands of Balmoral purchased by Queen Victoria.)

The other doleful fact of geography to be taken into account is the poverty of the land and the lack of valuable natural resources. Coal and fishes, yes, as in England and Wales, but little else save the semi-precious stones known as Cairngorms, a kind of topaz, and the freshwater pearls of which I am the lucky possessor of a pear-shaped example – a pearl from the River Ythan in Aberdeenshire – that embellishes a plain steel breastpin. Leave aside the sour, peaty soil (what little there is of it) over vast tracts of the highlands especially, and ponder the following notes from an account by a tenant on my family's estate. The reader will find in chapter 4 a summary of the oppressive and short-sighted system of nineteen-year leases operated in the second half of the eighteenth century by the 3rd Earl of Aberdeen, known to some as Lord Skinflint. His successor, the 4th Earl, gradually put right the policy of his grandfather which made improvements impossible. In 1820 he let, also on a nineteen-year lease, the farm of Fedderat to a Mr Mackie, great-grandfather of Sir Maitland Mackie, Lord-Lieutenant of Aberdeenshire since 1975, and his two brothers Lord John-Mackie, to whom I owe permission to quote his ancestor's notes, and Lord Mackie of Benshie. On entering this farm of roughly a hundred acres Scotch measure in extent, he found the arable half to be a light loam much encumbered by old and irregular stone dykes, and the soil completely exhausted, the previous tenant having been firmly told his lease would not be renewed. The uncultivated fifty-one acres that had never been under tillage consisted of peat moss, much of which had been cut for fuel, and of boggy and muirish ground producing reeds, bents and heath intermixed with a coarse and scanty herbage on which a few stunted cattle could subsist in summer.

First Mr Mackie built a dwelling house and farm offices – the old ones being too dilapidated to 'be inhabited in safety, either by my Family or Bestial'. Then he cleared old fences – undoubtedly of stone – in the arable part of the farm to

> admit of being cropped in some kind of rotation. I then resolved on adopting some measures for bringing my waste land into cultivation . . . I got the greater part of it divided into fields by means of open ditches . . . in general 4½ feet deep, 7 feet wide at top and 14 inches at bottom. Early in the Spring of 1823 I commenced the cultivation of four imperial acres of moss adjoining my infield land. . . . In this piece I put one hundred and seventy yards of drains of various depths, averaging fully 4½ feet filled with stones to the depth of 2½ or 3 feet.

Clay was carted to the extent of 600 cartloads on the surface as a mixture for the moss. 'Adjoining this portion of the Moss I found it necessary to trench and cover with mould ¾ of an acre, consisting of old roads, rocks and quarry holes, for the completion of my field.' That was just a beginning and one can only hope Mr Mackie was not covering up for ever some Aberdonian Scarabrae, that famous Orcadian neolithic village. It certainly reads like archaeology in reverse. Tenants all over Lord Aberdeen's huge estates were probably having to do the same, also on nineteen-year leases with no guarantee of renewal. At Mr Mackie's 'the Proprietor undertook only the boundary ditches and the cutting and straightening of the Burn of Fedderat'. Happily 'the Earl of Aberdeen, on account of the exertions I have made in improving my Farm, has agreed to renew my Lease, at the present rent for a period sufficient to enable me to recover the capital I have laid out'. All this was done in the parish of New Deer in Buchan, that easternmost district of Aberdeenshire, in a climate described by Mr Mackie as among the latest and most precarious in the area. Far from markets, the farms were small in size – forty or fifty acres – and 'a great proportion of the land let in crofts of from 5 to 15 acres in extent. Improvements are therefore in their infancy, drainage, except in very few instances, has not been resorted to, and the average produce of grain in the parish is under $2\frac{1}{2}$ Quarters per Imperial acre – $3\frac{3}{4}$ quarters are reckoned a good crop.'

Compare this with the South of England. Yet in many parts of Scotland the inhabitants would have regarded this as being favoured by nature. I can myself remember in the late 1940s going round with my brother to look at the covered byres for wintering cattle that he was building on his tenants' farms, and being invited into the house – not I hasten to add any occupied by a member of the famous Mackie family –and finding myself in quarters so primitively equipped, with no 'mains' of any sort (although warmed by a dram and a peat fire, with some valuable pieces put about), that a Sussex shepherd at that date on another relation's property would have turned his back upon the offer of such a dwelling.

I find it essential thus to put in its setting the sort of land I am writing about, and to show how values and standards are never absolute. One further example, possibly an imaginary flight but not without a grounding of veracity. I heard William Mann, the eminent music critic of *The Times*, contribute to a radio broadcast about the real Hans Sachs the fact that this shoemaker-poet of Nuremberg ultimately lived in a dwelling whose richness of appointment would have made a king of Scotland go green with envy. Sachs was an exact contemporary of Albrecht Dürer in the early sixteenth century. Mr Mann's king, therefore, refers to James IV or James V, neither of whom are believed to have lived behind cold stone walls with nothing to show for the eminence and luxury of kingship. Mr Mann has a point: there is a world of difference between showy living and real comfort. Montrose generously kept open house when he dared to be at home, yet on his famous forced marches across the nastiest, bleakest part of the Highlands he slept along with his men wrapped in his plaid on the cold, damp heather. They breakfasted off handfuls of oatmeal moistened by scooped-up snow. It is unlikely that he could have lived so hardily if his normal breakfast included kedgeree and scones spread with apricot jam.

In Queen Victoria's era the comments of Christian Watt, in *The Christian Watt Papers*, are most revealing of lowland attitudes towards the West Highlanders. She was born in 1833, the daughter of a Fraserburgh fishwife, brought up in a tiny house, and accompanied her mother as a young girl when the Fraserburgh herring fleet moved to western waters. The editor of her papers, Sir David Fraser, sums up her attitude by writing that

> Christian made clear how different from her own kind were the Highlanders. . . . The west coast people she clearly found attractive but supine. They tolerated, she reckoned, treatment which east coast folk would have vigorously rebuffed in any age. . . . But the Highlanders of the Upper Dee she found more akin. They spoke the Gaelic but 'the young ones could all speak Doric as well'.

This refers to about 1850, and it may well be that the 'supine' men and women whom she encountered on Skye were those who remained after the clearances, and who had not afterwards voluntarily cleared out themselves. In parenthesis, it may be remarked here that those who may question Professor Smout's reference to unconsciousness of class should read *The Christian Watt Papers*, if only to learn what Christian relates she said to Lord Macdonald of Sleat – 'a greedy man' – about his tendency to regard his clansmen as his slaves; and later on to a certain Lady Lovat when she and her husband summoned Christian to explain why marriage between her and a younger son of theirs was an impossibility. She was, in any case, a kinswoman, on the wrong side of the blanket, to Lord Lovat's Fraser kinsman, Lord Saltoun, and did not mince her words. She was unconscious of class in the sense that she was aggressively aware of her blood connexion with these grandees, and did not hesitate to let them know it. Yet for a time she served them as a housemaid. As a Scottish type, she is not unique. Neither were the Frasers.

Leaving aside the strength of blood and the zest for power in men and women whose claim to the former gave them the notion that they were born to rule so long as they had money, I decided, then, to limit my attention to a number of men bearing the surname of Gordon. The fact that most of them, except Byron's maternal ancestors, were connected by blood with my own family is not, of course, a coincidence. In the case only of Adam Lindsay Gordon was I unaware before I examined his background that he and I both descend from William, 2nd Earl of Aberdeen. This apologia being now concluded, I feel obliged to make a few autobiographical remarks.

Both my father and mother were the children of parents who had no doubt whatever that they belonged to the aristocracy of the late nineteenth century. This couple's adult experience, however, was a reflection rather than an emission of aristocracy. My father's father was John Campbell Gordon, 7th Earl and 1st Marquess of Aberdeen, who inherited a great acreage of ground and a fine house in Aberdeenshire in 1872 at the age of twenty-five. My mother's father, born in 1835, inherited as a young man the position of senior partner and later proprietor of Messrs Drummond, bankers to the quality and, some-time, to Royalty. According to *The Drummonds of Charing Cross* by Hector Bolitho and Derek Peel 'he became a Partner in 1859 at the age of twenty-four and, after the death of his cousin, Edgar Atheling Drummond, in 1893 was in sole charge of this bank until his own death in 1917'. Although I was rising four at the time of his death, I do not remember him. He appears to have been a considerable tyrant in his business affairs; however he was much loved by his four daughters, if not also by his three sons, possibly because he was very generous in replacing jewellery lost through carelessness by their mother and by the girls themselves. My maternal grandmother was 'Lizzie' Norman, daughter of the Reverend Canon Norman and Lady Adeliza Manners, a daughter of a Duke of Rutland. The Misses Drummond were known to boast that their parents between them mustered, amongst a hundred or so first cousins, no fewer than five dukes. The family of Norman emerged from the City of London, where they had been timber merchants, during the Commonwealth and made their headquarters at a charming house called The Rookery at Hayes Common, near Bromley in Kent. Its architecture is generally ascribed to the period of Charles II. In due course the Norman sons made a number of remarkably successful marriages to the daughters of dukes and earls, so that at one time in the nineteenth century whispers went round in exalted circles about a second Norman invasion.

When, in many long, probing conversations with my mother about her multitude of second cousins – she had none in the first degree – I chanced, as a beastly youth, to say that of course consciousness of these connexions was a necessity to a large, late-Victorian family which came from a long line of misters on both sides, she was not at all pleased.

Neither did the run-up to my own birth in 1913 give great pleasure to my mother, for in the photograph album embellished with water-coloured drawings that she made for all her five children as infants, she permitted herself the disclosure: 'I ought to say little Archie arrived a week before he was expected, but on the whole that was a very good thing, as his Mother had got rather tired of waiting for him.' In retrospect this seems a foretaste of a somewhat quarrelsome relationship, which perhaps we secretly enjoyed, despite some mutual verbal bruising. The home in which this summer event took place was itself far from aristocratic. It was a rented house on the edge of Bexley in Kent, at the opposite end of whose High Street was, and I hope still is, a stone saying 'London Bridge 13 miles'. This part of what is now known as Greater Bexley was then just Bexley and in 1913, and until 1939 at least, was a suburban village where there dwelt a number of bourgeois of considerable wealth, although the vast new housing estates were fast swallowing up the nucleus.

My parents' case was different from that of those rich bourgeois. Old Mr Drummond had always made it clear that any suitable young man was at liberty to seek the hand of any of his four daughters, but they must be in a position to keep and maintain them in comfort, as he offered no *dot* or dowry with his daughters. This meant a long engagement between Dudley Gordon and Cécile Drummond. My father on leaving Harrow School did not enter for Balliol College, Oxford, as his elder and younger brothers both did, but instead gladly put on overalls and took up an apprenticeship in Hall, Russell's shipyard in Aberdeen. He had long determined on a career in engineering. He lodged in Aberdeen during the week, and drove out to Haddo House for weekends, or when he could, on what he claimed to be the first motorcycle in the county. This primitive machine, after conveying him one winter gloaming so far out of Aberdeen as to traverse part of the Haddo estate, suddenly conked out with a loud explosion. From across the stone dyke he was greeted with curses by a cowman whose beasts had scampered in fright from the unaccustomed noise. Upon recognizing the Earl of Aberdeen's second son, however, he beamed a smile and called out in the Buchan Doric accent: 'Why, it's Doodley!' When its surface coating has been scratched, Scotland still is a familial or, if you like, a paternalistic society. By contrast to this good man's instant recognition, my father's elder brother Lord Haddo showed some alarm on one occasion when he was greeted in an Aberdeen street by a workman in greasy dungarees. He had not at first recognized his brother in this grubby garb.

The engagement of the young pair continued until my father found work with the marine refrigerating company of J. and E. Hall Ltd at Dartford in Kent. Marriage now became possible and took place in April 1907, after the rented Bourne Place, Bexley, had been suitably equipped to meet my mother's requirements and my father's taste for early electric cookers and the like. The house's architecture showed distinct signs of the influence of Norman Shaw rather than of Philip Webb, whose Red House at Bexleyheath nearby was designed for William Morris in 1859–60. My first home was described as being in the Queen Anne style, which puzzled me until I learnt that this 'Queen Anne' revival was the loose description given to the Norman Shaw school's ingenious use of Dutch and early eighteenth-century elements. There was a real rookery in the elms beyond my mother's bedroom, and this also dominated the view from our nursery on the floor above.

The young couple settled down to raising a family. I was their third child, born after more than six years of marriage. I was a most dislikeable brat, red-haired and bad-tempered, cruel to the cat and frightened, with reason, of the dog. Our nextdoor neighbours were Lord and Lady Churston at Hall Place, one of England's beautiful houses, built on an H plan, early Tudor to the roadside, visible from a great wrought-iron gateway and fence; William and Mary facing towards the south and to the little River Cray. There was a topiary garden on the western side. The Churstons' children were brought by their nanny to play in our garden sometimes, until the nurse reported to Lady Churston, who had been Denise Orme, actress, that she could not take her charges there any longer because of the little redhead's language. I had discovered the word 'bugger', and used it whenever I was angry, which was often. My grandmother Drummond and some vicar's wife thought it such a funny word when at teatime I refused to say my name when asked, and was told there would therefore be no cake during this drawing-room appearance. Thereupon I marched round the room declaiming the funny word. My mother kept blushfully quiet; my father had told her it was wicked. It was not until I became an adult that, when asked my name, I could say 'Archie' without embarrassment. The reason for this was that other children teased me with the phrase 'Archibald, certainly *not!*', taken from a popular song I have myself never heard. I can only hope it was sung by the incomparable Hetty King, for whom I later formed an admiration.

After my grandfather had been elevated to a marquessate, my

parents became, by courtesy and custom, Lord and Lady Dudley Gordon. Soon after I was nine I was dispatched to a preparatory school at Bickley, Kent, between Chislehurst and Bromley. I do not remember whether, on arrival, it was an assistant master, the matron, or a senior boy who escorted me to the far passage where my playbox – a kind of wooden chest where we boys kept our private bags of sweets, a book or two, and heaven knows what rubbish – was already in position. To reach this passage we had to pass through the boot room, where there sat on benches some of the sons of the rich merchants of Chislehurst. They called out, as though rehearsed, 'Lord Dudley *Gordon*! Lord Dudley *Gordon*!' I must have looked odd, with the shortened red hair, the round metal frames of thick spectacles, and a blush of shame. There then was added to my inability to say my Christian name the attempt to conceal the connexion with persons of title, except in company where the fact was taken for granted. This tendency has persisted. I lay no claim to being scarred for life by those assaults upon my sensitive self. At the time of my entry to St Hugh's, an otherwise excellent school with several men, including the headmaster, who had the genius of making boys want to learn, I had forgotten the word 'bugger', but after a few terms, and when I had become notorious in the school for the record number of canings I received, and probably deserved, I remembered it again and joyfully learnt other (four-letter) words as well. Here was a boy aware of his inadequacy of wealth and shortage of expensive toys by comparison with the children of the rich of Bexley and Chislehurst, growing up with a strong inclination to hide his aristocratic connexions, which his appearance did nothing to encourage anybody to believe in, and at the same time learning accurately from his mother the intricacies of her many relations amongst the nobility, and even on occasions meeting some of them. My father kept quiet about the vigorous and active titled persons amongst his closest relations, and I easily sorted out most of them for myself when the time came for me to meet them.

I do not wish to pursue these autobiographical flights; they are revealed only to illustrate a few general points about my groundings in the idea of aristocracy, or its inevitable absence, in the twentieth century. I have one more glimpse to offer. When I was about seventeen my mother and father and I were sitting in her upstairs sitting-room, known as the boudoir, when I was asked to fetch something from my father's desk in his study downstairs. Opening the rolltop cover I found what was wanted, but I also saw my father's calculations of his income and expenditure. This was in 1930, and I secretly returned to look at this sad paper again. He was by then chairman and managing director of J. and E. Hall Ltd at a salary of £3,000 a year with four sons, all having been or about to be educated at Harrow School, and a daughter whose bringing out as a débutante had been of the scantiest sort. They were six months in arrears with the grocer's bill – no wonder they looked frosty when we implored them to change to a more enterprising, more modern shop – and my father had agreed, at a time of world-wide depression, to accept a larger cut in salary than his fellow directors because he had married a rich banker's daughter. (That, anyway, was my mother's story.) The rich banker had left her enough money to buy the house and its 50-acre dairy and poultry farm where we now lived in place of the rented house in Bexley, but there was nothing left over to provide her with any investment income. My father's firm declared a nil dividend. I do not accurately recall my reaction to this knowledge; except that I now wanted badly to leave a school I disliked and try to find a job. I succeeded in both, but only at the cost of greatly upsetting my father, who was in love with Harrow School, which I was not.

We had moved from Bexley on my seventh birthday in 1920 to this small estate at Wilmington, nearer Dartford but still rural. On this patch of dairy and chicken farmland, with the newly stacked haybarn a favourite romping ground for mother and children, and with an attractive bank of woodland to one flank, our life was pretty self-contained. The undistinguished Georgian house had room for the family of seven and its attendant servants, including several active or retired nannies, and healthy walks could be taken on Dartford Heath, then an expanse of heather and grass, hawthorn and gorse, shallow disused gravel workings whose ridges made bicycle switchbacks, fun for us children but bad for the bikes. Many of the paths had names: Daddy's path on which he daily bicycled to the works in Dartford, Fagg's path along which Miss Fagg, a short-stay governess, and Mrs Burton, our laundrywoman, walked several miles from Bexleyheath every day in the early 1920s. A brother, Michael, who was killed in Italy in 1943 by a sniper's bullet, mapped this tract with great ingenuity when he was a schoolboy. Now it is scarred by the two-lane Rochester Way with an interchange built 'to motorway standards' on cheap land, albeit a public open space, hard by the Bexley Mental Hospital of the GLC. We were never taught to ride a horse – we had none – only bicycles. In the winter we never followed the Hunt. From 1928 to 1935 my father had no motorcar, borrowing a works runabout when occasion demanded. When I first went to work I cycled sweatily the three miles to the railway station at Bexley, often with a suitcase somehow balanced on it with clothes for a débutante ball in smartest Belgravia. Even then I enjoyed the sudden switches from a clerk's life to that of a rich girl's partner amongst *Tatler* people.

We seldom entertained at home, my mother being a reluctant and shy hostess who expected her young guests – our friends and relations –to fit in entirely with her arrangements. Perhaps that is the sign of an aristocrat? Our only continuing childhood friends from our Bexley days were a family whose father and mine had been contemporaries at Harrow, and whose five children more or less paired off with us. Surviving members of the North family are still beloved friends, though we seldom meet. I regard mine as a rather shut-in, bourgeois upbringing, due largely to my parents' medium financial resources, which restricted our pocket-money compared with that of school contemporaries, and not in the least bit even upper class, let alone aristocratic. It taught me easy adaptability, whether or not I took joy in such dissembling. Aristocracy, in my view, needs not only plenty of money, but the acceptance by a large segment of society of the idea that 'being born to rule' is a good thing and a proper principle. Wealth and a deferential society are the only bases on which aristocratic rule can flourish, whether or not an element of corruption is also needful. It was knocked out of me at an early age that I, or any of my closest relations, could possibly qualify for this delightful situation, by the taunts, superior abilities and more expensive toys of my middle-class child-hood neighbours and schoolmates. I think now that I am grateful to them, but it was a hard struggle for a long time to hold feelings of love for such boys and, a few of them, girls. The lesson I learnt from them is that aristocracy ceased to exist as a reality at about the time I was born and certainly by the time I was five, at the end of the First World War. The learning of it did little, however, to give me self-assurance, nor to modify my share in the national pastime of judging the social class of passers-by.

I feel now a confidence in undertaking an account of a number of men called Gordon, some of whom, except by their blood, had no more pretension to an aristocratic posture than I, though most of them seem to have had better manners. (Those of us who share my mother's Drummond blood will be inclined to agree that a talent for sudden rudeness comes from that half of their parentage rather than the other.) Yet even amongst those odd Gordons of whom I treat there were some who seemed hazy about their antecedents. Catherine Gordon Byron herself proclaimed, and her famous son seemed to continue to believe, that she was a 'true' Gordon, not one descended from the Seton strain, created Earls of Huntly and, ultimately, Dukes of Gordon. But this, as the reader will see at the beginning of chapter 1, is exactly her line and a good deal grander than she supposed. However, I must not knock this poor lady who has been so maligned, even during her lifetime, by her son Byron and by others. She lived in a world of fantasy created by herself and was surrounded by fantasists, not the least of them being her husband. A sympathetic study of her would, nevertheless, demand imaginative treatment beyond my reach. The illegitimately born William Gordon of Fyvie, on the other hand, never seems to have behaved with any recognition that he was 'the brat of Bell Black', and his mild, scholarly countenance portrayed by Beechey gives no hint of a character warped by the compulsion to be defensive of self. What it does show is a secretive nature.

I now turn briefly to George, 4th Earl of Aberdeen in this context. A believer in aristocracy, and with eighteenth-century confidence that he personified it, there is never a hint from him that his grandmother, the 3rd Earl's countess, emerged from the kitchen of a Wakefield inn and that her father shod horses. He certainly behaved as an aristocrat, in both public and private. He was one of the last to hold a private court to settle tenants' grievances and disputes. He distrusted the mild degree of democracy enshrined in the 1832 Reform Act because he thought it could lead in the end to universal suffrage, which he regarded as the equivalent of mob rule. Today's despairing democrats may be inclined to agree; is there no posture between mob rule and authoritarianism but the organized, though genteel, corruption of American 'fixing' in political institutions? And is it not possible that genteel corruption is as good a mortar joining governors to governed in mutual inter-dependence as the vote (in the USA generally on a low percentage poll), the universal vote, and nothing but the vote? That goes beyond the scepticism of my grandfather's grandfather, and those readers who wish to should find out more about a man whose eminence so greatly exceeded that of his predecessors and successors amongst the Gordons of Haddo. They may read two recent full-length studies of him: Lucille Iremonger's biography *Lord Aberdeen* and Dr Muriel Chamberlain's scholarly *Lord Aberdeen: a Political Biography*. Both these authors also write fully of his broad artistic, intellectual and antiquarian interests. Indeed, but for the accident of his early becoming an orphan and, according to Scotch custom, the appointing at a certain age of two politicians – Pitt and Dundas (later Viscount Melville) – amongst his guardians, it is possible that he would not have entered political life, for which he was in many ways ill-suited. He was too much the disdainful, sceptical scholar; his rhetoric was wretched. Apart from a fondness for actors and the theatre, and a capacity to yield unlimited passionate love upon his two wives, there was nothing the slightest bit wild about him. Yet if I were writing about aristocrats rather than about Gordons, he would merit an even longer chapter in such a book than the 6th Earl, his grandson, the cheerfully doomed 'Storm Petrel' as I call him, does in this. The 4th Earl of Aberdeen cannot be discussed in the present book with the brevity to which I have committed myself. My concern, in treating of my own family, has been to write about those antecedents whose lives have not hitherto been written.

The other notable omission from these pages is Charley, though he is mentioned in passing as a fellow cadet at Woolwich of Adam Lindsay Gordon. He was described then as a 'sulky little devil'. Charles George 'Chinese' Gordon, Gordon Pasha, Gordon of Khartoum, probably the most famous man of this name ever to have lived, was not only a soldier of exceptional merit, he was also a man of strange moral elevation and mysterious religious conviction. He had four generations of forebears in the army; beyond Captain David Gordon, who died in 1752, no further ancestry has been traced by the genealogists. His father, also a distinguished general with a strong commitment to British honour, found that Charles's acceptance of a foreign command – both father and son had probably not studied the tendency of Scots to serve as mercenaries abroad in a rather different setting from the Chinese undertaking – 'gave him little pleasure; he was proud of his son, but he did not like to think that he was serving among foreigners and not, as a Gordon should, with the men of his own race and faith'.* J. M. Bulloch, the foremost chronicler of the Gordon families, who is reputed even to have searched the Patent Office for the name of any patent-holder called Gordon, in *The House of Gordon*, vol. III, exclaims that 'an enormous literature has arisen round Gordon, filling several pages of the British Museum Library Catalogue'. That was written in 1912, and I do not propose to add to the British Library cataloguer's worries.

One phenomenon for which this remarkable man is principally responsible is remarked by Eilert Ekwall in the *Oxford Dictionary of English Christian Names*. He writes: 'The modern use of Gordon as a Christian name is due to the popularity of General Gordon (1833–85). It is now [1976/7] firmly established as a Christian name.' It is indeed, and I was sometimes stupid enough in the past to be angry when on being asked my name and replying 'Gordon', my inquisitor wanted to

* *The Story of Chinese Gordon*, A. Egmont Hake.

know my surname. Until General Gordon's martyrdom the name was rarely given as a Christian name, and then generally to nephews or godsons of girls who had married a Gordon. The pedigree of the Earls of Morton gives at least two such examples. I doubt if this popularity would have occurred had not Queen Victoria been so pleased at the great general's obstinacy and downright disobedience to his political masters, and so outraged and grieved by his death. The historian G. M. Trevelyan described him in his *History of England* as 'a strange and single-minded hero fit for any service except that of initiating retreat'. So famous was he, so violently was popular opinion of the same view as the Queen, that his death in January 1885 through the failure to relieve Khartoum led to the Gladstone government's defeat at a general election in that year, although Salisbury's Conservatives gained no clear majority and his government lasted only a few months before Gladstone was back again. The Sudan was taken for Britain and Egypt only after Cromer had toiled long and patiently, and Kitchener's campaign of 1898 had led to victory for Salisbury's re-established supremacy in the year of Gladstone's death. Kitchener is often dubbed 'of Khartoum', but how many boys, pray, are christened by that name?

Charley Gordon's label 'Chinese' tells me that he was simply a latecomer to the long tradition of Scotchmen, especially Lowlanders, turning their attention to Europe. The Highlanders were a more introverted society living under conditions even poorer than those of their lowland neighbours and rivals. This is due to the natural tradition of Celtic societies to cling to their customary chieftain, who in turn subjected himself to the clan chief. Both the lesser and the superior overlords tended to collect round them as many adherents as possible, the poverty of the land notwithstanding and, indeed, aiding the age-old custom of raiding rival neighbours' lands for cattle and victuals, for which a superiority of numbers was an advantage. Vigorous younger sons had little taste for looking beyond the Highlands or to Ireland for an outlet for their energies. However, to Ireland, especially Ulster, very soon after the original Plantation men there came many Scots, driven from every part by the hungry 1690s, the years of failed harvests and actual famine in Scotland. An exception to the Highland introspection may be Mackay's Regiment, originally raised by the first Lord Reay in 1626 to serve the King of Denmark. The emphasis quickly transferred to the United Provinces of Protestant Holland, where a Scots' Brigade already existed by 1572. The Mackay clan were pushed out of their harsh lands centred on Strathnaver's green sliver of a glen in northern Sutherland by the marauding Gordons, who acquired the Sutherland earldom through marriage in the sixteenth century. Dark tales that the Sutherland heirs male were done to death are countered by assertions that they were weak in the head as well as in the body and therefore, according to Highland custom, not fit to rule. The Scots' Brigade's recruits were mostly, in the end, of lowland stock, many called Gordon. This is not surprising. The younger sons of Lowland landowners and town burgesses often turned to Europe, where in mediaeval times men of their sort went as pilgrims to Rome or to Santiago de Compostela. Later such men sought fortune as Baltic merchants or as mercenary soldiers. Lowland Scotland was only marginally less poverty-stricken than the Highland areas, as I have tried to show. My stories of the Russian connexion and of Colonel John Gordon are only fragments of a recognized drift to Sweden, Poland, Germany and Russia in the north, and to Spain, in particular, in the south. Later, flocks of lowland people, following in the wake of those wretched Highlanders evicted by the savage clearances at the beginning of the nineteenth century, when landowners found that sheep were more profitable than men trying to survive on a subsistence economy long after the rest of the United Kingdom had become a cash economy, emigrated to the Americas and the British Empire, where the opening up of virgin lands and new industries offered larger and quicker rewards than Europe in constant turmoil. An unconscious pioneer of this movement was a Dutchman called Robert Jacob Gordon, whose family had settled in Holland in the sixteenth century. He discovered the Orange River in South Africa in 1776, and it was named three years later. Credit for the initiative in naming it is disputed. What is certain is that his father, at Volendam in Holland, made the most beautiful Holland's gin.

So, my claim is that we Gordons were and are not simply aristocratic, but also unconscious of class, designed for war. This particular Gordon claims none of these attributes in his person. As for class-consciousness, as my friend James Lees-Milne has pointed out, the British relish class distinctions and cannot do without them; what is odious and to be deplored is the erection of class barriers. My apparently random selection of subjects in the following pages is designed to show the wide variety of type that emerges from persons with a common surname. In degree the same might be claimed of families bearing any other famous name; all families are famous to their members and their cadet branches. It is simply that Gordons are more famous than others as beheld by others, rather than solely by themselves. If this judgment is held to be arrogant, or a silly pronouncement with tongue in cheek, let the reader make his own judgment from the ensuing chapters.

I

The Heron Leaves the Tree

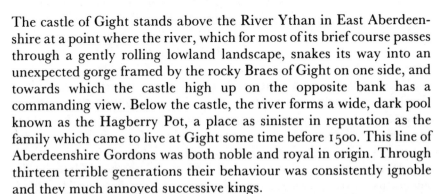

The castle of Gight stands above the River Ythan in East Aberdeen-shire at a point where the river, which for most of its brief course passes through a gently rolling lowland landscape, snakes its way into an unexpected gorge framed by the rocky Braes of Gight on one side, and towards which the castle high up on the opposite bank has a commanding view. Below the castle, the river forms a wide, dark pool known as the Hagberry Pot, a place as sinister in reputation as the family which came to live at Gight some time before 1500. This line of Aberdeenshire Gordons was both noble and royal in origin. Through thirteen terrible generations their behaviour was consistently ignoble and they much annoyed successive kings.

The 13th laird of Gight was the poet Byron's mother, Catherine Gordon, and he should have spent his childhood in this romantic place. Instead, in 1787, the year before he was born, she had to sell the whole property to my ancestor, her neighbour the 3rd Earl of Aberdeen, to pay the debts of her husband 'Mad Jack' Byron. The poet's early childhood was, therefore, spent in penurious discomfort in Aberdeen and at the farmhouse of Ballaterach in Upper Deeside, but he saw Gight as a boy, and recalls it, already a ruin, in the third canto of *Childe Harold*:

> Worn, but unstooping to the baser crowd,
> All tenantless save to the crannying wind,
> Or holding dark communion with the cloud.
> There was a day when they were young and proud;
> Banners on high and battles passed below;
> But they who fought are in a bloody shroud,
> And those who waved are shredless dust ere now,
> And the bleak battlements shall bear no future blow.

Byron's cynicism and talent for satire are not evident in writing about his maternal ancestors. Perhaps he never knew the truth about those who once were 'young and proud'.

Their line began with William, third son of the 2nd Earl of Huntly by his wife Princess Annabella Stuart, daughter of James 1 of Scotland. (Both the Earl and the Princess had been divorced from earlier spouses.) By 1498 this Sir William was confirmed in his lands of Gight. By a later marriage Huntly had a daughter who married Perkin Warbeck, the first of her four husbands. There is some evidence that there was a fifteenth-century castle on the Greens of Gight, but there is little doubt that the present ruin represents a building characteristic of the work of the same master mason who built Towie Barclay castle, higher up the river Ythan, in about 1580. A Russian descendant of the family that owned that castle, Field Marshal Prince Barclay de Tolly, commanded against Napoleon in 1812. It is still inhabited.

William started the Gight family's impressive record by getting into debt. Later generations feuded – who didn't? – pillaged the burghs, plundered their neighbours, murdered and were murdered, flouted the law, and disregarded all respected codes of conduct except for occasional bravery on the field of battle. There may be nothing exceptional about all these goings-on by the Gordons of Gight in the generality of the society of their times, both Lowland and Highland, especially in those parts where the Celtic and Anglo-Norman systems touched. Everybody was doing it some of the time. Their near kinsmen the Gordons of Abergeldie, next door to Balmoral, were often pretty hot stuff, and they are still in possession; yet the goody-goody Gordons of Lesmoir, who just accumulated land until they were owners in thirty parishes spread through five counties, have disappeared as totally as the Gordons of Gight, whose record is so consistently vile for so many generations. Yet most of the Gight sons married pretty well – the daughters of neighbouring gentry or even aristocratic girls. Perhaps fathers were willing to unlock their daughters in marriage to a line so high born in its origin, however base its reputation.

The 1st laird William became a burgess of Aberdeen, and in 1512 sold land to another burgess, Alexander Gray. Mr Gray had money to lend, William had needfully borrowed and this was his only way to pay off the debt. The following year William was killed at the battle of Flodden, which his elder brother, Alexander, survived to become 3rd Earl of Huntly and from which another brother, Adam, ran away and instead conquered by marriage the earldom of Sutherland, which remained in Gordon hands for over three hundred years.

William's son George, 2nd laird, was a minor in 1513, married a granddaughter of the first of my line, the Gordons of Haddo, and otherwise seems to have done nothing worse than to be arraigned together with his son before the Privy Council on 12 October 1564 for the 'crewale invassion of William Con of Auchry and hurting and wounding him in divers parts of his body to the great effusion of his blude; and striking and draging with a brydill three of Con's cottars and others'. They had probably gone short of chickens and malt and meal and this was the means to get what they needed. The son, 3rd laird and another George (like so many of them), married a daughter of the great Cardinal Beaton, who covered the land with his illegal offspring. The only child born in wedlock was a daughter, who resigned her interest in favour of her uncle John, the 4th laird. Her father had become heavily involved in the continual feuding between the families of Forbes and Gordon. He appears to have visited Charles IX of France and, whilst there, took part in the killing of a Forbes. Retribution came later on the shore at Dundee, where he lost his life to a Forbes in a formal duel. So ended the brief blood connection between Haddo and Gight.

John, the 4th laird, his eldest son William, who later became 5th laird, and a younger son, also John, were responsible in 1591 for the murder of the 'Bonny' Earl of Moray, successor to the Regent Moray. The story is confusing. Bothwell, in disgrace for having challenged in some way the great power of Chancellor Maitland, found out how to get into the Palace of Holyroodhouse, and intended there to beg the King to pardon him for his offence and to be secured against Maitland's oppression. In the course of gaining entry, servants and guards were killed, and Bothwell managed to lock the King and himself in a closet. Tumult broke out, the town became aware of goings on, the King was rescued, frightened and angry, and Bothwell fled to the island of Bute.

At the time of this outrage the King was trying to patch up the ancient quarrel between the two great magnates of the North East – Huntly, the leading Catholic, and Moray, who had promptly joined the Protestant Lords of the Congregation in 1559–60, soon after John Knox's famous Perth sermon of 1559 which had launched the Calvinist Reformation in Scotland. Rumours meanwhile spread that Moray had concurred in Bothwell's outrage. 'At which', wrote William Gordon, the apologist of the House of Gordon in 1726, 'the King flew into an extreme Passion, having as it was reported other just grounds of

Indignation against [Moray] besides; and calling for Huntly to go and bring the Earl of Moray with him.'

Huntly, therefore, with his three kinsmen of Gight and about forty men, crosses the Firth of Forth to Donibristle in Fife, where they arrive in the twilight. Whilst Huntly's men parley at the gate of the castle, one of Moray's men 'from the window fires' and gives young John of Gight 'a deadly wound'. His friends thereupon set fire to the castle. Moray escapes in the confusion and the dark, runs several miles to the seashore to find a boat, and 'is found out by a spark of fire which had stuck to the top [a silken tassel in another account] of his Helmet; and, refusing to be Prisoner, is killed by one who knew not what he was'. In fact he was brutally slashed and slain on this rocky shore of Fife. It will never be known by whom, though some said it was Huntly himself. This seems unlikely; more because it would not have been in his interests than because he was a scrupulous man. He then panicked rather, sent an emissary to tell the King what had happened and 'marches by Perth to his own country . . . Huntly left Captain John Gordon [younger son of Gight's laird] in his wounds at Inverkeithing, where he was seized, and brought to Edinburgh, and beheaded in his wounds tho' mortal: And to all this (the clamour was so great) the King was obliged to give way.' He had intended no killing of Moray, only that he should be brought before him, and the execution of a minor figure in the tragedy was not in his style.

Nevertheless, it is true that this was a political killing rather than a conflict of religious fervour, and the King had reasons to be doubtful of Moray, William Gordon's 'other just grounds of indignation' most likely being the considerable favour with which the Queen, Anne of Denmark, looked upon the bonny Moray. The King's attraction to his own sex would not in his sight justify his consort's also dallying with men, however noble and closely related to the throne. The King ordered a trial of Huntly, whose vassals and neighbours in Highland country were very angry with him and rose up, causing tumult which the Earl of Angus had to try to put down.

Determined that the highlandmen should be kept in order and within the law rather than that the noblemen who could achieve this most readily should be sacrificed by the Sovereign lawgiver, Huntly's trial was not much more than a formality, though maybe uncomfortable. Today we would say he was let off with a caution. He was needed to keep the peace in his own fashion in Badenoch and Lochaber and elsewhere. Curiouser still, in 1599 he was created a marquess. Most curious of all, his daughter was given in marriage to the murdered Moray's son and successor. The importance of this story, told more or less from the Gordons' standpoint, is that, whatever the *facts*, the *truth* it reveals is that Scotch noblemen, so soon before the Union of the Crowns in 1603, could tell the world, and especially Englishmen, how they could behave towards one another with apparent impunity and despite their acceptance of a wily, legalistic Sovereign placed over them especially to keep them in check.

The date of the 4th laird's death is uncertain, unlike that of his successor. William Gordon, 5th laird of Gight, remained firmly a Catholic despite the King's insistence that such families should submit to the presbyteries, and flouted the law in many other respects. He engaged in a feud which outlived him with the family of Mowat, had early in life killed a Fraser, a friend with whom he disagreed over a minor transaction between them, and, having undertaken to protect the town of Turriff from attacks by junior members of his family, suddenly one midnight attacked it himself. The biggest scandal he caused was his funeral, in 1605, after a lifetime of feuding and pillage and murder. He was buried, as his wife had been a year earlier, in the Roman Catholic rites. News of this came to distant Whitehall, where the new King of England as well as of the Scots reigned by Divine and Protestant right. In January 1607 James VI and I wrote to his Privy Council in Scotland:

> We are specialie to recommend unto you that exact tryall be taikin of these two verie heynous offenceis committed at the two severall buryallis and funerallis of the Lord Ogilvy and Laird of Geicht, quhairin ther wes sum superstitious ceremoneis and rittes used as gif the profession of papistrie had been specialie licenced and tolerated, and upon the knauledge of the authoris of those insolenceis, owre plesour and will is . . . that ye acquent us thairwith to the effect that we may returne bak unto you owre will and pleasour thairin.

Needless to say, William's son George continued in this recusancy, and it was complained of him that in 1607 'he careyed ane crucifix upon ane speir' at the funeral of a tenant.

Let it be clear that junior members of the family were no better at keeping within the law, both civil and ecclesiastic. Even some of the girls were wildcats. In 1618 one of them, Elspeth, who had married a Cheyne, joined her husband in a raid on a neighbour's house and took away all the corn and meat and meal they wanted. They then moved upon a tenant farmer and the first victim entreated Elspeth to 'forbear such unseemly form of doing'. Those words are taken from the pursuer's claim in the lawsuit that followed. The claim goes on: 'She thereupon conceiving a high offence against him in the height of his distempered passion and unruly humour, put violent hand upon him, and unhonestly struck and dang him with her hands and feet in sundry parts of his body, and left him for dead.' Perhaps she did not quite unman him. When her husband was brought before the court to answer for the behaviour of both, the pursuers failed to prove the charge.

Among the young men of the family there was little of tender boyhood. A nephew of the frightful Elspeth, John Innes of Leuchars, in December 1612, was ringleader in a series of riots, with some Gight cousins of course, at the Grammar, Song and Writing Schools of Aberdeen. The Council Register of Aberdeen reported that

> long before the superstitious time of Yule, notwithstanding that surety was found for them that they should not take the Schools at that time, nor any other time of the year; and that they should observe good order and discipline within the said Schools; they carried guns, and they went shooting there withal as well as on the night as on the day. In their great deeds and oppression and riots they made forcible entry of the citizens' houses, and breaking up their doors and windows, and masterfully taking of their fowls, poultry, bread and vivars.

They also looted the country carts bringing fuel and victuals to the burgh. For this they were imprisoned in the Tolbooth. For those Gight boys it was a natural initiation to the sort of thing the laird was doing. The 5th laird's fourth son, Patrick, would have excited the respect of anybody in the gangster line of business. When young he murdered someone else's farm servant, called Catto. Later, in 1615, he was involved in the avenging of his brother Adam's murder by Francis Hay, an account of which follows below.

Before that, in 1612, complaints were laid of Patrick's treatment of some Bannermans, whom he and friends chased into Aberdeen with guns blazing, wounding two of their servants. After the Hay affair, the Privy Council told him to leave the country, but six years later, in 1623, he was back, bristling with hagbuts and pistols and shooting at anything, man, beast or bird. He stole a horse and, when its owner remonstrated, trying to calm him, he 'gaif him ane cruell and deadlie straik and wound a little above his left eye, and thairby almost dammeist him dead'. The victim of this assault lodged a complaint, the defenders (for Patrick had a companion with him) did not appear and the Lords of Session ordered them to be denounced as rebels. Patrick had an illegitimate son William, and determined that the boy should marry Margaret Cushnie, daughter of John Cushnie in Culsalmond. The girl had set her heart on Richard Gordon, son of John Gordon of Clymies. (A man described as 'in' a place implies that he was landless, 'of' refers to a man of property.) So Patrick was not being greatly ambitious for his bastard. He was, however, so angry at the girl upsetting his plans -- the wedding to her Richard was imminent – that he sent his son, with some companions, to ravish the girl. You may suppose his reasoning was that, thus defiled, Margaret's parents would perforce abandon their plan for her to marry Richard and accept the man who raped her. So they carried her away, having offered violence to her parents, and 'the said William verie barbarouslie did force hir'. Nevertheless, with the protection of the justices of the peace, she married her Richard. The Gight blood was now up, and they determined to put Richard on the spot. Richard was no mean fellow, having killed a man at Inverurie a few years before his marriage, and when it now became necessary for him to protect his own life he shot Patrick, whose prayers for peace and 'quarter' went unheeded. Patrick's dying words were to the effect that it was all his fault, and he pardoned his slayer. Margaret's father, John Cushnie, asked the justices for and was granted one year's protection from the Gight family, but for some years various people kept on shooting at each other, especially upon 'the linkes' (or sand dunes where golf courses were laid out later) of Aberdeen, but there seems to be no record of fatality.

George, the 6th laird, was a militant Catholic and carried on a constant battle against 'the trew religion'. He harboured priests and he broke his sword upon the Protestant laird of Leask's head, so the Ellon Presbytery continually complained. Then, in 1615, his brother Adam fought a friendly sword duel with Francis Hay, a cousin of the Earl of Erroll; Adam won and Hay, out of pique, shot him dead. This affront to the Gordons is briefly referred to above; it had to be avenged. There had also been trouble with the Hays over marriage settlements and other matters. Although Gight had been banished abroad in 1614 for refusing to dismantle the oratory in his castle (the remains of an ambry can be seen even today), he captured Francis Hay with the help of friends and relations, including Patrick, only three days after Adam's murder. They rigged a mock trial in Aberdeen, refused legal advice to Hay, condemned him to death and killed him 'with so butcherly mangling the poore gentilman with sex severall straikes upon his shoulderis, hind head and neck, as the lyke has nevir, or seldome, bene sene or hard', or so the King's Advocate advised the Privy Council the following year, 1616. Naturally the Hays now tried to avenge themselves for the murder of their Francis. James VI and I, who must have been tired of having to reprimand the troublesome Gight family, then commanded Lord Huntly, and the head of the house of Hay, the Earl of Erroll, to put an end to the feud. They failed. Furthermore, Gight's trial in Edinburgh for usurping the law was a fiasco even there and was stopped in its eighth day. In the end King James personally intervened to settle the matter. The surviving Gordons and Hays, one of whom was Gight's son-in-law, submitted to a 'royal decreet arbitral' (a Sovereign decision) and 'in testification of their willing obedience to His Majesty, they chappit hands, one with another, and promised to bury all former griefs, displeasures, and unkindness standing amongst them and to stand, and underlie, and fulfil the decreet and sentence given and pronounced by His Majesty betwixt them'.

That was in August 1617, but the quarrel simmered on until 1623, when at last it cooled. However George, 6th laird of Gight, was not finished yet. He tried to blackmail his second wife's mother, the ancient and dying Lady Saltoun, who was rich, into making a will in his favour. He did not succeed, but the Privy Council had to intervene to stop his assaults upon her. He was desperate for money and tried anything. It is a surprise that such a brute should have had a French governess for one of his daughters. It is not a surprise that he failed to pay her wages. An Aberdeen lawyer, Mr John Paip, complained to the Privy Council, who wrote to Lord Huntly specifying the amount as being 'the proper debt due to a stranger, a Franshewoman, who these divers years before has had and still has, the charge of education of one of the laird's daughters, and entertains and furnishes her very honestly in her apparel and diet, and brings her up in all virtuous exercises beseeming a young gentlewoman of her birth'.

This turbulent man had some awareness of his spirit. A record of the Privy Council declares that he had once said to his wife: 'I can tak no rest. I knaw I will die upon a scaffold. Thair is ane evil turn in my hand.' He just avoided this fate. In 1639 he rode past the kirk of Ellon on the Sabbath in a scandalous manner, and although he began to fortify his house against the inevitable coming of the Covenanters, he was arrested by a Captain Beaton, and taken to the Edinburgh Tolbooth where, already ill, he died in 1640.

24

His successor George, the 7th laird, whilst still a young boy, had helped his father to worry Lady Saltoun and was imprisoned in Edinburgh for his trouble. Later he got into debt, and for three years from the time of his father's death was in Germany. Notwithstanding this absence King Charles I in 1642 wrote a fulsome letter in his praise, making him a colonel. He appears to have come back home more to prevent his creditors from seizing his property, which the Court had empowered them to do, than to serve his King. In 1644 the inevitable happened. After he had taken part in a raid on Aberdeen the Covenanters sacked his house and captured him, along with his neighbour Sir John Gordon of Haddo, who, according to the book of William Gordon, 'was put in the nastiest Prison in Town, ever since called Haddo's Hole'. This was an airless cell let into the thick wall of the Tolbooth adjoining St Giles's Cathedral. Haddo was quickly tried and executed, the first of a long line of Royalists to suffer this fate at the Mercat Cross at Edinburgh. Gight was luckier; his trial was postponed and he meanwhile escaped by the simple means of bribing his guards. In 1647 Parliament surprisingly pardoned him, possibly because his eldest son had married a Covenanting Keith of the Earl Marischal's family. The hereditary office of Great Marischal of Scotland had been held by the Keith family (originally Hervey, which owned the lands of Keith) from the twelfth century. Their descendant was created Earl Marischal in 1458. The last holder of the title, and the office, suffered attainder for his part in the 1715 rising. He died, aged eighty-six and unmarried, in Europe in 1778.

Nobody will ever know the truth of the story that was told of George Gordon, 7th laird, through many generations, often improving in the telling down the years. He knew his house would be sacked by the Covenanters and himself taken, so he packed all his silver and plate in fine linen, put the bundles in a secure chest, and lowered it into the depths of the Hagberry Pot, the pool in the river Ythan below the castle. On returning to his desecrated place after his pardon in 1647 he found a diver to go down to retrieve his treasure. After a long wait the diver surfaced, green in the face and bleeding. He said he had seen the devil himself and other monstrous creatures, sitting by a smooth rock spread with a fair cloth and all the laird's treasure put out. They were waiting for dead babies to be cooked for their feast, and they had set upon the diver, shrieking: 'Keep away from here. This is our domain; we have no other. Keep you to your ain.' The disbelieving laird would have none of this. The man would secretly come back and take the treasure for himself. He must go down again. He refused. He was taken to the castle to be persuaded to return. First his fingernails were drawn. No, he still would not return. Then the pins were stuck in. At this he yelled: 'Better to face the Devil again than the Laird of Gight.' So he submerged for the second time. At this the waters swirled and seethed and at last the diver's quartered body surfaced, a knife impaling his still quivering heart.

The story is well founded on many myths of treasure in a watery hiding-place being guarded by devil monsters, but nobody need doubt the practice of torture of a crude sort at that date. One thing is certain: the hagberry, the name in Scotland for the bird cherry, *Prunus padus*, still grows at this place. Its fruit, small, hard and bitter, less comforting even than a raw sloe, was always supposed to be the main ingredient of the favourite fermented brew of witches. The pool, alas, is not nearly as deep as the story is tall.

Whatever the laird's opinion of the diver's tale of the devil, it may have helped him in 1650 at last to succumb to the 'trew religion'. In his case the swearing of adherence to the League and Covenant had to be undergone twice. After his first appearance in the Kirk at Fyvie, barefoot in sackcloth upon the penitential, or cutty, stool, the Presbyters were not satisfied with his behaviour, and ordered the ceremony to be done again. The Turriff records make this clear; equally clear was his reluctance to come abroad from his place in case a writ was served upon him.

His son and successor, George, the 8th laird, distinguished himself by trying to seize the property for himself whilst his father was in Germany in 1642, took part in Royalist skirmishes, killed one or two sleeping soldiers attached to Forbes of Craigievar, and appears to have accepted the Kirk as the right place for his two children's baptism. His son, George, the 9th laird, had only a daughter, Marie, and his is one of the few names, with his wife's, inscribed on the tombstone in the churchyard of Fyvie.

Marie, the 10th laird of Gight and the first woman owner of the property, married in 1701 a Davidson. The daughter of generations of lawbreakers married into a family which had practised as advocates in Aberdeen for at least a century. He soon fell in with the conventions of Gight. Part of the marriage settlement was that Davidson should pay his mother-in-law's debts. Before the contract was registered, he borrowed her copy of the document and tore it up. By now we have reached the eighteenth century, not necessarily the age of reason and enlightenment in these parts, but at last the Gight tendency to violence was stayed and there were no killings; in the place of exciting feuds a web of boring lawsuits and always, always the restless search for cash.

The Gight estate, throughout its occupation by this family, seems to have varied in extent between 4,000 and 4,500 acres. This was its size at an inventory of 1762, and farms referred to then are also mentioned as being part of the property in records of the family during the sixteenth and seventeenth centuries. At the time of the Civil War, the neighbouring estate of Sir John Gordon of Haddo was probably not so extensive. An account of the removal from Sir John's House of Kelly of his valuables and furniture allows the guess that Gight Castle was more richly appointed. These lairds, at this time, had some luxuries but few comforts: well-fashioned chests, tapestries probably, and for apparel a silk shirt and furs for the winter, both denied to the less elevated in society. Their general living condition and their food, would, however be as rough and unrefined as that of the meanest of their tenants and servants. Their method of avoiding shortages is demonstrated in the incidents mentioned in this chapter. At times of poor harvests and of actual famine they would survive, just. There must have been a great gulf in material well-being between such families and the great ones, such as Montrose. Yet Montrose must have been schooled in rough living to survive, with his followers, his astonishing marches across the harshest highland wastes.

Marie and Davidson had seven children; the youngest son was chosen to inherit Gight and changed his name to Gordon. All the others stuck to Davidson. Alexander 'Gordon or Davidson', as he is described in the Service of Heirs, the official register of property holders, married a Duff from a family both clever and successful, and fathered fourteen children. All but the eldest son reverted to the name of Davidson. Alexander 'Gordon or Davidson' was drowned in the Ythan in January 1760. There was a pretence that he was bathing in the river when melted snow overwhelmed him. J. M. Bulloch, who worked on his great chronicle of the Gordon families from the 1890 to the 1930s, suspected suicide. 'Scotsmen in 1760', he wrote, 'had not become slaves to the tub so much as to induce them to bathe in ice-covered rivers in the depth of winter.' The names of this laird, his wife and children are also inscribed on the tombstone in Fyvie churchyard.

We come now to the last male laird of Gight: George the 12th. He revived the association between the Gight and Innes families by marrying an Innes. Of their three daughters only Catherine survived.

This last George Gordon of Gight seems to have come to Bath for his health, and having made a precise will in 1777 bequeathing the whole estate of more than 4,000 acres to his daughter Catherine, drowned himself in the Bath Canal in 1779. A modest tablet commemorates him in Bath Abbey, inscribed 'an honest man'. In Catherine's own testimony in a later letter to her lawyer written at the time of her son's succeeding as Lord Byron, this also was a suicide. Within a few years this vain, muddle-headed, plain young woman with provincial accent and manner then began to show off in Bath society, itself by now pretty seedy. She liked to boast, and later taught her son likewise, that she was a 'true' Gordon, not of that ducal strain that was really Seton, not Gordon at all. In fact her descent came from the same Seton root. It was in Bath that she met and married Captain John Byron, 'Mad Jack', the widower of the Marchioness of Carmarthen, who was in debt because the £4,000 a year he had enjoyed in that ladyship's lifetime ceased at her death in January 1784. So in May 1785 he married the dumpy heiress from Aberdeenshire, who had probably exaggerated her fortune to the handsome libertine, and was silly enough at the age of twenty to marry without a settlement that would protect her interests. Very soon his creditors fell upon her income, and a farm, and much timber, had to be sold. Peter Buchan's collection of ballads, printed in 1828, included one which goes:

> O, whare are ye gaein', bonny Miss Gordon?
>   O, whare are ye gaein', sae bonny and braw?
> Ye've married, ye've married with mad Johnny Byron
>   To squander the lands o' Gight awa'.
> This youth is a rake, frae England is come,
>   The Scots dinna ken his extraction ava',
> He keeps up his misses, his landlords he duns,
>   That's fast drawn the lands of Gight awa'.
> The shooting o' guns, and the rattling o' drums,
>   The bugles in woods, the pipes in the ha';
> The beagles a howling, the hounds a growling,
>   These soundings will soon gar Gight gang awa'.

The gentry of Aberdeenshire could not stand his showing off, and in 1786 Catherine and Mad Jack departed, first for South Warnborough in Hampshire, then for the Isle of Wight, then to France. In 1787 a forced sale of the whole property to the Earl Aberdeen realized £17,850. All except the tiny jointure of Catherine's Duff grandmother, living in

Low Street, Banff, and £3,000 for herself, were mopped up by Mad Jack's creditors. When Catherine became pregnant she came to London from Chantilly alone, and George Gordon Byron was born on 22 January 1788 in a furnished room in Holles Street, London. It is the short street between Cavendish Square and Oxford Street. The baptism was at the Marylebone Parish Church, the Duke of Gordon and a Duff cousin were the godfathers, and probably to please them and to ensure economies of her meagre income she lived from 1790 to 1798 at various houses in Aberdeen. Until his death at Valenciennes in 1791 the Captain continued to plague her for money, which yet further reduced her income. She was freed of these worries after her son succeeded in 1798 to the Byron peerage and the Nottinghamshire estate, and lived either at Newstead, or at Burbage Manor near by when the Abbey was let for a few years.

Her appearance had always been unsatisfactory and her temper uncertain. She flew into rages with her sensitive son and her stepdaughter Augusta Leigh, and then as suddenly covered them with kisses. Pouring profane abuse on the boy, she called him a lame brat. His icy reply was: 'I was born so, mother.' Later he wrote to Lord Sligo that it was impossible for him to love Mrs Byron as a son ought to love a widowed mother. To his half-sister Augusta he wrote confessing to hurricanes of real hatred, 'to me most terrible'. Nineteenth-century anthropologists, both professional and amateur, loved to hang theories of degeneracy on the examples of mother and son, and what they knew of their immediate forebears, not only Gordons of Gight but Byrons and wild Trevanions from Cornwall as well. One of these anthropologists, an American called Dr Kiernan, wrote only a hundred years ago a series of articles in the *Alienist and Neurologist*:

> Mrs Byron's features had that exaggeration of the Scotch type which constitutes arrest of facial development. She was by no means devoid of the shrewdness and ordinary intelligence of inferior femininity. She was capable of generous impulses to persons whom, in her frequent fits of uncontrollable fury, she would assail with unwomanly violence. Mrs Byron's early education was remarkably neglected at a time when Scottish young ladies of her station were exceedingly well educated, and the contrast between them and the women of the lower class [whom Dr Kiernan says Mrs Byron 'reached'] was enormous. Her husband did not hesitate to leave her penniless, burdened with her own infant and the daughter of his first wife, whom she seems to have treated with all the kindness possible to an ill-regulated nature.

Even J. M. Bulloch, the Gordon chronicler, writes that 'there can be no doubt that she came of an utterly impossible race, and came at the fag end of it, when mere ebulliency of spirit had passed into a form of actual insanity on the one hand (as illustrated by her father) and of enfeebled physique on the other (as shown by the rapid decay of the family)'. By this I suppose he means the failure to breed. But who knows how many descendants survive, in well-educated health and showing no signs of Scotch arrest of facial development, from the numerous progeny of earlier generations, not to mention Davidsons and Duffs and persons called Innes.

When Catherine died at Newstead in 1811 Byron was away – her final illness was sudden and swift – and he was genuinely anguished, hurrying home to moan at her bedside. He had other causes for grief in that year. No fewer than four of his men friends also died, three of them drawn from the romantic attachments of his adolescence at Harrow and Cambridge. He gave his mother decent burial in the Byron family vault in the church at Hucknall Torkard, and remained at Newstead for some time. She had preserved intact for her son her own capital of £3,000 and the £1,100 odd which, since the old lady's death in 1801, represented her grandmother's jointure. On the inscription in the church, perhaps Byron's final ironic twist once he had recovered from his well-advertised grief, there is acknowledged her descent from the 'Earl of Huntley and Lady Jane Stuart'. He once wrote: 'My mother was as haughty as Lucifer, with her descent from the Stuarts and the "old" Gordons, not the Seyton Gordons as she disdainfully termed the ducal branch.'

And the Gordons of Gight? They have utterly vanished, as the prophecy implied they would. An allegedly ancient rhyme, as usual credited to Thomas the Rhymer, went:

> When the heron leaves the tree
> The laird o' Gight shall landless be.

In 1786 herons which had for years nested by the Hagberry Pot flew over the Braes of Gight to Haddo. The young Lord Haddo instructed that no harm should be done to the birds, for the land would soon follow. It did, the following year. Lord Aberdeen and his factor had, of course, already started negotiations for the purchase. All that is left now of that 'young and proud' race is a tangle of farm tracks leading to a hulk of a ruin; a path down through trees to a dark pool; a discreet tablet in Bath Abbey; a burial vault in a Nottinghamshire church; a tombstone in Fyvie churchyard, and an immortal who turned his back on the Gothic barbarities of his northern race, and faced the sun.

2

Mercenary : Cavalier

Among the numerous younger sons and remoter progeny of the family of the Gordons of Gight two stand out as participants in events which have a major place in history. They were near contemporaries, but they never met. The elder one, Lieutenant-Colonel John Gordon, had his moment of fame by being party to the assassination of Wallenstein, Generalissimo of the forces of the Holy Roman Empire, in 1634, some years before the other, Nathaniel Gordon, cast his lot firmly, more firmly than Huntly, the head of their House, with Montrose in his campaigns in Scotland on behalf of Charles I.

John was the only recorded child of the second son of the second son of the 1st laird of Gight (William, who was killed at Flodden in 1513). The date of his birth is uncertain. He was almost certainly born in Holland, where his father served in the Protestant Scots' Brigade, purposely formed of volunteer mercenaries and permanently stationed there. The father was 'killed before Antwerp' in 1584. John's mother was closely connected with the Innes family, and married again twice after her first husband's death. She had two daughters by her second husband, and by her last husband another, Anna Weache, who married Alexander Petrie, son of the minister of the Scots' Church at Rotterdam. Instead of going into the Protestant Scots' Brigade John had some military training in France, and may have served as an officer in the French Army. He then took service in the pay of the Holy Roman Emperor, the Habsburg Ferdinand II, although himself not undergoing conversion to the Roman Catholic faith. This was to be his career, and like so many men from Scotland scattered throughout the armies and navies of European powers, he made a success of his trade.

This was well within the tradition, explained in the introduction, of junior members of landed families in Lowland Scotland going abroad, serving either in the armed forces of European powers, or seeking mercantile reward, principally in the busy Baltic trade based on the towns of the Hanseatic League, or in Spain and the Spanish Empire. In John's case, being born in Holland, he was spared the initial impulse necessary to leave Scotland, and he was an accomplished linguist, speaking Dutch, German, French and English. It was not even considered eccentric or particularly adventurous, let alone dishonourable, for such a man, of genteel birth but of no fortune, to hire himself out as a mercenary. If successful, the rewards were great; the booty of war, the ransom that could be claimed if you captured a prisoner, were both very attractive, and it did not disturb a man's ambitions in these respects to contemplate the opposite condition, of being taken prisoner or even being killed. Without the backing of more than a pittance of family wealth, John Gordon's life as a civilian, either Scotch or Dutch, would have been pretty brutish, and probably short. He saw his service in the savage conflict which ravaged much of Central Europe, known to history as the Thirty Years War. It is a mistake to regard this conflict solely as a religious war of Catholic versus Protestant. This was an important element in it, and sparked it off in 1618 when the Protestant Council in Bohemia threw two interloping Catholic grandees out of the Hradčany Castle – the famous defenestration of Prague – and retribution had to be exacted. Two years later, in 1620, the imperial forces attacked in the Battle of White Mountain, near Prague, when the Protestants, including the King and his English Winter Queen, were sent packing, and the capacity of the Bohemian Czechs to use military force, even in their own defence, seemed to be extinguished, apparently for ever. The irony is that the two Catholic nobles thrown from the castle's steep bailey, Martinitz and Slawata, escaped with only small hurt and lived on to play their parts in the complex game of imperial political manœuvrings.

This religious spark lit many fires. The French used it as an excuse to recover territory in their eastern lands, and King Gustavus Adolphus determined to turn the Baltic into a Swedish trading pond, subordinating the German Hanseatic cities and his Catholic kinsman the Vasa King Sigismund of Poland to Sweden's interests. Lutherans and Calvinists hated each other just as much as either hated the Catholics. The odd Bethlen Gabor, the Calvinist Prince of Transylvania, made sure nobody could be certain of his allegiance, and Wallenstein, a man of genius, turned out in the end to be concerned principally with personal aggrandizement. He came of a modestly noble Bohemian family, being born Count Albertus von Waldstein, later becoming

Prince of Friedland – a huge tract of Bohemia which he ruled as a model estate – and Duke of Mecklenburg, which was more or less his own idea. He raised an army of great strength for Emperor Ferdinand II, and asked for no pay for his services. He would see to that. He even at one time lent money to the Emperor. It was in this man's army that John Gordon became in due course a Lieutenant-Colonel.

To attempt briefly to describe Wallenstein is to invite disbelief from those who do not know, and accusations of 'disinformation' from those who do. A contemporary account of his character begins: 'A meditative and melancholic, ever restless, generous, resourceful, magnanimous gentleman, though hard and harsh of temper.' That he was an able strategist whose military tactics and ruthless speed of movement were exceptional, at a time when that king of military genius, Gustavus Adolphus of Sweden, was his principal opponent, are proven in any history of the Thirty Years War. He had a Catholic education in Germany, where he and his friends were a bit of a menace, and he inherited his initial family estates at the age of nineteen, returning hurriedly from Padua to claim his inheritance. He married a rich, ugly widow and, having consolidated the economy of his enhanced estates, offered his services to the Emperor. He stood at the centre of a group of familial and political alliances, German Catholic at one end –Eggenburg, Harrach – and Bohemian Protestant at the other – Trčka, Kinsky. Here there were shifting sands, and lack of trust just as intense and complex as the affairs of the nobles, lairds and chiefs of Scotland at about the same time. Wallenstein was addicted to astrologers for guidance; nothing unusual about that. Everybody, the Jesuit-trained Emperor included, had his astrologer. Later Wallenstein's health showed signs of breaking and, both in his lifetime and through subsequent history, he was accused of resorting more to scheming, 'diplomacy' and political intrigue than to getting on with the business of soldiering at which he excelled. All this is true, but his latest biographer, Golo Mann, is also convinced that amongst the mixture of motives that led to the final accusation of treachery – of being prepared to take his forces and his command over to the Protestant side, an accusation that led to his death in 1634 – was his desire in the last year of his life to keep Germany – the Empire – from being involved in the imminent war between France and Spain.

This, then, was the world in which John Gordon was a willing participant. In the interests of securing popularity amongst his troops, the aloof Wallenstein often preferred the appointment to colonelcies of

Protestants because they were accommodating to him. He also liked the Dutch, because they could be relied upon to attack the cities of the Hanseatic League, and so relieve him of the need to do so himself. Gordon fought under Wallenstein against the Swedes at Nuremburg in 1632. The imperial forces won the battle, but Gordon was taken prisoner. He was a popular prisoner and would have met a number of compatriots, since Gustavus is estimated to have acquired at least twenty-eight officers who were Scotchmen. After six weeks he was released without ransom, a most unusual occurrence, but not before the Swedes were ready to fight again.

Lützen, a small town to the south-west of Leipzig, became the site of the next battle. It also figures in the Napoleonic campaigns. In 1632 one of Germany's best roads ran between it and Leipzig, where Wallenstein was resting, nursing his ailments, issuing orders and trying to keep the shifty Lutheran Elector, John George of Saxony, on the Emperor's side, or at least neutral. The battle with the Swedes took place in November 1632. Wallenstein's plan had been to lure Gustavus into Saxony, and there destroy him. The Swedes in fact won on a technical knockout, because at the end of a day's hard, inconclusive fighting Wallenstein retired his troops to Leipzig during the night, leaving the surprised Swedes the next morning in their original position, before they had attacked. But by one o'clock on the day of the battle the great Swedish Lion from Midnight had been killed, set upon by a posse with pistol shot and sword thrust, all his valuables stripped from him, and his naked corpse left bloody on the ground. This became quickly known on both sides soon after the event, and it did Wallenstein politically no good that he failed to follow through and destroy the Swedish army, though it was superior in numbers to his own, after the death of their great commander and king. There is no record of John Gordon being present at Lützen. Wallenstein had only recently been recalled after the death of General Tilly in April 1632, consequent on Gustavus having seized Augsburg, and then swiftly marching to Saxony, whose elector, John George, a man who wobbled about on the shores of advantageous neutrality, sent the Emperor a cry for help. Probably Wallenstein, on his recall to service, had sent Gordon as commandant of Eger (Cheb in Czech), a Bohemian border town at a key point on the route from Bavaria to both Bohemia and Saxony. The old castle had been converted into a citadel, another of the General's commanders having described the townspeople as an evil-minded lot, more trouble than the foe. Now it was in the reliable hands of the

Protestant Dutch Scotchman; or so Wallenstein thought.

Between the end of 1632 and February 1634 there was much coming and going by the ailing Wallenstein between Prague, his home estates of Friedland, and Pilsen (Plzeň). There is little doubt he was hoping to negotiate a settlement with the Swedes in order to keep the Empire out of the conflict between Spain and France that many people knew was coming. There is no doubt that the Emperor in Vienna was being persuaded that Wallenstein must be removed from the scene. The move by Wallenstein from Prague to Pilsen, then Eger, accompanied by Field Marshal Ilow, Counts Trčka and Kinsky, with a force of about a thousand men, had 'diplomacy' as its objective. Vienna had decided otherwise, and it was Ilow who first got wind of the plot to kill Wallenstein. Nevertheless preparations to move to Eger went ahead. An old Catholic friend of Gordon's, Walter Leslie, was with him in the citadel, garrisoned by Count Trčka's Regiment of Foot. After Wallenstein's arrival in Eger, they were joined by a Catholic Irish mercenary, Walter Butler, recently promoted Colonel by Wallenstein, and a certain Captain Devereux, an Englishman, I presume. Butler's function was to persuade Gordon and the others to fall in with the imperial decision to kill Wallenstein, and to organize the carrying out of the act.

At this point it should be made clear that Schiller's great poetic drama *The Death of Wallenstein*, written at the end of the eighteenth century, is a play, not history. It appears to fuse together Gordon and Leslie, and makes delightful fiction by also fusing Wallenstein's two wives – the second was young, and not rich – and makes the one fictitious wife sister to Countess Trčka, or Tersky as it is given in the German form. He also kindly has Gordon saying to his fellow conspirators:

> Seize him and hold him prisoner; do not kill him;
> Murder's a black deed, and Nature curses it.

There is no evidence that Gordon was reluctant, and there is certainty that Butler told him of the rich rewards that had been promised by Vienna, whether he was authorized so to suborn Gordon or not. Schiller makes Gordon hesitate. Butler, in real life a fiery Irishman, characterizes him as

> Poor, weak Gordon . . . who prizes above all his fealty.
> His conscious soul accuses him of nothing
> In opposition to his own soft heart.

A much earlier piece, rushed out by one Henry Glapthorne in 1639, *The Tragedy of Albertus Wallenstein*, played to good audiences at the Globe on London's Bankside. It is poor rubbish, but it makes Leslie the principal villain (Butler's rôle in real life), and this was clever politicking by Glapthorne, since he makes great play of Leslie's Catholicism, hardly the most fashionable religion in the London, or Scotland, of that time.

So in February 1634 the scene was set in this small town on the Bohemian border. Gordon and his fellow mercenary officers were lodged in the commanding citadel; Ilow, Trčka and Kinsky scattered in the town; the General carried in a litter to the first floor of a house in the town formerly occupied by Gordon. Wallenstein knew he had been deserted. He had failed in his attempts to negotiate with the Swede Count Oxenstierna; he had failed to make himself intelligible to Vienna. He was ill, and even money was running out.

Butler and Gordon had not met before, and the plot demanded immediate action. Butler had a good idea that it was known already to Wallenstein's staff. Wallenstein held a staff meeting on Saturday morning at his house, after which Ilow summoned Butler, Gordon and Leslie to give them routine orders. Leslie later reappeared on Gordon's behalf to invite Wallenstein and the others to a banquet at six o'clock in the citadel. What could be more natural than to give a party on the Saturday before the commencement of Lent? Wallenstein did not leave his room; the others, Ilow, Trčka, Kinsky and Colonel Niemann, attended the dinner. They all sat down, started with pike garnished with snails, and agreeable wine to relax any tension there may have been. Later the three mercenaries rose up and cried: '*Vivat Ferdinandus*', as though to a prearranged signal. Captain Devereux chimed in and they all set about their guests with sword thrusts. Trčka, a big man, protected by an elkskin doublet, was the last to die. There was then the rounding up of the various Countesses by dragoons, and the progress to the General's lodging. The gallant Lieutenant-Colonel Gordon stayed downstairs, presumably nursing 'his own soft heart'. Captain Devereux went up with six protectors. There was a storm raging, but the hubbub in the street was audible above the noise of thunder and Wallenstein had dragged his frail body to a window to see what was going on. Devereux and his men burst into the room. His victim in his nightgown had no means of defence, spread his arms wide in the traditional plea of 'Quarter!' – surely a mere reflex – and was stabbed in an upward jerk from stomach to throat. His corpse was bundled into a red rug and dragged down the stairs, his head bumping on every tread,

36

and taken into a carriage to the citadel where the others lay.

Butler that night posted off to the Emperor's representative at Pilsen to say that he alone had killed them all. Leslie was quickly sent to Vienna as spokesman for Gordon. The object here was to maximize the reward; all Wallenstein's immense possessions, as well as those of his rich, dead entourage, would be parcelled out. They knew the plums would go to Ferdinand's high commanders. The murderers would be rewarded on a lower level, mostly in land. Friedland, worth half a million gulden, went to Field Marshal Gallas. Butler, made a count and a chamberlain, was awarded land worth 225,000 gulden: not bad for a mercenary.

John Gordon's share was worth 178,000 gulden. One account says he was created a marquis, Bearer of the Gold Key, and a chamberlain. *Vivat Ferdinandus* indeed. He remained a Protestant; a friend wrote to Father John Seton in 1638 saying: 'Colonel Gordon is not yet a Catholic'; as if strenuous efforts had been made to convert him. His soldiering days were nearly over and he resigned his commission in the Imperial Army in 1644. He had made his pile and had no further need of battle honours. He visited his cousin Innes in Leuchars in Fife with a view to buying an estate in Scotland. He even inspected one that was available, but 'the intesten trouble of Scotland diverted him' from buying. It may seem a surprise that a soldier who had seen so much of the battle horrors, and the 'politicking', of the Thirty Years War should be nervous of the state of Scotland at the time. But it was his first visit to this northern land, so different from his native Holland. He was admitted burgess of Elgin on 27 February of that year, so probably he was looking at a property thereabouts. His part in the assassination of Europe's most formidable soldier made him for a time a celebrity, but he retired to Holland, as Lord of Schmydar and Scrivan. He died, still unmarried, at Danzig in December 1648, and was buried in the Nieuwe Kirk at Delft. To this church ten plain silver beakers were presented in his memory.

John Gordon made his will at Lübeck less than two months before he died. He left two communion cups to the Scots' Church at Rotterdam, where his half-sister Anna Weache's husband, Petrie, had been brought up when his father was minister there. By 1902 these cups, much battered, were on loan to the Scots' Church in Brussels. Most of his wealth, in money and land scattered all over Europe, was left to Anna, but a good share also to his mother's two daughters by her second marriage. The legacies caused rows between the ultimate legatees of the next generation, and so late as 1687 lawsuits were pursued by disputing parties in the Edinburgh Court of Session and in the Dutch courts. The chief contestants were Sir William Binning, lately Provost of Edinburgh, and Lady Hope of Carse. The total costs were enormous, because visits to Lübeck were also involved. One estimate was 40,000 Rix-dollars (£6,000 approximately) – and Binning wasted more than £1,000 sterling on the process and in journeys to Holland.

John Gordon seems to have had a straightforward, soldierly character according to the tenets of his time, and it is hard not to applaud a man who, from small beginnings, amassed a fortune in a manner considered perfectly respectable in the seventeenth century which was large enough to be worth quarrelling about forty years after his death.

In the same year – 1634 – that John Gordon reached the climax of his career on the Continent in the slaying of Wallenstein, there occurred the first recorded event in the career of John's kinsman Nathaniel Gordon. He was the third son of John Gordon of Ardlogie, who was the second son of the 5th laird of Gight. Ardlogie must have brought up his sons to expect a warlike passage through life and, being far away from the source of family wealth, although Ardlogie House was often appointed for a laird's widow, there was little choice for Nathaniel. John of Ardlogie had been responsible in 1601 for forming the 'Societie and Companie of Boyis' or 'Knights of the Mortar'. They went about as champions of Rome, but their real object was plunder. They became such a nuisance that in 1607 the Privy Council wrote to Huntly to call them to order in a letter which has a note of menace in it should Huntly not succeed in disbanding the Boyis, or at least in bringing their thieving to a halt. The newly created marquess was only too glad to oblige. Then in 1630 Huntly tried to settle a dispute between Crichton of Frendraught and another laird. He could satisfy neither party, and the offended laird went away swearing vengeance on Frendraught. Huntly thereupon arranged for his son Lord Aboyne and others in his entourage to accompany Frendraught from Huntly Castle to his own place not far away. This man was no minor laird. He was heir male to the great Lord Crichton, who had been Lord High Chancellor of Scotland, and he thus had importance, even though only reflected. Frendraught persuaded Aboyne to stop the night, against his better judgment. After they had 'supped merrily' they were taken to the tower of Frendraught Castle and went to bed joyful. At about midnight a raging fire leapt up the stone stairs – there was only one room on each floor – and Aboyne and his party perished. It was reported that the laird of Frendraught and his lady looked on, and did nothing to offer help. That was the story told by one of Aboyne's retinue, who escaped. It seems to have been a wanton killing for no discernible purpose or gain, and of course it had to be avenged. Crichton of Frendraught's wife was a daughter of the Earl of Sutherland, head of another branch of the Gordons and a close kinsman of Huntly. The Sutherland Gordons were inclined to support the Covenant, whereas Huntly was Royalist. This may have been the cause of the killing.

Huntly went at once to Edinburgh to petition the Council, which appointed two bishops and others to form a commission of inquiry. By 1634 nothing much had happened except that Frendraught was obliged to stop in Edinburgh awaiting the decision about a trial. The Gordons then pounced. A number of them fell upon Frendraught Castle. An unfortunate named Thomson, found drinking in the alehouse, was taken for a spy and hurried to Strathbogie, where he was hanged. Meanwhile others let loose 260 nolt (cattle) and 360 sheep and burned 80 cornstacks in the cornyard. They then commandeered a large number of sheep for immediate eating. Nathaniel Gordon was in the party which carried out this jolly foray. That is the Gordon side of the story. Crichton denied murder, saying that the fire was accidental, and it may be supposed that he thought he had a reasonable chance of living down his rash and stupid act. Although much shaken, and not until 1636, he was allowed to go with a caution.

During the course of these long-drawn-out proceedings Nathaniel was amongst those ordered to appear before the Privy Council to answer for their act in letting loose all those sheep and cattle, and for burning the corn. Of course they did not appear and were consequently declared rebels. They were 'put to the horn', as outlawry was officially described.

There were two distinct causes of the frequent pillaging and raiding of supplies between neighbours. The standard of farming was so wretched that those with the skill and the strength took such action when it was necessary, in their view, to avoid going hungry. That was one good reason. The other was that it was part of the conventional practice of revenge; it was normal procedure in the course of a feud. The violence of these sudden attacks was probably necessary as the only way to carry them to success.

After being declared a rebel, Nat took refuge with the lady of Rothiemay on her Banffshire property, well within the province of Gordon patronage. He was a handsome young man and a great favourite among women, which may have endeared him to his great commander, the amorous Montrose, whom he served with distinction a few years later. A contemporary ballad collected by the author of *Buchan's Ballads* may have had its origin in this incident:

> Widow are ye sleeping yet?
>   Or widow are ye waking?
> Ye'll open the gin, let me come in
>   And me your only darling . . .
>
> If I promised to marry you,
>   My dow, but an' my dawty;
> And if I promised to marry you
>   I'm sure I'm nae sae fauty.

It is a long ballad from which these two verses are extracted. The lady of Rothiemay was imprisoned for harbouring this rebel, who then himself escaped to Germany, where his father had already gone. He was back in Scotland in 1638, went in 1639 to Berwick with Huntly's eldest surviving son, brother to the burnt Aboyne, and almost certainly sailed from Berwick to France, where he probably had formal military training. He does not again appear in the records until 1644, when he was back in Aberdeenshire out plundering with some friends, loosely serving under Montrose, when they came upon a band of Covenanters, likewise engaged in reducing the estates of some persistent Loyalists. The Covenanters were routed and disarmed and as Spalding records in his *Troubles* 'cam shamefully back againe to Aberdene'.

Encouraged by this a bolder venture was planned in which, as Sir Walter Scott recorded in *The Minstrelsy of the Scottish Border*,

he assisted at a sharp and dexterous *camisade* (as it was then called), when the Barons of Haddo, of Gight, of Drum, and other gentlemen, with only sixty men under their standard, galloped through the old town of Aberdeen, and, entering the burgh itself about seven in the morning, made prisoners and carried off four of the covenanting magistrates, and effected a safe retreat, though the town was then under the domination of the opposite party.

Nat's next exploit got him into trouble with his chief, Lord Huntly. A Danish fishing buss, engagingly so described by Sir Walter, which an

English pirate had seized, drifted into Aberdeen Bay. Nat and twenty musketeers seized the prize and clapped the only man on board, an Englishman, in the Tolbooth. Then the pirate ship arrived to claim its prize. Nat arrested pilot and skipper, who turned out both to belong to an English man-o'-war. Muddle, and trouble fullfart, as the Danes describe full speed ahead on a ship's telegraph. The pirate, thwarted, harassed local shipping and even raided on land at Belhelvie. The fishermen complained to Huntly, who reproved Nathaniel 'veray bitterly' for acting without his permission. The accused, hitherto a soldier obedient to his chief, was 'so angrie that he hastellie took his leive and left the Marques' service'. In April 1644 he offered his services to Huntly's heir, Lord Gordon, who was inclined towards the Covenant, but was rebuffed. He was on his own. Had he been as wise as he was brave he would have cleared out of the country, for the forces of the Kirk – the Covenant extremists – were quickly closing round the Cavaliers. At the beginning of May they took Sir John Gordon of Haddo's House of Kelly, and the neighbouring Gight Castle. Haddo and Gight themselves were marched off to Edinburgh. Haddo was executed on 19 July 1644, the first in a long list of Royalist killings, and Gight escaped from his prison, as described in Chapter 1. Meanwhile a reward of 18,000 marks had been offered for the capture of Huntly 'quik or deid', and another sum for Nathaniel, who then resolved to fight to the death. He quickly attacked the Aberdeen and Dundee merchants assembled on 24 July in Elgin for St James's Fair, who thereby returned home 14,000 marks the poorer. Lord Gordon was sent to arrest him, but failed; possibly he did not try very hard. Nat's next move was made not only to gain time, but also to avoid the penalty of excommunication, which he dreaded. So he agreed to a truce with the Covenanters, and even allowed the Reverend Andrew Cant, described by Scott as 'the famous apostle of the Covenant', to reprove him. Spalding says this was 'politique'. It was indeed about time that Nathaniel learnt the uses of guile. Nevertheless this was on the surface an effective desertion of Montrose, who had favoured him because he had proper military training, and in November he carried it to the lengths of releasing from prison a leading Covenanting laird, Forbes of Craigievar. So his conversion may have been more real than the word 'politique' implied. And why not? Huntly and his heir were at odds – Huntly's wife was the sister of Argyll, undoubted leader of the Covenant throughout the kingdom – and even the great Montrose himself had changed sides. So how was a young man of no estate, literally a soldier of fortune, who relied on pay and booty to support himself, his patient wife and child and one or two other women, to stay constant to a cause, in those days when it was unwise to trust your brother or even your best friend?

'Politique' indeed: in February 1645 he signed the Royalist Bond of Union and wrote a scarifying letter to Mr Cant which, wrote Spalding, 'nigh frightened him out of his wits', and very soon, for other reasons, that divine's power crumbled. In March Nat stormed into Aberdeen with a hundred Irish dragoons – the same sort whom Butler brought to Eger – seized the keys of the Tolbooth, freed the prisoners and seized much arms. The Covenanters' General Sir John Hurry came into town, caught Nat and friends carelessly drinking in their lodgings, and killed some of them. Nat escaped, at the cost of losing Huntly's best horse, which he had been lent, for they were now reconciled. He could not really escape, for fighting was in his blood and events now moved with speed. In a series of battles he commanded Montrose's right wing and was described as colonel. Scott attributes his apparently siding with the Covenant to 'an artifice, to arrange a correspondence betwixt Montrose and Lord Gordon, a gallant young nobleman, representative of the Huntly family, and inheriting their loyal spirit, though hitherto engaged in the service of the Covenant'. He fought at Auldearn, near Inverness, in May, then helped young Graham (Montrose's son) to rescue his sister from Linlithgow. At the battle of Alford (2 July) on the river Don in Aberdeenshire he hacked his way through the enemy by ordering his men to ignore their muskets and use their dirks to hamstring the horses. He escaped but Lord Gordon lay a corpse. On 15 August he fought at Kilsyth. It was not all disciplined warfare, the Gight spirit being lively in him. In early September he and young Lord Ogilvie were quartered on the minister of Nithsdale in Dumfries. They 'brake up his cofferis, chistis, almries, carried away his whole bedding'. They 'brunt and spoiled his buekis, chistis, chyres, stoolis, and uther timber work' – for a camp fire had to be kept going. Of course they ate all the reverend's glebe corn. The quotations are taken at second hand from a book called *Earls of Sutherland* which cannot be traced.

On 15 September he was taken at Philiphaugh, and marched off to Edinburgh. Sir Walter Scott wrote:

He was one of ten loyalists, devoted upon that occasion, by the Parliament, to expiate, with their blood, the crime of fidelity to their King. Nevertheless, the covenanted nobles would have probably been satisifed with the death of the gallant Rollock, sharer of Montrose's dangers and glory, of Ogilvy, a youth of eighteen, whose crime was the hereditary feud betwixt his family and Argyle, and of Sir Philip Nisbet, a cavalier of the ancient stamp, had not the pulpits resounded with the cry that God required the blood of the malignants to expiate the sins of the people. 'What meaneth,' exclaimed the ministers, in the perverted language of Scripture – 'What meaneth, then, this bleating of the sheep in my ears, and the lowing of the oxen which I hear?' The appeal to the judgment of Samuel was decisive, and the shambles were instantly opened. Nathaniel was brought first to execution. He lamented the sins of his youth, once more (and probably with greater sincerity) requested absolution from the sentence of excommunication pronounced on account of adultery, and was beheaded 6th January 1646.

Scott was eloquent and concise, and his account needs filling out. The deadly charge was that Nathaniel had taken upon himself 'to rise in arms, and remain with, fortify, assist, and supply James Graham Montrose, the avowed enemy of this Kingdom, leader of that rebellious army, which lately this year by-gone has infested this Kingdom and troubled the peace thereof'. He parleyed with the Presbyterians, which was unusual, and there is a sadness in that on the back of his written submissions he had scribbled texts from the Scriptures, though probably not from the book of Samuel. The Court was not open to entreaties, for they knew it only meant more trouble, so they condemned him to die as a traitor.

Morland Simpson in *The Deeds of Montrose* uses modern English in quoting Bishop Wishart's account of Nathaniel's ending:

When he saw death so near he bitterly lamented the sins of his youth. Just before his death a paper was thrust into his hands to sign, in attestation of penitence. To this he readily put his name. At the same time he called God and his angels and all who were present to witness that, if there were anything in that document derogatory to the King and his authority, he utterly disowned it. He was then absolved from the sentence of excommunication laid upon him for an adultery he had committed long before. Amidst the profound pity of the spectators he laid his head upon the block.

Apart from Byron, Nathaniel was probably the only attractive man to come from the house of Gight. Save for the wounded John Gordon, executed five days after the murder of the 'Bonny' Earl of Moray, he was the only member of that family to die upon a scaffold. He deserved a better fate where many of them deserved a worse. Scott's opinion in his time was that he was one of 'the bravest and best soldiers in Europe'. Had he ever written an Aberdeenshire romance, which he did not, he would probably have taken Nat as his hero. Life, and death, are real, however, and as with Byron there was not universal praise for a gallant cavalier after his demise. There was dispute over his estate, which had hardly any ready money in it. He had claimed that a widow called Janet Gordon owed him 500 marks, which he instructed should be paid to his wife Grizel, whose patience over his infidelities is a marvel. Dame Gordon, however, refused to pay. Long after his death these entanglements beat on the conscience of the Strathbogie presbyters, who had charge of the soul of one Jean Gordon. They persecuted her on the grounds that she had borne one child to Nathaniel and another to his comrade Captain Mortimer. In consequence she was known as 'Lady Alter'. Nat had a legitimate son, Adam, who was probably at Königsberg in 1659, and was most likely the messenger who brought letters home from General Patrick Gordon of Auchleuchries, the first subject of chapter 3. Bishop Wishart's final epitaph is that Nathaniel Gordon had great influence in his own country.

3

The Russian Connection

The long and honourable tradition of Scotchmen, generally of Lowland origin, serving as mercenaries in the armies and navies of Europe, starting in the sixteenth century, reaching its zenith in the seventeenth and quickly dying out in the eighteenth, is here exemplified by three men: Patrick Gordon of Auchleuchries, his nephew Thomas and his son-in-law Alexander of Auchintoul. They all served under Peter the Great of Russia; Thomas the sailor, besides being in the navies of Scotland and England, served in only one foreign country, Russia. Alexander, who also served his own country in the 1715 Jacobite uprising, from which he survived with his life and his lands by a narrow squeak, provides a clue to the waning of the mercenary's way to fame and fortune. The Union of Parliaments of 1707 fanned the spark of the concept of nationhood into a small flame; it was considered an aristocratic treachery by many humble people. The Hanoverian succession and the two Jacobite risings, although they intensified the distinction between Lowlanders and Highlandmen, set on a course the idea of one Scottish nation because of the punishment meted out by the English to all Scotland indiscriminately, and this tendency became irreversible only after George iv's famous visit to Edinburgh in 1822. Queen Victoria's acquisition of Balmoral completed the realization of the dream of William Wallace – one Scottish nation – 550 years earlier. That was partly because of the response of the gentry to what A. G. MacDonell amusingly called 'Balmorality'. The evidence of the Christian Watt papers, however, is that the sturdy fishwives of Buchan and their daughters thought little of the West Highlanders whom they seasonally visited. Her observations show clearly two cultures side by side.

Patrick Gordon of Auchleuchries most particularly demonstrates how modes, morals and emotions have changed in three hundred years, for he served Poland and Sweden alternately before accepting service under the Russian Tsars and reaching high rank. All this was achieved without anybody questioning his motives or calling him a turncoat. Not even Byron was retrospectively sniffy, as only he could be, when he wrote of

> . . . General Gordon
> Who girded his sword on
>   To serve with a Muscovite Master,
> And help him to polish
> A nation so owlish
>   They thought shaving their beards a disaster.

The last line is a reference to Tsar Peter ordering the boyars of Muscovy to adopt, and adapt to, the modern ways he had learnt in the West and was determined to force upon his reluctant subjects.

Patrick was born in 1635, the second son of an impoverished laird who descended from one of the early Gordons of Methlick and Haddo. The Auchleuchries family was Catholic but kept pretty quiet about it. Adherence to the old faith meant, however, that his education, in Aberdeenshire or anywhere else in Great Britain, came to an abrupt end at sixteen, there being no question of his being able to enter a university. So in 1651, two years after King Charles 1 had been consigned to martyrdom, he sailed from Aberdeen to Danzig. From there he entered the Jesuit college at Braunsberg, but 'his humour could not endure such a still and strict way of living' and he attempted to return home. There was no money for the younger son of an impoverished laird to achieve a passage to Scotland, and after two years' harsh wanderings, at the age of twenty he entered the service of a young Polish nobleman. In 1655 they were in Hamburg, where he was persuaded to join as an ordinary trooper the Swedish army about to invade Poland. Stettin was the bridgehead from which this invasion was launched, and Patrick soon found himself near Cracow, where he suffered a leg wound when his horse was shot under him. In January 1656 he was captured by the Poles and, there being no ransom attaching to such small booty, after seventeen weeks he was persuaded to join them. In July he was recaptured by the Swedes and, after explaining satisfactorily his service with the Poles, was drafted into the force of Marshal Douglas. (Douglas and Hamilton are still big names in Sweden. Wherever you can look for them there are connections. Many years ago I knew well a Polish count married to a Swedish Douglas.)

Patrick seems to have been as thistledown, for in 1657 he was again taken by the Poles, urged by his namesake Patrick 'Steelhand' Gordon to rejoin their service, but was exchanged instead and so remained under Swedish colours until he was, believe it or not, captured by the Austrians. Enticements to enter the Holy Roman Emperor's service were unavailing and he managed to escape to the Swedish camp. At this point, he demanded his discharge because he had not so far received a farthing for pay or equipment. The response was at last to give him an ensign's commission in a Colonel Anderson's regiment. After a disastrous venture when he lost a handful of hair attempting to chase some Poles who had made off with horses from his garrison, and was threatened with shooting by his colonel for not awaiting orders, he was again captured by the Poles. Offers of exchange were refused and, reasoning that service with the Swedes risked death by starvation if not in battle, he took service in 1659 under Lubomirsky, who promoted him in the following year to be Captain-Lieutenant of his bodyguard. He had already, during his several seizures, become proficient in the Polish language.

In 1660 he also wrote to his father hoping to return home to serve under the restored Stuart King, but his father quickly disabused him. He next tried the Austrians, who were no more encouraging, so in July 1661 a soldier frankly in search of fortune decided to make his way to Muscovy. There, making sure that Tsar Alexis became aware of his past kindness to Russian prisoners in Poland, Patrick was appointed Major in the regiment of Colonel Daniel Crawford. Quickly promoted Lieutenant-Colonel, and tiring of the frivolity and wenching of his fellow officers, he arranged a marriage with the thirteen-year-old daughter of the Catholic Colonel von Bockhoven, then a prisoner in Poland. Bockhoven's release took some years to accomplish, and Patrick hung about with little to do – certainly with no mission to make the Muscovites shave, a process only begun by Tsar Peter at the end of Patrick's lifetime. His marriage at last took place in 1665 in the absence of the bride's father.

Meanwhile an incident of a kind familiar to us today was making a long but barely noticeable scratch on the face of history. Somebody called Charles Howard, who had been in the brief Barebones Parliament of 1653 and then in Cromwell's House of Lords, secured ennoblement as Earl of Carlisle from Charles II in 1661. Two years later he was sent on an embassy to Moscow to reply to the Tsar's congratulations to the restored monarch, and to advance English trade.

He complained to the Russian authorities of his reception in Moscow, refused to accept the Tsar's presents and stayed in a huff in his embassy. The Tsar sent an envoy to London who was himself cold-shouldered until Carlisle returned from Moscow and told the London officials not to be silly. He had recovered his temper. Nevertheless the Russian counter-complained when he returned to Moscow and the Dutch meanwhile increased their stranglehold on the Moscow trade at the expense of the English. By this time none of the available Russians was willing to go to London, and it was decided that Patrick, a foreigner, should be the Tsar's emissary. He was delighted, for it meant that this time he could visit his home with all expenses paid.

Patrick had to leave his wife behind as a guarantee of his return, and arrived in England with her brother as aide in October 1666 just after the Great Fire of London. He delivered the Tsar's letter, collected the King's reply and, after amusements in the course of which he met again Patrick 'Steelhand' Gordon, he set off on the return journey at the end of January 1667, not reaching Moscow until June. King Charles's letter was not well received, being unhappily phrased as regards the Tsar's degree of serenity. Patrick was held responsible and ordered not to leave the foreign, or German, quarter of Moscow, the Sloboda, where his regiment was stationed.

Whilst in London Patrick had pressed Charles II to ask the King of Poland for the release of von Bockhoven, and this must have been effective, because in 1668 he sent this effusive letter to the Earl (later Duke) of Lauderdale, the 'L' in the Cabal and quite certainly the King's favourite Secretary of State:

> Right Honourable,
> Though from the almost frozen zone yet with a most torrid affection ushered by my humble duty, I send thes addresses to your Lo^p. All humane actions, constitutions, complixions, and all terrestiall Creatures, yea even vegetives, being tyed and owing a sort of duty to the Celestiall Creatures by reason of their influence upon them; even so, wee who crawle in the lower Orbs cannot be but sensible of the duty wee should carry for those persons and spirits that move in higher spheares. The many undeserved favours yor L. was pleased to confer upon me while I was in England have put ane inviolable ty and engagement upon all my faculties. I am ignorant only of the meanes and want sufficient ability to give evident testimonies of my real professions. My father in law having been released befor I came from England doth acknowledge his engagement never the less to his Royal Matie as likewise to yor Lo. for yor trouble in his behalfe; he being made Major

Generall is gone from hence, and is to have a kinde of absolute comand over ane little Army against the Cosaks and Tartars whither I am to go with my Regiment also very suddainly. I send by this occasion to yo' L a piece of unsophisticated Cavear in its Mothers skine which will make a cup of good liquor tast the better, and hath besides an extraordinary strengthening quality. if there be anything which this Countrey affords and may be usefull to yo' L. let me know your will and it shall be duely fullfilled; and lest I prove tedious, with the tender of my most humble respects to yo' L. most honourable Lady and Family, I take leave contining

      Right Ho*ble*

      Yo' L.

      most faithfull and humble servant.

To the 'Cosaks and Tartars' Patrick indeed went, in 1670, to subdue their activities in the Ukraine. He was so successful there that he remained seven years, and was able to study the mechanics of warfare and fortification. Meanwhile, his elder brother having died, his father provided him with the life rent of some Auchleuchries lands so long as he provided for his younger brother in the event of his inheriting the whole property, and in 1670 he had been made an honorary burgess of Aberdeen in the resounding style of '*Honorabilis vir Patricius Gordoun Miliarchus sub imperio serenissimi et illustrissimi imperatoris Russie Magni ducis Muscovie*'. After an attempt to reprimand him because of the behaviour of some of his troops in Southern Ukraine, he tried again to quit the Russian service in 1678. Tsar Feodor was advised against letting him go and he was promoted Major-General and appointed to the Kiev command.

In 1682 two events occurred that greatly altered his life; yet this remained on the surface the same. In that year Patrick's father died and in Russia Peter, aged ten, succeeded Feodor as Tsar. The Regency was put in the hands of Peter's elder sister Sophia (his brother Ivan was insane) and her chief minister Prince Vasili Galitzin. They thought well enough of Patrick to promote him Lieutenant-General, but kept him firmly at Kiev. In 1685, hearing of the accession of James II and fearing for his inheritance of Auchleuchries, he applied for six months' leave, eventually granted on the same terms as before, that is on condition he left his wife in Russia as hostage for his return. He was able to take up his son James (who later became a brigadier in Russian service) at Memel, where he was studying at the Jesuit College, on the grounds that to leave the boy there would open him to subversion from the prevailing Calvinistic atmosphere of the place. In April 1686 he

arrived at Margate at night and departed for Scotland in the company
of Lochiel after several audiences with the King, who agreed to write
asking for his release from Russian service.

In Scotland the Duke of Gordon, at that time Governor of Edinburgh
Castle, was gracious, and Patrick then went north to his affairs in
Aberdeenshire. He had made the acquaintance of the lawyer 1st Earl of
Aberdeen's father, George Gordon, in London during his visit of 1666
and describes their meeting with other friends when 'wee mad merry,
remembring ffriends, till neer midnight'. Now, on this visit to
Aberdeen, he consulted his exalted kinsman, already retired as Lord
High Chancellor, about his property. At that time it was not practical
to be an absentee owner if you were a small man, so the bulk of the land
was made over to Patrick's son, reserving to himself a small portion of
the ground and some money as a fallback for himself and his wife. Lord
Aberdeen gave him the full weight of his professional advice; Patrick
also met Lady Aberdeen in the town and only 'mad merry' with the
Earl Marischal – head of the Keith family – after the Aberdeens had
gone home. He had already visited Lord Aberdeen at his House of
Kelly, makes no mention of its condition forty years after its sacking,
'had large discourse of many things, and spoke at length of my own
particular'. Both soldier and lawyer must have come to the real point of
the conversation without too much formal dancing round the subject,
or of resorting to merrymaking. Patrick rode away next day to visit the
neighbouring laird of Schivas, crossed the River Ythan by boat but got
soaked in 'a very great raine' once across this modest river.

After seeing other relations and friends and receiving a civic welcome
in Aberdeen he set sail for the Baltic and arrived back in Moscow on 1
September 1686. Galitzin was displeased by his repeated requests to
the Regent Sophia for release, so it was back to the dreary campaign
against the Turks and the Crimean Tatars. This was at one time active,
at another called off, and Gordon was able to spend a good deal of time
with the young Peter. Whether the Tsar's talent for great joyful bouts of
drunkenness in low company had yet seized him, and if so whether
Patrick was required, willingly or no, to join in, is not recorded. Patrick
was not slow with a bottle, but may have been less inclined for low
company. Russian society was still in a state of oriental mediaevalism,
and it is a tribute to the impecunious son of a minor Aberdeenshire laird
that he was able to rise so high amongst people so strongly disliking
change and distrusting foreigners. Peter was yet too young to shake
them out of their stodgy conservatism.

By 1689 there was trouble in Moscow arising from a different quarter. The Regent Sophia was determined to keep the reins of government and, afraid of her younger brother Peter, ordered in August the Streltsi (the imperial Russian guard formed by Ivan IV in 1568) to march on Peter's residence and seize him. Peter, warned in time, fled to Troitsa, away from Moscow, and sent word to the troops to join him. His orders were countermanded by Sophia, and he then appealed to the foreign officers, stating that his life was threatened. Patrick showed the message to Galitzin, who laughed at his fears, saying that he would consult Sophia. On hearing this Patrick decided to go to Troitsa, his brother officers joining him, and four days later Peter entered Moscow in triumph. Galitzin was banished, Sophia confined in a convent, and the imbecile Ivan resigned the throne in favour of his younger brother. Peter the Great was on his way.

General Gordon, now fifty-four, naturally was in high favour with the young Tsar who owed him his accession, for it appears that it was due to Patrick's influence and arguments that the other officers supported him in responding to Peter's appeal. Nothing of much consequence occurred during the next three years, the new government being engaged in consolidation. In April 1694 he accompanied the Tsar to Archangel and, acting as Rear-Admiral of the fleet, made a voyage along the west coast of the White Sea. In 1695 he took part in the siege of Azov but the affair was badly conducted and two assaults, made against his advice, were repulsed so that the siege was raised. In June 1696 Azov was again besieged and, through his advice to push forward a rampart of earth overtopping the town walls, it fell by the end of the month. This was the real beginning of Tsar Peter becoming the Great, for it was the first victory ever gained by the Russians over the Turks. In addition to other awards for a famous victory, Patrick gained an estate with ninety serfs. In 1697, when the Tsar set out on his travels through Western Europe, General Patrick was left as second to the general-in-chief of military affairs. In June 1698 some Streltsi companies that had grievances broke out in mutiny; he marched on them and by skilful tactics forced their surrender after they had refused his offers to look into their complaints. A bloody suppression followed. He received the thanks of the Tsar, who had returned hurriedly on hearing of the outbreak, and this was the last service Patrick was able to render, for his health began to fail and by the following summer he was too weak to leave his bed. He died on 29 November 1699 in Peter's presence by his bedside, and was accorded a state funeral attended in person by the Tsar. Peter finally abolished the Streltsi in 1704.

To have lived into his sixty-fifth year was not a great achievement by the traditional standards of the Gordons, but is remarkable in view of the frequency with which he was wounded in the earlier part of his career. Certainly his portrait does not show a man who had endured the rigours of Aberdeenshire fare (pretty primitive in that era) in his youth, and the starvation of the Swedes. Certainly at that time Russian food was not all 'unsophisticated cavear'. He was remembered by his hosts, who for some reason held celebrations in his honour a few years before the Second World War.

In 1699, the year of Patrick's death, or in 1700, his elder daughter Katherine Elizabeth, already a widow, married Alexander Gordon of Auchintoul, the eldest son of another Roman Catholic laird of a property near Banff. A later part of his story is tinted with the romance of his having taken a prominent part in the Jacobite Rising of 1715. He was born in 1669, and after attending a country school he was sent at fourteen to complete his education in Paris, his family circumstances allowing for this richer outlet than that forced upon his future father-in-law at about the same age. The Glorious Revolution of 1688 caused him to become a cadet in one of the companies raised at the wishes of James VII and II to assist in the French attacks on Catalonia. Although he was given a captain's commission in the French army by Louis XIV, he returned home and stayed for a year or two with his father. The Auchintoul family lived, however, under a cloud of disapproval and he again went abroad in 1692–3, this time to Russia, where he at once became acquainted with General Patrick Gordon.

His first Russian commission was not due to Patrick's influence but to his own extraordinary behaviour. He was present at a wedding feast where he was so angered by some of the young men present speaking contemptuously of all foreigners and of Scotsmen in particular that he raised his fists to one of them, whereupon five others came to their friend's assistance, but Alexander beat them off so thoroughly that they bore the marks of his punches for some time. A complaint was made against him to Tsar Peter, who sent for him. When he had heard Alexander's account of what had happened, the roisterous young giant characteristically said: 'Well, Sir, your accusers have done you justice in allowing that you beat six men. I also will do you justice,' and thereupon gave him a major's commission, followed very soon by a lieutenant-colonelcy. In 1696 he was present with General Gordon at the successful capture of Azov.

At the disastrous defeat of the Russians by the Swedes at Narva in 1700, Alexander was taken prisoner. No exchange having been arranged by 1704 he wrote in desperation to the Earl of Seafield, Lord High Chancellor of Scotland, hoping for Queen Anne's intervention on his behalf:

> No doubt your Lordship can well remember the memorable passage of raising the siege of Narva in November an. 1700 where I had command of a regiment of Russes. Would to God they had been of my own countreymen. Then haply our ennimies had not bought their victory so cheap; but so it was finding myself abandoned by them and slightly wounded, many of our generall officers shewing me the way, I submitted on tearms which I thought would have been accompanied with a totall liberty for to goe off for Moscovy or at least a treatment more becoming a cavalier, to be a prisoner att large, suffered abroad on paroll; but instead of this I have ever since been confind to my lodgings under a guarde, and have rarely or never leave to take the air out of doors . . .

It was not until 1707 that the Swedes agreed to an exchange for a Livonian, Livonia being still in Swedish hands. In September of that year he presented himself to the Tsar, and was swiftly appointed first Brigadier and later Major-General. He was given the command, or was associated with the command, of a series of key engagements against the Swedes and those Polish forces which allied themselves with the Swedes, and added to success against this combination a drive into Hungary, which obliged the Polish Prince Lubomirsky to retire to Vienna. He was next ordered into Transylvania to assist Prince Rakoczy, Francis II of Transylvania, who was in rebellion against the Austrians. This Prince of Transylvania, evidently a less mercurial figure than his weird predecessor during the Thirty Years War, Gabor Bethlen, so liked Alexander that he asked successfully for his services until 1711, and on Gordon's departure in that year for Poland presented him with several tuns of the best Tokay. Alexander arrived in Poland to learn that his father had died the year before, and he was allowed to resign his commission in the Russian service and return to Scotland, bringing with him several hogsheads of the delightful Tokay.

He was served heir to the family property of Auchintoul and set about improving the house, living meanwhile partly in Edinburgh, partly in Aberdeen. He had no intention of again going abroad. In June 1715 he was summoned to Gordon Castle by Lord Huntly, who succeeded his father as 2nd Duke of Gordon the following year, 'to concert methods what they are to do afterwards', as it is expressed in *Stuart Papers*. In August he attended the Earl of Mar at Braemar, where on 6 September the Jacobite Standard was raised. Alexander was sent to the Western Highlands, where he mustered 4,000 men, unsuccess-fully attacked Fort William, showed himself at Inverary to give Argyllshire Jacobites a chance to join him, made his way to Perthshire and on 13 November commanded the centre of the first line at the Battle of Sheriffmuir, which broke through the government troops but alas, to no avail. After the disastrous defeat he accompanied the Chevalier, or Old Pretender, son of James VII and II, also called James, and the remnants of his army to Montrose, where the unhappy Stuart who had never been King set sail for renewed exile in February 1716, leaving Alexander to disperse the forces under his command quietly in the Highlands, where himself also sought refuge.

By July 1716 he had arrived at Roscoff in Brittany from Uist, two months before the Jacobite packet *Hope* arrived to take off those whose absence from Scotland was now a necessity of life. After stopping first at Avignon and then at Toulouse, where he had a little grange, he was strangely and unjustly accused of sacrilege by some French rivals jealous of his success as a horse dealer. He arrived at Bordeaux in 1719, in time for the proposed invasion of Scotland from Glenshiel far away in the North West, by Loch Duich and the Sound of Sleat. When the Spanish ships that formed the vanguard of this attack were blown to smithereens off the castle of Eilean Donan, Major-General Gordon conveniently found he was too ill to follow in one of the two Swedish ships that were due to take part in this venture, and remained in France, refusing an offer of a lieutenant-generalship in the Spanish service.

He was, of course, under attainder, but in 1720 the House of Lords ruled that his attainder was invalid since it had been made out in 1716 in the name of Thomas Gordon, probably mistaking him for the admiral of that name in the Russian service whose story follows. Nevertheless he prudently remained in France until 1727, when he felt it safe to return home, since the Hanoverian King had 'the universal consent and approbation of the people'. He crossed from Boulogne and quickly settled at Auchintoul, becoming a burgess of Banff in 1728 and interesting himself in local affairs. His wife, Katherine of Auch-leuchries, died in 1739, their children having all died young, and he married secondly Margaret, a daughter of Sir Thomas Moncreiffe of that Ilk, by whom there were no children. She lived on until 1788. He busied himself founding a new village – Aberchirder – and with the writing of his *Life of Peter the Great*, published at Aberdeen in 1755 four years after his death. He took no active part in the 1745 rising, being then seventy-six, but there was much communication with those who

54

were active at that time.

General Patrick Gordon's nephew Thomas, a sailor, had his first experience of the sea in 1693 in the merchant vessel *Margaret* of Aberdeen, probably in connection with the Holland trade. He later transferred to the Scots' Navy, in which he served with sufficient distinction to be appointed a captain by 1704. In the following year Queen Anne requested the Treasury to reward him suitably, out of the war prizes taken by him, for faithful service and 'good behaviour'. The prizes in question concerned a Dutch ship bound from the Canaries with a cargo of wine and equipped with French papers. His capture of this ship was the subject of a diplomatic wrangle so late as 1714. In 1707 the English Admiralty took over the navy of Scotland, and Thomas was lucky in that his captaincy was made to date from 1703. He did, however, have doubts, which he expressed to the Earl of Erroll as hereditary High Constable, about taking the oath of abjuration to be imposed on all officers in consequence of the Union, but thought better of quitting the service and going to France. In 1715–16 he refused to take the oath of allegiance and was promptly dismissed. Being a nephew of General Patrick Gordon of Auchleuchries, and acquainted with Alexander of Auchintoul, his Jacobite sympathies cannot be doubted.

He went to Holland, being already a fluent speaker of Dutch, and was certainly in touch with Peter the Great very quickly, for in November 1716 the Earl of Mar, according to the *Stirling-Home-Drummond-Moray Papers*, wrote to him:

> I hope you have got [a letter] I wrote to you the 21st October, in which I told you the pleasure Mr Brown [Prince James] had in the assurances you gave him by our friend of Mr Buckley's [the Tsar's] good intentions towards him, and how reddy he would be to do all that he possiblie can to cultivate that friendshipe betwixt Buckley and him which may certainly tend to both there advantage.

Mar was a great one for codes and code names, which probably deceived nobody. He was not the only one to devise ciphers. During the preparations for the 1715 rising Major-General Gordon of Auchintoul had been variously referred to as 'The Skipper', 'Dr Anderson', and 'Mr Gilbert'. 'Mr Buckley's' response to Thomas's overture was to commission him to attract naval officers from England to join the Russian service. Perhaps it was easiest for Thomas to do this in Jacobite circles in Paris, where, however, he was not greatly approved of. Mar was informed by Ogilvy that the latter's cousin considered Thomas an empty, airy nobody – a windbag we would say – and Ogilvy was of much the same opinion. It appeared that Thomas had put on airs to Ogilvy, announced that he was the 'famous' Captain Gordon and expected a frigate to be waiting for him. Ogilvy advised the Earl of Mar to observe him narrowly. Perhaps he was not a typical sailor, who is traditionally not talkative; perhaps he was the victim of those Jacobite courtiers who found it agreeable to busy themselves being disagreeable to each other and doing little else, whereas the famous captain was bent on action. This soon came his way, for in 1717 Tsar Peter appointed him a captain commander in the Russian navy.

Success came more quickly to Thomas than it had done to his uncle Patrick. Both men were in it to make their fortune, and Thomas rose quickly to command the battleship *St Catherine* in 1718, and later to take a squadron of six ships on cruise in the Baltic to train the crews and keep a watch on the Swedish enemy's movements. In 1719 he was promoted to Rear-Admiral and enjoyed a salary fixed at 600 roubles per annum. In 1721 he was in command of the Kronstadt squadron consisting of six battleships, three frigates and two smaller ships. The Tsar's liking for him excited the jealousy of some of his contemporaries and, at a banquet attended by the Tsar, a violent altercation broke out between Thomas and Rear-Admiral Sievers, who was Danish. The details of this row are confused, but Thomas does seem to have been very pompous in accusing Sievers of not consulting him, of handing out the best jobs to Danes and Dutchmen, and leaving Thomas's men so wretchedly provided they must inevitably suffer should they be ordered out to sea. General-Admiral Apraxin tried to interrupt and then, failing to restore calm, tried to persuade the Tsar to stop enjoying the row. The ensuing conversation, in Russian, obliged Thomas to keep quiet, for he did not understand a word of the language, and Sievers did. The General-Admiral took Sievers's part and declared his view that Gordon and his associates were fugitives from justice in their own land and were now trying to cause divisions in Russia. What a mercy that the gallant Scotchman could not understand all this. Count Apraxin probably knew that Thomas had been in receipt of letters from Jacobites in France over a long period of time. The Tsar eventually threatened everybody with the loss of their heads if the row led to any damage through maladministration. Perhaps they were all more than a little tipsy. Later Peter tried to effect a reconciliation, but the two rear-admirals continued to dislike each other. Peter continued to appreciate Thomas, however, and at the end of the year 1721 promoted him to

Vice-Admiral. This was after peace had been signed between Russia and Sweden.

In 1724 he was appointed Acting Commander-in-Chief at Kronstadt. In 1725, the year of Peter the Great's death, he investigated a strike at the Sestroretsky Works (one may imagine the word 'investigate' to be a euphemism) and in November was invested with the Order of St Alexander Nevsky, with the Red Ribbon. He was promoted Admiral in 1727 and appointed Governor of Kronstadt. He retired from this post after a few months, the succession to Tsar Peter being a bit wobbly, to say the least, but took up the governorship again in 1733, the Empress Anna having consolidated her power, and he received as a hereditary freehold estate the Delegate's House at Kronstadt. Thus he was settled for the rest of his life. In 1734 he was sent with a large fleet to Danzig, which the Poles had besieged with French naval and military help. The Russian land forces aided by Saxons could not dislodge them, but the mere appearance of Admiral Gordon's fleet from Kronstadt, and the bombardment of a fort outside the city, were enough. General Keith*, writing to him in February 1735, assured the Admiral that all the Poles he had spoken to were certain that the city's surrender was entirely due to the appearance of his ships.

News of this achievement travelled quickly to Aberdeen, because there was always much traffic of merchandise between the two cities, and he was made an honorary burgess of Aberdeen on 30 June 1736, with the resounding encomium 'from his early years a most worthy citizen of Aberdeen; that this same brave man, when in the British Navy, strenuously defended the commerce and ships of this city from pirates and enemies of every kind; and that he being on account of his great valour deservedly promoted to the highest honours by the Empress of Russia, still befriends this city'. During the remaining years of his life more roubles flowed in, and after his death in March 1741 770 roubles were due to him for salary. The Admiralty desired to know whether this should be paid to his children, who wished to visit Scotland, together with 1,070 roubles outstanding of his allowance for entertainment and expenses in connection with his office. Surprisingly the Russian Household Department approved release of the money.

Thomas was twice married; first to an Elphinstone, second to Margaret Ross. This second wife died in 1721, and was buried beside the unwilling nun, the former Regent Sophia. One son also predeceased

*His career was truly international. From being a colonel in Spanish service from 1719 to 1728, he graduated to a generalship with the Russians between 1728 and 1747, when he switched to Prussia as a field marshal under Frederick II and was killed in action, unmarried, in 1758.

him, the second returned to St Petersburg as a merchant, and died only in 1806. Two daughters married in St Petersburg: the elder, Anna, to Sir Henry Stirling of Ardoch, the other to an English resident in Russia called Elmsal.

As indicated above, the Jacobites continually tried to persuade him to assist in their proposed descent on Great Britain, and there are recorded nine letters from the Pretender himself, even to the point of sending him in 1729 his own and his son's portraits. Admiral Gordon knew better than to respond to these overtures, however; 1,000 roubles in the hand with annual regularity was worth more than plotting and planning with people who, he knew, did not especially like him. More practically, he did write to Scotland at the Tsar's request in 1718–19 to find two men 'that knows how to find stone cole by the marks they find on the surface of the earth'. The only response to this by the clever Scotsmen was to offer Tain marble, and to invite the Tsar to send some 'knowing men' to test it so that 'His Majesty might make a better bargain by taking the quarries for a term of years until his great palace was finished'.

This character of intercourse is a pointer to the ending of the era of the great mercenaries. Here was a great admiral approaching the height of his career being asked to fix a bargain of trade in lumps of stone, even though they be marble rather than coal. Later in the century commerce, through the early onset of the industrial revolution, grew at such a rate that there must have been many more outlets for younger sons of landed families than the traditional Baltic trade and ventures to the Americas, or the alternative of serving in their own or a foreign army or navy. Again, improvements in agricultural methods made the provision of young sons' portions easier to arrange by the greater reserve of value for securing a bond on the entailed property. Lastly, the growing sense of nationhood, and the formation of regiments which quickly attracted a loyalty to themselves so fierce that it exceeded even loyalty to clan or nation, reduced to a memory of history the idea that a mercenary's calling was honourable. Of course there remains the importance of all those Scotsmen from many families who played such leading roles in the battle honours of the countries which accepted their service. Many men, also, descended from those who had settled in Holland, France, Sweden, Poland, Spain and Russia especially, continued to serve those countries of which they had become citizens. But for anybody taking the initial step of leaving his homeland to become a mercenary seeking honour as well as fortune, the game was over.

4

Earls of Inheritance

William, 2nd Earl of Aberdeen (1679–1745) and his eldest son George, 3rd Earl of Aberdeen (1722–1801) line up as adults to fill the entire eighteenth century. Either succeeded with extraordinary ease in achieving the kind of domestic and familial regime he favoured: William by three marriages, each grander than the one before; George by marriage to an irresistibly pretty cook and then, having started the business of legitimate procreation by her, by assembling at least three households of mistresses. It is necessary first to describe the provenance of these remarkable men.

The Gordons of Methlick and Haddo, after spending nearly two centuries quietly accumulating land in Aberdeenshire, emerged as a family of national significance during the seventeenth century. Sir John Gordon was prominent and steadfast as a supporter of the Royalist cause against the Cromwellian Covenanters, held an important command under the head of his house, the Marquess of Huntly, and fell victim to a ruse to persuade him to surrender his fortified House of Kelly when Argyll and his men besieged it in 1644. He was brought to Edinburgh, and defended himself at his trial so skilfully that he was held on remand, in a cell known as 'Haddo's Hole' in the wall between St Giles's Cathedral and the Tolbooth, until the Edinburgh Parliament passed hurriedly a measure from which his guilt of treason could be inferred, and was executed with customary ceremony at the Mercat Cross on 19 July 1644. This is an early taste of retrospective legislation.

His son George, born in 1637, was therefore seven when his father became one of the first of many such victims. He was the second boy. He entered King's College, Aberdeen, in 1655. In 1657 General Monck, in charge of the Commonwealth forces of occupation, issued an order that Lady Gordon and her brood were not to be molested, and that the House of Kelly should be no further despoiled. The family was of necessity living in Aberdeen. The General also gave permission for George to travel to France. He stayed in Aberdeen, however, to take his master's degree in 1658 and became a professor the day after he ceased to be a student. He resigned his post at King's College in 1663, three years after the Restoration of Charles II, to study law abroad. His elder brother died childless in 1655 and he returned in 1667 to take up his considerable inheritance of land in that part of Aberdeenshire known as Formartine and to practise in Edinburgh as an advocate. He married in 1671 Anne, heiress of a prosperous lawyer named Lockhart. In addition to her father's fortune she later acquired the wealth of an even richer Lockhart relation, also a lawyer. Crawford, an eighteenth-century apologist of the great and the good in Scotland, wrote in his *Lives of the Lords Chancellors [sic] of Scotland* that 'he never took any fee as an Advocate, tho' he had an Abundance of Clients, and many of them Persons of the first Rank in the Nation'. This posthumous encomium may be treated with some reserve. He may have acted in a few *causes célèbres* without fee, and for 'several noble Persons' with whom an amiable relationship might be of more value than money. In due course he became President of the Court of Session – comparable to the English Lord Chief Justice – and in 1682 Lord High Chancellor of Scotland. The appointment of a mere gentleman and lawyer to this office infuriated the ancient nobility who had monopolized it for so long. Besides, those with Civil List pensions could not draw them from the exchequer without his signature. In the same year he was created Earl of Aberdeen with subsidiary honours. For two years all went well. In London he had told the King that in Scotland he got the character of a Whig, and in England of a Papist; he was neither of them, he said, but a true orthodox Protestant. Such a remark was as soon likely to make him enemies as friends in Scotland. It was to the Duke of York, the King's brother, that everybody in Scotland looked for preferment, and Aberdeen found himself at a disadvantage when the 1st Duke of Queensberry, over some matter of procedure on state business, successfully complained about Aberdeen's methods to the Duke of York. There was also, at that time, a move to penalize men for their wives' non-attendance at church, as well as their own, and to this Aberdeen objected. This intensified the quarrel between Queensberry and Aberdeen, who thus lost the duke's patronage. Later it was revealed that Queensberry and Perth had between them raised £27,000 for the Duchess of Portsmouth to use her influence to get rid of Aberdeen.

It was allowed to appear that he resigned over the issue of the proposed fines; he was in fact dismissed. None of the parties to this dispute – the King, his brother, Queensberry, Aberdeen and the Earl of Perth, who succeeded Aberdeen as Chancellor – was a Presbyterian. All of them, except Aberdeen, favoured any measure that would bring money into the treasury. Perth, in particular, was of the opinion that the Presbyterians 'could not be governed, but with the extremity of rigour'. Aberdeen dismantled his Edinburgh house and must have lived thereafter at Kelly, probably in some discomfort. Despite Monck's leniency it was, after all, one of the ruins Cromwell knocked about a bit through the agency of Argyll. As shown in chapter 3, the Russian General Patrick Gordon twice visited him there. The lawyer Earl advised his émigré kinsman on the disposition of his inheritance of Auchleuchries, and surviving correspondence from Patrick, written after his return to Muscovy, indicates gratitude beyond the elaborate deference of the time. It may be safely assumed that for this kinsman, who, despite his handsome pay as a general, was far from rich, the Earl of Aberdeen did advise without fee. The early papers of the Haddo family did not survive the sacking of Kelly in 1644, and the 1st Earl's papers, and very nearly himself and his wife, were burnt in the 1680s when his house in Aberdeen caught fire. Letters to him published by the Spalding Club in 1851 are, therefore, fragmentary survivals.

Later, Aberdeen refused the oath of allegiance to William and Mary and for this *lèse-majesté* was imprisoned in Edinburgh Castle, where the Earl of Leven and Melville was Governor. He had no difficulty in swearing allegiance to Queen Anne. He seldom attended the Scottish Parliament and took no part in the final proceedings which led to its extinction in the Treaty of Union of 1707, although as a young politician he had advocated an ill-considered plan of union. In 1705–6 he certainly did not oppose union, much to the annoyance of ancient friends and former political colleagues. In that same year of 1707 his wife Anne, who had brought him so much Lockhart money, died. In 1708 he secured for William, his eldest surviving son, the seat of Aberdeenshire in the Commons House of Parliament at Westminster. In this year William, Lord Haddo married a daughter of the Earl of Leven and Melville, the same who had been governor of Edinburgh Castle whilst his father was imprisoned there. William's parliamentary election was quickly disallowed on the grounds that, as the eldest sons of Scottish peers had had no place in the Edinburgh Parliament, so it should be at Westminster. The real reason had more to do with Lord

Haddo's well suspected Jacobite sympathies. William's first marriage lasted little longer, his wife dying in 1709 leaving him only a daughter.

At the time that his father had put him forward for the parliamentary seat and before his election was disallowed, an anonymous wag, not the greatest versifier of his age, penned the following lines:

> *To the Friends of the Rt. Hon. Lord Haddo*
> Rouse, gentlemen, townsmen all, arouse
> Lord Haddo's come your Freedom to espouse
> Behold him hear him, He, the Man,
> Who will support you, deny it if you can,
> In Freedom's cause, stand firm, be bold
> He is a Patriot not lukewarm or cold
> If artful Man with venial intrust
> Attempts frustration of your Cause, so just,
> Come forward then, Join Haddo, Heart in Hand
> As Champion in so just a Cause
> Long may he shine with Honour, and Aplause.

Still under thirty, William the widower must now have decided to go in for dynastic politics, a dangerous occupation at any time, rather than to seek a second wife at once. Like many second-generation grandees he was a thumping snob, but he was not yet a great catch. His father, although retired from all public activity, was still busy increasing his estate, and perhaps William was kept on short commons. The outlet for his political leanings was the 23rd Earl of Mar, a representative peer of Scotland at Westminster since the Union of 1707, and a near contemporary. Mar had the love of conspiracy so strongly implanted that by 1710 he had sent William a list of officers of state, peers and MPs, each numbered as if for a simple code. In a sequence of letters starting in 1709 he indicates men at Westminster who were 'safe'. Except for a couple of innocuous letters from Haddo to Mar, written early in their correspondence, none of William's side of the correspondence has survived. In the reverse direction fifteen of Mar's letters have been preserved for us by William. Queen Anne died on 1 August 1714; already suspicious fingers were pointing at men who viewed the Hanoverian succession with distaste. Mar had been appointed a Secretary of State in 1713, and was not without influence. A warrant was out for Lord Haddo by 7 August; Mar expressed his vexation and by 10 August the Lords Justices had made inquiries about the warrant, and the tension was relieved. On 7 September Mar wrote to the Earl of

Aberdeen from Whitehall about the election of the sixteen Scottish representative peers. The letter is not in his own hand: it is beautifully scripted and the clerkly purity of the English is not his. Despite the accession of George I he still had ambition at Westminster:

> Some people seem resolved to endeavour to have some of us who were in the Queen's Service secluded at this Election, but I hope that the majority of the Lords will not think that a ground of objection among us, and that we have done nothing undeserving of the Trust the Peers put in us, but done what was in our Power for the service of Our Country.

Mar was not only expecting re-election by his fellow Scottish peers to serve a further term at Westminster; he was hoping to continue as a Secretary of State, and appears to have made overtures to the King's advisers to this end. They would have none of it; hence the tone of his last letter from London to William, Lord Haddo, dated 23 December 1714:

> My dear Lord,
> I had the pleasure of yours of the 14th some days ago, by which I understood you was going north [from Edinburgh] I hope upon a good design.
>
> There is great expectation here of what you are to do in Scotland at this time. Now is the time or never, and I assure you some who were long of changing their mind of what they were once fond of, are now perfectly cured and will stick at nothing that can get a riddance. There ought to be good advice taken about the way of doing this and I doubt not but those who have it will take it.
>
> They say now that the writs for the Parliament are to be immediately after the Holy Dayes, so I fancie the time of our meeting will be about the end of June, and I hope before that time things will be so far advanced that it will not be in the power of any f——t [faintheart?] to put a stope to it. We are now in for it. Let us act like men, wch is all I'll now trouble you with so my D. L^d. Adieu.

Mar went on to act like a man the following year. His impulsive, ill-thought-out 'raising of the standard' at Braemar in September 1715 led quickly to the untidy disaster of the Battle of Sheriffmuir in November, and to his attainder. William, Lord Haddo, stayed put. Some form of warrant was still available to be issued in his case, as a postscript referring to it, in Mar's letter of 23 December 1714, indicates: 'Your lo'p may be sure I shall do what's in my power, tho' at present that's not much.' What he could do, and did, was to destroy all incriminating correspondence from his friends. This, as much as his own inaction, probably saved Haddo from grave trouble. Mar, known to his many detractors as 'Bobbing John', was incautious and indiscreet, but maintained influence in the Old Pretender's exiled court, even to the extent of suggesting the marriage of Prince Charles Edward to a daughter of the Regent Orléans.

In 1716 Haddo married again. His bride was Lady Susan Murray, daughter of the 1st Duke of Atholl. Susan's mother was a daughter of Anne, Duchess of Hamilton, and her Douglas consort, created Duke of Hamilton: a most satisfying arrangement. Meanwhile his old father, the 1st Earl of Aberdeen, was still increasing his estate. He bought the substantial farmland of Cairnbrogie in 1714, and in 1717 he acquired from the Forbes family the barony and Castle of Tolquhon, thus bringing his mother's home into the family. In 1720 he died in his eighty-third year. William was now 2nd Earl of Aberdeen.

In 1721 and in 1722 William secured election as a Representative Peer of Scotland; he had a son and heir, and a daughter, Catherine, by his wife Susan, who died in childbed in 1725. In 1727 he was not re-elected as a Representative Peer, having meantime taken a decided part against all government measures. His contemporary the 2nd Duke of Gordon agreed that William should take one of his daughters as his third wife, so long as he bought a suitable property to be entailed on the issue of the marriage. Hearing of this Lady Eglinton, a caustic dowager, who was a connexion of William's by marriage, wrote to a friend: 'It disturbs me not. No doubt his ambitious vews will give his fancie wings. Take care to lope them as he may soar quite out of reach.' The Duke died in 1728, and in 1729 William, in his fiftieth year, married Lady Anne Gordon, who was not yet nineteen. He now looked round for a suitable property to keep to his bargain with his late father-in-law. He had already begun to acquire property on a large scale in West Aberdeenshire since his father's death, taking advantage of the very large Lockhart fortune he had inherited. The only house of any consequence in that part of the country had once been the home of the Coutts family, who had long since sold Auchtercoull House to set up as bankers, and this was far too modest for his 'ambitious vews'.

It came to his knowledge that Fyvie Castle was for sale. This had for more than one hundred years belonged to the earls of Dunfermline, who had added a tower to an already extensive castle. The last earl had had the misfortune, however, to be on the Stuart side at the Battle of Killiecrankie. This was foolish of him as he had hitherto supported the

Prince of Orange, being himself a Protestant. He was attainted and his estates forfeited. He fled to Paris, where he died in 1694 in penury, the jostling Catholics round the Stuart court in exile not even contriving for him Christian burial. There was no heir, and those who represented the forfeited property agreed in 1733 to sell to William, 2nd Earl of Aberdeen and his new brother-in-law, Cosmo, 3rd Duke of Gordon. For a knockdown price of £26,000 between them Cosmo got the lands of Urquhart and the valuable fishing on the River Spey, and William took as his share Fyvie Castle and its three or four thousand acres. It is very close to Haddo and that was a convenience, for he was now building a fine mansion to replace the House of Kelly, to the designs of William Adam. He had been persuaded to this course by Sir John Clerk of Penicuik, a paragon whose advice in matters of taste and culture was sought by many. His taste was indeed impeccable, and Adam, father of the more famous brothers, was renowned for his skill in designs carried out in the manner of Palladio's villas of the Venetian countryside. Adam appears never to have visited the site, the work and its supervision being left to the master mason John Baxter.

Baxter's correspondence with Sir John Clerk shows that Earl William was not easy to work for, did not see the need to pay promptly, and at one stage must have believed Adam's complaints about Baxter. It is not possible to disentangle the cause of the quarrel. This was overcome during the second season's work on the new house. Baxter wrote to Clerk in July 1733:

> My lord is better to worke to this year then he was the last . . . he seis plainly now that the Story Mr Adams advanced to him is false and without foundation for the house stands weill without Crack . . . but if his lordship be not generous to me for my two years worke I never intend to return to the north again.

In September 1734 he made sure he got his wages for that season's work 'for when I lett it by two years unpaid he thinks it a great soum'. All ended well after further ups and downs, including the replacement of inferior timber by first-class wood from Scandinavia. William approved Baxter's carving of his coat of arms to be placed above the entrance doorway. It is easy to sneer, with Lady Eglinton, at William's ambitions, but much of his personal correspondence reveals an attractive and naive anxiety to do the right thing. He was very much a plain provincial magnate who drove a hard bargain. There is something endearing about a letter he wrote to Sir John Clerk as work on the house was reaching its final stages. Right from the start he had made Baxter alter Adam's plans. These were alterations of convenience in the plan of rooms; he felt confident of his decisions in that respect. The aesthetics of the roof line, however, demanded advice, so he wrote from Edinburgh to Sir John on 30 December 1735: 'In this Town Mr Adams is making out a Sketche of my Rooffe, which I beg leave to say that I may have your Approbation of it, if you think it deserves it, or otherways will hope you will be pleased to give your directions how you will have it done.' He refers to Sir John's past good advice and ends: 'please let me have it as to the Rooffe which will make me and my operators quite easie and at a certainty'.

Although many of William's letters are addressed at this time from Kelly or Haddo – he varied the form at will – he and his young Countess Anne were probably living at Fyvie when they were not wintering in Edinburgh. There was also a town house in Aberdeen. Countess Anne's sister Lady Elizabeth Gordon, calling at Haddo in July 1738, wrote to William in Edinburgh about the poor appointments at Haddo. She sent a list of things wanted: 'for instance there is scarce a gret, tongs or shufel. There is not one looking glass excepting one or two above the chimneys and several other things which I will not trouble to mention.' This Lady Betty was a handful of trouble, and already was heading for disaster. She had formed a passion for the chaplain to her brother the Duke of Gordon, the Reverend John Skelly, and whilst in London with her mother Henrietta, Duchess of Gordon, contrived to write to him, signing herself variously 'E.G.', 'Fidelia', 'your constant Arabela'. She wrote in November 1737:

> We were not presented to the King and Queen until the Monday after we came. The Queen stayed about ½ hour in the Drawing Room and I am sure talked 25 minutes of it to Her Grace and made her prodigious compliments and asked her 100 odd questions but there was one I resolved to remember which concern'd Lord Aberdeen. After saying to the Dutchess how dos my good friend Lord Aberdeen etc. I hear his lady is a very prittie woman, but I think my Lord Aberdeen should not call her wife he should call her Grand Daughter, which was prodigiously good in the Queen and I own I'd almost burst out laughing.

This was Queen Caroline's last Drawing Room, for a few days later she fell ill, and died on 20 November 1737.

It was not long before Lady Betty's mother, who was a daughter of the Earl of Peterborough, received anonymously a packet of love letters, accompanied by a letter in a careful copperplate, saying 'the enclosed having fallen into my hands I thought it my duty to send it to Your Grace'. That was received in July 1738. In September Jean Perth wrote furiously to the Duchess of Gordon that it had been 'given out that my Johnny was privately married to Lady Betty Gordon yr. Grace's daughter'. Whoever had 'given out' had got the wrong Johnny, because John Skelly, who had by now left Gordon Castle and was in Newcastle, where he had family connexions, was busy writing in July 1738 to Lady Betty at Gordon Castle, variously describing her as 'my sweetest Eloisa', 'my inexpressibly beloved Spouse', and signing himself 'Till Death most faithfull Husband'. Undoubtedly a handfast marriage had taken place. Later a secondary ceremony, in conformity with English practice, took place in Newcastle before proper witnesses. Her brother Cosmo's wrath knew no bounds and he wrote to William in January 1739 that Betty was 'the most ungrateful wretch to you and to me . . . more fit for Bedlam than anything else. The Lord pity her deplorable condition.' He made sure that Skelly had no financial advantage from the misalliance. Duchess Henrietta's English relations were of one view: 'She has all along been acting the hypocrite with your son.'

She had been indeed: in April 1738 she had written a most ingratiating letter to Cosmo: 'Upon some occasions I have been able to vindicate you and altho' I am very sensible I have got many enemies to myself by it I think it was so much my duty.' A month later she wrote: 'Surely a young man like you cannot live without a Wife to keep House. I must incline to say Her Grace and I differs much about you as about other things.' She offered to keep house for him at Gordon Castle meanwhile 'and prevent servants from imposing or cheating you'. They were not a small family. Duchess Henrietta had four sons and seven daughters, and had brought them all up strictly to impose upon them adherence to the House of Hanover, in opposition to the tradition of her husband's forebears and his own inclinations.

At the same time that Lady Betty's disgrace was looming, another match of a different character was cautiously coming to maturity. Duke Cosmo used 'the trifling gift of a handkerchief' to his brother-in-law William, 'the first of its kind made and now the tip top fashion', as an excuse to write showing annoyance that an earlier letter of his to William had been seen by his sister Countess Anne. The letter 'was in relation to her and the rest and which I never Dream't could have come to her ears'. Where Betty was flighty Anne was a nosey parker, for in

December 1739 Cosmo writes from the Canongate, Edinburgh, to William's daughter by his second marriage, Lady Catherine Gordon – 'Katrine' he calls her –:

> Madam, Tho' contrary to my inclinations this is the first letter that I ever had the Happyness to write to you because the Countess of A—— might as well her scurilous Curiosity to open and read all letters Directed for you as well as to your Worthy Father and my good sincere friend.

There follows an involved reference to honour and honesty and then: 'It is evident all bad qualitys take their rise from Dishonour and Dishonesty and from the latter, Female Curiosity is a very near Relation.' This letter and later correspondence were addressed through a third party and Cosmo declared his love for his Katrine with wordy fervour.

It has been generally accepted that Earl William was kept in ignorance of the love that was speaking its name between his daughter and his brother-in-law, but this is not true. Nor was it in any way against the laws of consanguinity that they should marry. William was keeping his son and heir George, Lord Haddo, studying in Holland at the University of Leyden, posted of the progress of the affair. He referred to it as 'Kettie's impending Marriage to the Duke of Gordon', and finally wrote from Haddo House on 7 September 1741: 'I can now acquaint you that your sister Kettie I bless God was married to the Duke of Gordon on Thursday 3 Sept. at Dunkeld; I have had letters from them both by an express acquainting me of it.' Dunkeld was Atholl property. She married from her mother's home there. In a letter to Holland in November William tells George: 'I am making ready to pay the Duke of Gordon your sister's portion.' Provincial he might be, but he was not to be caught napping over such a matter as this. Before the end of 1741 letters between Duke Cosmo and Earl William make clear that William had the Duke tied up in knots over financial affairs. He was pleased to have the same duke for brother-in-law and son-in-law, but he was not to be found to be second best over money matters. Cosmo signed himself 'Your Lop's most obedient servant and Son'. The final memorandum about the marriage contract, Catherine's uncle James, Duke of Atholl, being a party to it, is dated 23 November 1743. This delay may in part be the cause of the erroneous entry in *The Complete Peerage* that the marriage took place 'without [William's] knowledge or approval'. 'Kettie's' marriage contract stipulated that

Earl William her father infeft* her with lands worth a rental after deduction of all expenses and taxation of £800 sterling. Duke Cosmo agreed a widow's bequest of £400 sterling, one third of the household furniture 'with the exception of her parapharnalia as said is'. The contract's fourth part lays down that Cosmo 'shall instantly receive from the said William, 2nd Earl of Aberdeen . . . £2,000 sterling as a portion and provision' in satisfaction of any claim she may have had on her mother's inheritance (referring to Countess Susan, the Duke of Atholl's daughter who had died in 1725).

Now at last the busy Earl William could take his ease. Fyvie was entailed upon the heirs of his marriage to Anne; the large estates in East and West Aberdeenshire, which he had inherited and later extended to include an area round Boddam near Peterhead, were entailed upon his heir George and his successors; he had bought extensively in West Aberdeenshire centred on Tarland and the Howe of Cromar, thus becoming a neighbour of his fellow Gordon peer, the Earl of Aboyne; and two of his closest connexions were dukes. Could any man ask for more? There was a residual desire for the return of the Stuart kings, but so long ago as 1734 he had yielded to his young wife, who had written: 'my vast pleasure that you had the resolution not to comply with the strong solicitations of your Friends the Patriots upon this occasion. I'm sure so far as my Dearest has had the goodness to shune it on my account (as you may believe it would have been the greatest hardship upon me).' Even in 1741 he refers to Jacobite intrigues in his letters to George in Holland, but only hints at any active interest. More important was the drawing up of the strictest possible entail upon his remotest heirs, and the making of his will. He died in Edinburgh in March 1745, three months before Prince Charles Edward sailed from France to embark on the Forty-five. He requested that the smallest possible sum should be spent on his burial. Throughout his life he had been prudent as well as acquisitive; there had been no extravagant lashing out. From arguments with the merchants of Aberdeen over the price of meal and victuals, by bargains with powerful neighbours and the cunning exploitation of weaker ones, he had made steady progress through continuous material enlargement, and he was determined that his posterity should not let it go. He had also bankrupted a few small neighbours by letting out loans and, by timely foreclosure, acquiring their land.

When George Gordon, Lord Haddo, became 3rd Earl of Aberdeen a

*In the preferred modern spelling to 'enfeoff' means to put in possession lands or tenements in fee simple or fee-tail.

few months before his twenty-third birthday, the family he now presided over, in which his sister was married to his stepmother's brother, may have caused him to consider the world somewhat odd. Or maybe not. His years at Leyden University had possibly taught him lessons unknown to his less sophisticated father. Leyden, anti-Catholic and leaning towards a religious toleration the Spaniards had never dreamt of, was ready game for the new ideas coming out of France. Montesquieu's *Persian Letters* of 1721, the religious scepticism of Pierre Bayle, who lived in exile in Holland, probably, amongst others, had a strong appeal to the teachers of Leyden. The *Persian Letters* described the impact on two imaginary travellers from that country of the French Court, barely disguised, and its attendant *salons* where the talk was of toleration and social reform. In real life the *philosophes* were tolerated in the salons of Paris so long as their criticisms, even in conversation, were phrased with care. Thus many conflicting messages reached a circle, however restricted, which would soon spread to universities receptive of scepticism. The libertarian ideals of the *philosophes* did not dispute the rights of the owners of property, though they might accept that all men had common needs. In their optimistic theories of natural rights there was contained the seeds of libertinism in matters of sexual love. Or so it seemed. As Kingsley Martin observed in his *French Liberal Thought in the Eighteenth Century*, how people reacted to the teachings of the *philosophes* and, later, to Diderot's Encyclopaedists, was more important than what they may in fact have taught and written.

George started conventionally enough, being elected a Scottish Representative Peer at Westminster from 1747 to 1761, and he bought the lease of a spanking new house in Tilney Street, Mayfair. He had inherited his father's counting-house mentality, but with it went a cosmopolitan spirit entirely different. He extended the outlying parts of the estates in East and West Aberdeenshire, and he bought valuable lands in East Lothian at East Linton. This property included the farm called Phantassie, where the celebrated engineer and architect John Rennie was born in 1761. It was sold after Earl George's death, according to the instructions in his will.

Sometime in 1759 George, 3rd Earl of Aberdeen, set out to visit friends in Yorkshire. Arriving at Wakefield too late to travel further, he put in for the night at the Strafford Arms. He was so pleased with the mutton chops served him for his supper that he demanded to be taken to the kitchen to congratulate the cook. Thus he met Catharine Hanson, a handsome person aged twenty-nine, and immediately took her by the hand and led her to his bedchamber. The story goes that on the way back from visiting his friends the Hatfeilds, he again stayed the night at the Strafford Arms, expecting to enjoy a repetition of the first encounter with Miss Hanson. We do not have to believe everything we read, but J. W. Walker's *Wakefield: Its History and its People* clearly states that this cook, daughter of the blacksmith Oswald Hanson, entered Lord Aberdeen's bedchamber brandishing a loaded pistol and demanding marriage or his life. The compliant Earl preferred marriage, and thus came about the first English infusion of blood into the line of the Gordons of Haddo. There were two sons and four daughters of this shotgun marriage, but George was not going to deny himself the pleasures of life, which he had taken from what he had learnt at Leyden to be a man's natural right.

Whilst his Yorkshire Countess must have been kept busy with childbirth, Earl George was not slow to initiate and maintain other loving attachments. In fact it is likely that his libertarian lordship had started to exercise a man's natural rights even before his marriage in 1759. The house in Tilney Street favoured these exercises; contemporary records and chatter passed down the generations orally relate that his housekeeper there was either a sister of Catherine Hanson, or of a lady who came later into his life, Mrs Forrest. What is undoubted is that there grew up at his Mayfair house one Susan Gordon, whose letter to him of 2 March 1773 shows both an adult hand and adult sentiments.

Honored Sir,
I should not so long have deffered answering your Kind Letter had I not waited in hopes of having an opportunity to inform Peggy of your intentions but have seen nothing of her for so long a time that I fear she has accepted her Brother's invitation and is pursuing her Voyage in expectation of better Fortune than that of Servitude. Your still continuing in your intention of Visiting London makes me very happy indeed it is the only circumstance in which I distrust your promises and you must allow that I have some reason as You have often disapointed me.

There has lately been a Masquerade at the Pantheon you will hardly believe when I tell you that we saw Masks in Bow Lane you know its fashionable among the Great but I'll instantly unriddle this to your Lordship by informing you that Mrs Watkins gay Indian Brother and Sister came on purpose to exhibit themselves to us and paraded up and down our humble Apartment with great self-satisfaction no doubt pitying us poor domestic souls who were contentedly siting at home when tout le monde was at the Pantheon. I was greatly diverted by going with them to choose their

Dresses the Woman at the shop was so obsequious: 'Indeed ma'am you must have this Dress it becomes you charmingly that suits your complexion'. She told me that she should take particular pleasure in making me up a Dress to assume the Character of a Pilgrim. I told her I had made no Vows and Therefore thought that a Pilgrimage was useless. I read in the news papers some Days past that Lord John Murry was dangerously ill at Ireland an't he a relation of yours I think I remember to have heard you say so? [This must have been his mother Countess Susan's brother, who had in fact succeeded as 3rd Duke of Atholl in 1767.]

    I can say no more than that I am
Honored Sir

Your very affectionate dutiful daughter

S Gordon

This mysterious Susan seems to have remained unmarried and became important after her father's death in 1801 as one of his trustees. She must have been a lady of strong character, unafraid even as a natural daughter to reprove her father for neglecting to visit her in London more often.

 In 1775 the 3rd Earl of Aberdeen bought Cairnbulg Castle near Fraserburgh. It had passed out of the hands of the Fraser family* in 1703 and had been acquired in 1739 by Alexander Aberdein, a well-known burgess of Aberdeen, whose son sold it to Earl George. His object in making this purchase was to install Mrs Forest, by whom his son John of Cairnbulg was born in 1787. The castle appears to have been in a pretty ruinous state, the wind blows hard and cold on this north-eastern promontory of Scotland, and it is not surprising that John moved soon after his father's death to Mormond House near by. He had nine children by his wife Catherine Forbes of Craigievar, and moved eventually to Countesswells, where he died in 1861. Cairnbulg was then sold.

 A glimpse of the original purchaser's tough policy with his tenants can be seen in *The Christian Watt Papers*, where she quotes from her Granny Lascelles' written account of

> Geordie Gordon, the bad Earl of Aberdeen who lived [at Cairnbulg] for a fewe years with the English wifie, Whom he marriet her sister ... Lord Aberdeen was a go-ahead mannie who didn't lippen to the smoothe flattering tonge of Tyrant Factors but did the job himself and made a lot of siller. He gave out a lot of short, improving leases on the sides of Mormond Hill for crofters, to the backbrucking task of breaking in land from the heather.

*It was bought back into the Fraser fold only in 1934, by the 19th Lord Saltoun.

Apart from Cairnbulg, Earl George was extending the huge property left to him by his father Earl William and, following his father's drawing up of strict entails soon before his death in 1745 to make sure that the properties passed to his remotest posterity intact, George similarly drew up fresh entails in 1765, and again in 1798. His system of leasing to tenant farmers was so complex and strict that he must have had the services of tyrant factors – Cairnbulg was but a drop in his property, and very near the ocean – to oversee if not to take over fully as tacksmen. A tacksman held leases as a middleman between the proprietor in chief and the tenant and customarily enriched himself thereby. The Bad Earl would not allow much of that. Where his father had been hard, he was sharp. He needed everything he could screw out of the land and its tenants, and it is not surprising that a lost pamphlet or broadsheet characterized him as 'Lord Skinflint'. At his death in 1801 the estates were under the management of four separate factors.

His policy might yield quick returns at the expense of the poor, but the system of management employed was short-sighted, and made it impossible to improve the land. Farms were leased for nineteen years, with the right to sub-let; the rent payable in money and in produce. Principal tenants screwed up their subtenants to the maximum, but were afraid to improve the land they retained for themselves for fear of an increase in rent at the next break in the tenancy. On the Cromar estate cattle were sent thirty or forty miles away for summer grazing. In other parts of the estates green crops could not be raised for want of enclosure and because common pasturage was allowed after harvest. The minister of Tarland parish stated that if the last farthing's rent was not paid the tenant must remove at the next Whitsunday. When a tenant foresaw difficulty looming he would sell grain forward to men in the Tarland marketplace, some of whom were notaries public, payable nine months hence. These middlemen could thus grow rich on the ruin of the poor. Towards the end of the 3rd Earl's life, leases specified the number of subtenants allowed by limiting the quantity of grain they might sow. Parcels of land thus became so small that the subtenants were reduced to beggary or at the best to a very mean condition of living. No wonder his grandson and heir, the 4th Earl, momentarily thought of abandoning the properties and living as an absentee landlord.

George, the 3rd Earl, in 1752 had bought the Ellon estate, separated from his Haddo properties by the estate of Esslemont, which was half-heartedly claimed by Adam Lindsay Gordon a century later (see chapter 7). On this estate he doubtless employed the same management system as he had done on his other properties. Before dealing more fully with this we must return to Haddo House itself. Here from 1760 onwards was a young family growing up, warmed one hopes by a 'gret, tongs or shufel' in every room as recommended by their disgraced aunt Lady Betty, and provided with looking-glasses. Earl George had been a representative peer of Scotland from 1747 to 1761, which must have afforded him plenty of opportunity to be in Tilney Street, and again from 1774 to 1790. During those years dutiful daughter Susan's wish to have her father visit her more often would have been gratified. Her letter of 1773 was addressed to him at 'Haddo House, Edinburgh', so she was kept well away from too close a knowledge of his northern abode. Whether he did not seek re-election in 1761 or failed to be re-elected, is not known. His eldest son, Lord Haddo, born in January 1764, must have been unusually precocious, for he was sent by his father, under the tutelage of a Captain Livingstone, to go on the Grand Tour in 1773. Livingstone's instructions were that 'you allwise take particular care of everything that respects my son's morals and honour, these go allwise hand in hand . . . the Next thing is his health Education and Company . . . that he be constantly directed by your advice . . . and of course to account for all money to pass through your hands'. The boy wrote to his father from London 'Sunday night 1773' to say they had stayed at Hatfield the night before because it was getting too late to proceed to London. Lord Seaforth had just been robbed in the dark between Barnet and London. In the same letter Livingstone apologizes: 'We dined this day at the Star and Garter in New Bond Street. We had only a fowl boiled, some beef and a bottle of wine. The Bill came to 18 shillings which certainly was very dear. I trouble your Lordship with this detail to show you how the money goes fast away.' Comparing this figure with the excellent dinner for two at L'Etoile in Charlotte Street in the 1930s for 28 shillings, including a glass of cognac each and unlimited coffee, it makes one wonder whether Livingstone was not exaggerating and keeping the change. In due course they progressed to Italy, where Haddo soon became proficient in the language, being already well schooled in Latin, and was painted by Pompeo Batoni, whose full-length portrait of an apparently full-grown man still hangs splendidly at Haddo House. The date given for this portrait is generally 1775, but there is evidence that its true date is 1785, three years after Haddo's marriage.

In 1778 he was commissioned a captain in the Northern Fencibles, being raised by the 4th Duke of Gordon, chosen perhaps to snub

Colonel Gordon of Fyvie, raising a rival regiment. There was nothing unusual in a young nobleman becoming an army captain aged fourteen and nine months. By the time he was eighteen he had a furious row with his father over his debts, and Lord Skinflint made stringent conditions to tie him down financially as the price of settling. Haddo had to give up his house and most of his horses. He wrote to a friend complaining of his cruel treatment, and that he would have to resign from the ducal regiment and go abroad again. Instead he promptly married, at the age of eighteen, a girl no older than he, Charlotte Baird, youngest sister of General Sir William Baird – as he later became – a famous soldier of Wellington's time. Baird had entered the army at fifteen. Haddo promptly resigned his commission and started to raise a family, probably living at Haddo House with his neglected mother. Charlotte disliked her father-in-law.

The years 1786 and 1787 are, in retrospect, years of high drama for the Haddo family and for the neighbouring Gordons of Gight. In 1786, when Catherine Gordon Byron's first attempt to sell her estate to pay her husband 'Mad Jack' Byron's creditors had failed, herons, which for years had nested below the Castle of Gight, flew over to Haddo. The twenty-two year old Lord Haddo is supposed to have ordered that the birds should not be disturbed 'for the land will soon follow'. He was remembering the curse of Thomas the Rhymer:

> When the heron leaves the tree
> The laird o' Gight shall landless be.

In fact Lord Aberdeen and his factor, as described in Chapter 1, had already started negotiations for purchasing the property from the bankrupted Catherine Gordon Byron, but her advisers withdrew the sale in December 1786, the highest bid being below their figure. In 1787 Lord Aberdeen bought the castle and its estate of more than 4,500 acres for £17,850. The Gight family had been the subject of many couplets and longer jingles, but Lord Haddo either assumed the second couplet to apply only to the Gight family, or did not know it:

> At Gight three men a violent death shall dee
> And efter that the lands shall lie in lea.

For the moment all was well; Haddo, Charlotte and their young family moved to Gight, which they called Formartine House, and Charlotte went on openly disapproving of her father-in-law's manner of living.

As we have seen, the 3rd Earl had bought the estate of Ellon in 1752, and by the early 1780s had found an agreeable use for it. He had formed an attachment for a lady of charm called Penelope Dering. She came from Pett (there are villages in Kent and Sussex of that name, and the original Ordnance Survey map of 1819 gives, suitably, a Petting Grove in Kent), and there is a story that she and the Earl met first through her friendship with one of his four daughters. From this union was born first a daughter, Penelope, who did not marry, then a son, Alexander, born in 1783. His birth must have inspired the elderly Earl to rebuild Ellon House between 1784 and 1787, which thereupon gained Castle status. It is shown in a watercolour of 1841 by James Giles as a plain mansion of five storeys, with round towers ascending to cornice height. He stopped there as often as possible and it was probably more comfortable than Haddo, and certainly more agreeable than Gight, which may have been a subsidiary cause of Charlotte's disapproval. This busy Earl still found time to go to London to attend the House of Lords, and to enjoy whatever company there was at Tilney Street. He voted against Pitt's Regency Bill in the 1788–9 session and showed some foresight in doing so, because the King suddenly recovered from his mental malady and the bill had to be abandoned. The Earl ceased to be a representative peer in 1790.

At a date which cannot be judged with certainty he had set up yet another household, at Wiscombe Park in Devon. Some think that Susan Gordon was an issue of his union with an unknown lady installed at Wiscombe, but this is very unlikely since Susan was adult by 1773, living in London then, and was still in London in 1798 when the Earl made his final dispositions and appointed her one of his trustees. He had a son, Charles, at Wiscombe, who married twice. It may be he who held a commission in the East Chudleigh (2nd) Devonshire Militia, gaining a captaincy in 1809. By his first marriage he had two daughters and a son, also called Charles, who died unmarried in 1878, when the male line of the Gordons of Wiscombe Park died out.

No sooner had the Earl's back been turned on Westminster than he suddenly lost his son and heir, now installed at Formartine House with seven children after nine years of marriage. There are conflicting accounts in the family papers of exactly how Lord Haddo became in 1791 the first of the three men who 'a violent death shall dee', but all the stories have the common factor of a fall from his horse near a wellhead on the Greens o' Gight. He seems to have been able to remount the animal, which had been startled and had reared dangerously. He then collapsed and fell dead from the horse, now quietened. The second and third deaths occurred to farm servants after the castle had been left ruinous. As soon as she could arrange it, Charlotte Haddo took herself and her seven infants south to Potter's Bar, where she died in straitened circumstances in 1795. Henry Dundas, Pitt's Home Secretary and, although much the older man, a friend of the late Lord Haddo, came to the orphans' rescue and took them into his house at Wimbledon. Meantime the Earl in November 1791 named 'for tutors and curators of my grandchildren, sons and daughter of George, Lord Haddo, he not having named any' all his most imposing relations, including his cousin the Duke of Gordon, his younger son William, his half-brothers General William Gordon of Fyvie and the judicial Lord Rockville and, at the tail end, Lady Haddo, so long as she did not remarry. Dundas found this insulting to Charlotte, but maybe he was working towards extending his influence over George, the future 4th Earl of Aberdeen, who indeed, on reaching the age of fourteen in January 1798, took advantage of ancient Scotch custom by appointing his own guardians: amongst them William Pitt and Henry Dundas. The 3rd Earl in his turn indignantly announced that he wanted his grandson and heir of line to be 'partly educated in Scotland that he do not despise his own country'. Dundas had sent him to a school at Parson's Green near his home at Wimbledon, and he was destined for Harrow School, his grandfather being reluctant to pay the fees. When the sixteen-year-old Haddo entered St John's College, Cambridge, in 1800 it seems that his grandfather refused point blank to pay up.

The Earl was nearing the end of his days, but he was just as sharp over his dispositions in favour of his numerous descendants as he had always been over the letting of land. In 1798 he drew up a complex will, appointing amongst other trustees his legitimate son William, his natural daughter Susan, an advocate of Aberdeen, Alexander Crombie, who later became his successor's factor, and his son-in-law Edward Place, a Yorkshire squire who also held the lease of Haddo Farm, which is quite distinct from Haddo House and Haddo Mains Farm. The workings of his mind shine through; whilst behaving honourably towards his countess and their six younger grandchildren, whose portion was a mere £2,000 each, he was generous to his two surviving married daughters, to his surviving bachelor son William and to Penelope Dering and her children at Ellon Castle. It was an odd arrangement. William was bequeathed Ellon Castle and its plate – that is, silver – and Mrs Dering's elder son had the reversion of it should William leave no children. William was also left the much more extensive collection of plate at Haddo House. Countess Catharine was to receive a modest jointure from Haddo rents amounting to £750 a year, and a bit extra in place of her share of the household furniture. It must be assumed that she also had a right to her 'parapharnalia'. There was nothing he could do to interfere with his eldest grandson's inheritance by virtue of the entails set up by himself in 1765 in confirmation and extension of Earl William's entails of 1745. At least he could prevent his having the Haddo silver. Mrs Forrest's son John was bequeathed Cairnbulg Castle. He also was to receive the rents from outlying parts of the Haddo estate at Boddam, near Peterhead, and provision was made for his younger son by Mrs Forrest from the same source. Mrs Forrest herself was provided for and their daughter Isabella Gordon was left an annuity of £100 and a furnished house at Peterhead. Miss Susan was left £6,200 and was to receive £200 on each occasion that she visited Edinburgh or Aberdeen for meetings of the trustees. The house in Tilney Street and a piece of ground attached to it were to be sold after his death.

After settling his affairs to his satisfaction, drawing out of the estates entailed on his eldest grandson as much borrowing power as his advisers thought prudent to provide for his natural families and Charlotte's younger children, he relaxed at Ellon and there died on 13 August 1801. The trustees met at Aberdeen on 28 August and began the long process of unravelling his affairs. The legality of the late Earl's appointment of trustees and 'curators' as they are described in Scotland, and of using the entailed estates to make provision for his younger grandchildren, was at once questioned. The Lord Advocate and the Solicitor General gave their opinion in this sense. In addition, the young heir having chosen curators of his own choice at the age of fourteen in 1798, who were in several cases different people from those appointed by his grandfather in the same year, it looked as though there would be a divided and quarrelsome management of the estate for the duration of the 4th Earl's minority, if not for longer. Accordingly Miss Susan and Edward Place resigned their trusteeship. They took this step only because one of the Aberdeen advocates (not Mr Crombie) opposed the young 4th Earl's choice. They two at least wanted to avoid wrangling. Dundas at first advised the 4th Earl, who as a minor could do nothing on his own account, that the will should be contested. It soon had to be accepted that the will was good in law, however, and this was just as well, because the grounds on which it could be contested might have disadvantaged the heir's younger brothers and sister, and possibly the dowager Countess Catharine, rather than Uncle William and the natural families.

The 'bad Earl', as Christian Watt's Granny Lascelles described him, or the 'wicked Earl', as he came to be known at Haddo later in the nineteenth century, was able to dictate from the grave. Owing to the date of his death and the priority accorded to annuitants the heir of line could not, as a minor, draw any income until Whitsunday 1802, when, because of the annuities due to certain adults, there was a deficit in the estate accounts. It was not until Martinmas 1802 – Christmas Day in fact – that a small amount of money was received by the new Earl from his theoretically large inheritance. That would have pleased the old Earl. Meanwhile his grandson asked Dundas to inform the other trustees that he did not intend to continue his grandfather's policy of letting the estates upon 'grassums', the term used for the short, sublettable leases; he would gradually, as the grassums fell in, have his property divided into suitable-sized farms and encourage the tenants to improve by giving them allowances for enclosure, drainage and the building of proper farmhouses. The whole property, except the Gight estate which was not so affected, was to be professionally surveyed on instructions from the trustees. It must be recorded that the real hero of the young Earl's remaining years of minority is his uncle William. With Mr Crombie, especially, and with the professional survey, William Gordon, now of Ellon Castle, managed and advised with thoroughness and honesty. Who knows – he may even have restored to Haddo the silver bequeathed to him by his father. Younger sons have been known to carry out such acts of doing good by stealth.

The young heir had spent his first year at Cambridge giving full rein to his taste and aptitude for scholarship; not only the classical humanities, but Byzantine and Renaissance studies also were opening up a receptive mind. By the end of 1801 he was writing to friends, and to William Pitt, of his desire to travel, to visit the scenes of his studies. He had to wait. Whitsun, 1802, must have been a disappointment, but by the autumn of that year, when he knew some income would be forthcoming, he was on his way. The temporary Peace of Amiens (March 1802) made travel through France possible. Two Cambridge friends came with him, for the first part of his travels at least. Italy, Greece and Turkey, possibly farther afield, were the objectives, well beyond the confines of a Cambridge college. The nineteenth century dawned bright for the earldom of Aberdeen.

5

'They are Wise and Honourable'

Within the Gordon families there were during the second half of the eighteenth century a select number of men, closely connected though not always by blood, who became members of the House of Commons. One of them was General the Honourable William Gordon of Fyvie, eldest son of Earl William of Aberdeen by his third, ducal marriage; another was Lord George Gordon, the notorious anti-Catholic who was acquitted of constructive treason in connexion with the London Riots of 1780, and who later converted to Judaism, dying in that faith. These two were not only twice over closely related; they were also friends who became sworn enemies.

First in date amongst these members of Parliament is Lord Adam Gordon, fourth surviving son of Alexander, 2nd Duke of Gordon, and a brother of Countess Anne of Aberdeen and Lady Elizabeth Skelly. He was the member for Aberdeenshire from 1754 to 1768, and for Kincardineshire from 1774 to 1788. He was in 1789 appointed C.-in-C. Scotland with the rank of Lieutenant-General, and Governor of Edinburgh Castle as a full General from 1796 until his death in 1801. He had married Jane Drummond, widow of a Duke of Atholl. He seems to have had a steady temperament by comparison with his brothers and sisters and other close siblings with ducal blood, but he was tough and unyielding in his attitudes to the American colonies, which he visited extensively whilst both in and out of Parliament. He had been on a military rather than a parliamentary assignment to the West Indian colonies in 1764–5, and then visited Florida, which in 1763 had been ceded to Britain by Spain. (The Spaniards retook it in 1781, relinquished West Florida to the USA in 1801, and ceded all Florida to the new nation in 1820.) A strong subsidiary motive for this journey was to acquire land, which he later did, in order to qualify the better for his ambition to be appointed a colonial governor, which did not occur, the King writing: 'There is a very improper warmth in Lord Adam's letter that would undoubtedly be a very good reason never to promote him.' Of East Florida Lord Adam wrote: 'Was I ever to apply for any land in America it should be in this province.' Despite this affection, and expressions of even greater fondness for the company and climate of Virginia, it was eventually, however, in the back country of New York that in 1767 he acquired 10,000 acres, and sent out two Lincolnshire farmers to advise him about settling upon the New York estate 300 families as his tenants. At home he was adequately provided for by his father, by the will of his mother and by his brother Cosmo, 3rd Duke of Gordon.

Back in Westminster his political attitude towards the restiveness of the Americans was harsh – even before he had an interest to defend – but at least he knew the land whose taxworthiness he was voting. On the 1765 Stamp Act a friend wrote that 'he seems to be as sanguine about laying it thick upon the Colonies as they are to throw off everything'. At this date he also deplored Boston's 'ancient rugged spirit of levelling'. He voted in 1766 against the repeal of the Stamp Act. He avoided voting for the Land Tax of 1767 – as would be expected – but at the crisis of the War of Independence in February 1783 he voted against Shelburne's peace proposals. He seems to have kept quiet during the heated exchanges between his nephews, General William Gordon of Fyvie and Lord George Gordon, over the London Riots of 1780, and his parliamentary activity gradually decreased. His leaving Parliament and acceding to the Scottish command brought him into close contact with Henry Dundas, the virtual ruler of Scotland, and he died in 1801 apparently as steady as the Edinburgh rock on which is built the Castle he governed in his last appointment. Whilst he had the Scottish command he became fully aware that riotous outbreaks that occurred at several places in the east of Scotland as well as in the Highland west were not politically motivated but resulted from fears, only too well founded, that landowners were already thinking of letting the land to sheep farmers and evicting the crofting tenants, mostly dependent on subsistence farming.

Another member of Parliament having close connexions with the ducal Gordons was Cosmo Gordon of Cluny. The given name Cosmo became attached to some men called Gordon because Alexander, 2nd Duke of Gordon, was very friendly with Cosmo or Cosimo de' Medici III, Duke of Tuscany, and passed on his friend's name to his eldest son, who succeeded him as 3rd Duke of Gordon. John of Cluny, the father of

Cosmo of Cluny, was paying a compliment, rather than toadying, to his erstwhile employer, through whom he had grown rich, by so naming his son. The name quickly spread outward, which is a common happening, and, though J. M. Bulloch's and Mrs Skelton's 1912 *Gordons Under Arms (House of Gordon* vol. iii) lists only eight men in the British forces whose first given name is Cosmo, and none on the Continent, in the United States or as Jacobite soldiers, the name is frequently to be found still among Aberdeenshire farmers and others, whether or not their surname is Gordon. Cosima as a feminine name is not unknown.

John of Cluny had been factor to Cosmo, 3rd Duke of Gordon, Lord Adam's eldest brother, and leased from the duke as tacksman, or factor, the Spey salmon fishing which Duke Cosmo had acquired at the break-up sale of the Seton (Dunfermline) forfeited lands of Fyvie and Urquhart referred to in chapter 4, and became so enriched that he was able to buy the estate and castle of Cluny in Aberdeenshire. The son Cosmo acquired an estate in Nairnshire from a bankrupt family whose former owners had an electoral interest in the county, which was exhausted by 1772. Cosmo Gordon stood for the constituency in an opposed election in 1774, and won it by the astonishing majority of eleven votes to two. Nairn is a small county. In a brief parliamentary career he showed himself enthusiastic for North's American policy, but on a technicality opposed the sending of Hanoverian troops to form the garrisons of Gibraltar and Minorca, which he claimed was illegal. He 'disapproved of introducing foreigners into the dominions', he said. When Townshend alleged that the ministry had intended to secure a vote for the payment of foreign troops in Ireland Cosmo said, 'had he believed it, no man would be more ready to join in a vote of disapprobation and censure'. In 1777 he was rewarded with an appointment as Baron of the Scottish exchequer, which removed him from the House of Commons. Cosmo Gordon of Cluny had become very rich. He is credited with character and ability, using his money to good purpose by introducing the new-fangled agricultural improvements to his estates, sadly overdue in the poor and strife-riven country of Scotland. He was amusing enough to be a close friend of James Boswell and, politically, kept in with the Dukes of Gordon and with Henry Dundas until his death in 1800.

Cosmo's successor, John Gordon of Braid and Cluny, claims attention although he never entered Parliament. In 1826 he became Lieutenant-Colonel of the Aberdeen (55th) Militia, and in 1836 honorary Colonel in succession to the Earl of Aboyne. In 1841 he bought from the representative of the bankrupted Macneil of Barra the whole of that Roman Catholic chief's estate. This consisted of the southernmost island of any size in the Outer Hebridean chain, and some attendant small islands. It may be guessed that the Macneil Chief had done well out of the kelp trade during the Napoleonic period, like all landowners with a sea shore accessibly fringed by this valuable seaweed. Kelp ash was a satisfactory substitute for soda ash, normally imported from Spain, necessary for the glass and soap industries. After 1815 the trade rapidly dwindled and the swollen rents of the crofters who collected the kelp could no longer be paid. The Macneils may have gone on a spending spree of some kind, either to try to maintain their Catholic clansmen or to enhance their social position by the showy hospitality traditional in the Highland clans. Professor Smout, in his *A History of the Scottish People*, writes:

> By 1830 the Highlanders had become a society of smallholders living in great poverty either on crowded islands or next to extensive sheepfarms. . . . Given the high fertility of the Highlanders combined with the low fertility of their country . . . it is tempting to say that nothing in the end could have been done that was not done to avert the collapse of the Highland economy.

The potato failure of the 1840s put an end to any idea that pockets of subsistence economy could flourish alongside a predominantly cash economy. So the Macneils were forced out of Barra, the Macdonalds of Clanranald kept a mere toehold on South Uist and Benbecula, and Gordon of Cluny came in to all three islands. He joined enthusiastically in the movement that had started a generation earlier on the mainland and favoured sheep rather than people by the rigorous eviction of a population nearing starvation. So far as he was concerned the purchase of three Hebridean islands, so distant in culture as well as by miles from his corner on the edge of lowland Aberdeenshire, was an investment. Colonel Gordon of Cluny died in 1858 and there was lengthy litigation which concluded only in 1863, when his illegitimate son John inherited the property. That John married, made a trust settlement upon his wife, who outlived him – he died in 1878 – and married again. By 1937 trustees were able to make dispositions in favour of the Macneil of Barra, residing in the state of Vermont, USA. The land of Barra is let, or feued, in virtual perpetuity to others, a much reduced population of relatively prosperous crofters and farmers, but the chief of Clan Macneil holds the superiority again.

We come now to the career of Lord George Gordon. This weird man was ill-fated from birth. His father Cosmo, 3rd Duke of Gordon, had married Lady Catherine, daughter of William, 2nd Earl of Aberdeen; there is evidence, of which he is the principal witness, that a double dose of Gordon blood can be a troublesome inheritance. As to inheritance in the material sense he was still less lucky. The marriage contract between his parents stipulated precisely a stated sum to be divided between daughters and younger sons, but by the time Lord George was born in December 1751 there were so many children older than he that the money allocated was all apportioned and he was totally unprovided for. His father died the following August at the age of thirty-three when George was only seven months old. By the time he was three, his eldest brother Alexander, 4th Duke of Gordon, had agreed to set aside a sum ranging from £150 a year at once, rising to £250 as he grew older until he reached the age of twenty-one. The Duchess Dowager also had a few pounds a year allotted for George's keep. Detailed accounts for clothes, education, doses of medicine and the like were to be kept by John Gordon of Cluny, acting as factor for these purposes.

Meanwhile Duchess Catherine set about determinedly looking for a suitable second husband. Her first thought was for Stanislaus Poniatowski, aged twenty at the time of her husband's death, and not yet King of Poland. There is an absurd story that the duchess invited him to her house and presented her two youngest children, George and a sister only a year older, dressed as Cupids, and instructed them to shoot darts from their toy bows at the object of her attentions. Nothing came of this eccentric overture. By the time George was five she had lighted upon a young American colonial serving in the British Army, good looking, ten years her junior, with the fancy name of Staats Long Morris and a determination to marry well. The match succeeded. He quickly achieved a colonelcy, and they soon set out on a long and pleasurable visit to America. Later, in 1774, he became Member of Parliament for Elgin. Any idea that Lord George and his nearest brothers and sisters enjoyed a happy childhood romping about at Gordon Castle can only be true if the nurses and senior servants, and John Gordon of Cluny with his account books, gave them free rein. Lord George was dispatched to Eton at eleven, his mother having arranged for his appointment as an ensign in the 89th Foot at the age of eight. This army commission notwithstanding, she entered him for the Navy, without protest by him, by the time he was fifteen. He was probably glad to leave behind a wretched childhood.

For three years, from 1766 to 1769, he served in the West Indies, where he took an unconventional interest in the poor negroes, whose plight roused his quick emotions, but in America he noticed none of this and was much pleased by the even treatment of all that he saw. This was the beginning of his deep interest in penal reform at home. His mother and Colonel Long Morris were also in America in 1768–9. Returning to home waters he became lieutenant in 1772, the year of his majority. He must have been conscious of his exclusion from any permanent portion from a very rich family and perhaps this helped him to identify with poor suffering slaves. Gordon of Cluny had kept accounts so meticulously that whilst George was at sea he had been able to advance £1,500 in Lord George's name from his allowance to help his eldest brother Duke Alexander to pay off some mortgages. By 1772 Lord George had this money returned to him, and he received an additional bond for £1,000 from his brother. It must have been about this time that he started to cultivate the parliamentary seat of Invernessshire. He did this with a thoroughness that frightened the sitting member, General Fraser. He visited Skye, learnt to speak Gaelic and to play the bagpipes, found out the concerns of fishing communities, and never wore a wig to conceal his ginger-coloured hair. Fraser got together with George Selwyn, wit, patron and friend of Horace Walpole, and paid enough for Lord George to be installed, in 1774, in Selwyn's pocket borough of Ludgershall in Wiltshire, which returned two members. Here was a ducal scion of no fortune, newly elected to Parliament entirely through patronage and by having given General Fraser a good fright. He was determined to place his mark on history.

He attended the House regularly, formed an admiration for Edmund Burke and generally voted with the Opposition. He made no speech, however, until after resigning his naval commission in 1777, but was already a conspicuous figure amongst his fellow members; he dressed darkly and his lank, long red hair gave the appearance of a Puritan except when he occasionally wore bright tartan trousers. It was rumoured that he had resigned his commission because in somebody's house he had so vehemently defended the riotous behaviour of some Maryland colonials, that a gentleman from Maryland who was present and whose house had been despoiled remarked that an officer who could so take the rebels' part ought not to wear the King's uniform. An odd twist to history is the fact that he neither spoke nor voted against Sir George Savile's bill in February 1778 to remove certain penalties from Roman Catholics. This bill in fact sparked off anti-Catholic agitation. Still Lord George stayed any feelings he might hold on that matter and his first reported speech – do not call it maiden – was on 13 April 1778, still on the theme of the Americans' right to their freedom. He appealed to North to 'call off his butchers and ravagers from the colonies – to turn from his wickedness and live; it is not too late to repent'. This ranting combination of piety and violence, of which he was not the first exponent, echoes down the generations to our own day, especially if the hair is red. In Lord George's case the speeches were always accompanied by long periods of incoherent irrelevance. Nevertheless he was credited with occasional shafts of debating skill. In the following year, 1779, he made an extensive visit to Scotland and there was mutual enthusiasm between him and the various Protestant Associations that had been formed to oppose the Savile Bill. Namier and Brooke's *History of Parliament 1754–1790* states:

> From this time onwards alarming tendencies began to reveal themselves in his Parliamentary utterances. In May 1779 he told the House that the Scots were ripe for rebellion. . . . In the debate on the King's speech on 25 November he boasted that he had 'one hundred thousand men at my back: the Scots are convinced in their own minds that the King [who was his godfather] is a Papist'.

Duchess Catherine was probably spared knowledge of her son's verbal extravagance; she died on 16 December.

Before continuing Lord George's story it is necessary to introduce his cousin, the Honourable William Gordon of Fyvie, born in 1736 and fifteen years Lord George's senior. He had a more comfortable and certain childhood than his close relation. His father Earl William of Aberdeen had purchased Fyvie as a condition of his marriage to Anne, daughter of the 2nd Duke of Gordon, and as their eldest son he stood to inherit it. He entered the Army as cornet in the 11th Dragoons. He first entered Parliament as member for New Woodstock in 1767, and transferred in 1774 to Heytesbury, in the patronage of the 4th Duke of Marlborough, who had already obtained for him the position of a Groom of the Bedchamber. He was a man of high spirit. Just before Christmas 1777 he raised the 'Aberdeenshire Highland', the 81st Foot, of which he became colonel. His cousin-german and nephew by marriage Alexander, 4th Duke of Gordon, wrote from London an ill-tempered letter on New Year's Day 1778 (Hogmanay is the name given to the last day of the old year) that Fyvie 'had not the civility to offer me one officer' for the Northern Fencibles the Duke was hoping to raise. Fyvie's brother, the future judicial Lord Rockville, delivered William's reply to the Duke in Edinburgh, which made His Grace very angry. Fyvie, said the Duke, had got a regiment through his interest, and had not given him the nomination of a single officer. Rockville answered in a huff: 'Well, by God, we can raise it without you.'

(This Lord Rockville was a great lawyer, becoming a Lord of Session in 1784, and took his life title from a small estate near North Berwick, where his garden produce was renowned for its high quality, especially his peaches and pears. He was also a great drinker. On arriving one night in Edinburgh for a convivial evening with friends he excused his dishevelled and bruised appearance thus: 'Gentlemen, I have met with the most extraordinary adventure. As I was walking along the Grassmarket, all of a sudden the street rose up and struck me in the face.' To go down smack on your face is one thing, but on a snowy night early in 1792 he slipped backwards. At first it was thought that only an arm was broken, but concussion set in and in three days the judge was dead.)

Colonel William Gordon's royal appointment allowed him at first to skip round the wrath of his important nephew the Duke of Gordon. An enemy, Pryse Lockhart Gordon, wrote: 'Never was a more perfect prototype of Polonius than our Groom of the Bedchamber and, though the King sometimes hit him rather hard, yet he was a great favourite.' North was informed of the jealous squabble over the raising of the regiment and wrote to the King:

> Colonel Gordon, by taking this method has made it HIS regiment and not the Duke's, and has obliged many of the Duke's friends, as he supposes, to gain their interest at a future political contest if [he] should again oppose, as he has already done once, the Duke's candidate for the county of Aberdeen.

The King ordered Fyvie to be reprimanded, but was so pleased with his spirited reply that instead he was commended. The Duke, still angry, was only mollified when the sovereign allowed him to raise his own 'Northern Fencibles'. It was to lead to a lasting estrangement between the Gordons of Fyvie and the ducal line. Colonel William of Fyvie, although a Member of Parliament, took his soldiering seriously and was in Ireland on and off during 1778 and 1779 with his Aberdeenshire Highlanders, but was back in London in January 1780 seeking military promotion. He must, meanwhile, have noticed the dangerous development of his cousin's career.

Lord George's utterances in the House were becoming more and more peculiar, lengthy and irrelevant to the business of the day. If these had any rational origin they lay in the Protestant Association in London inviting him to become its president in November 1779. On one occasion early in 1780 he read out, for the second time, the Declaratory Act of 1718 and all members present left the chamber. In March 1780 he told the House he had 160,000 Protestant men in Scotland at his command and that if the King did not keep his coronation oath they were determined to cut off his head. In another debate he was interrupted by a fellow member, who could no longer stand his description, entirely irrelevant, of popery in Ireland in 1626. This Charles Turner said: 'The noble lord has got a twist in his head, a certain whirligig which runs away with him if anything relative to religion is mentioned.' The noble Lord then read out yet more rubbish and assured the House that his supporters had not yet determined to put the King to death: they only considered they were absolved from their allegiance. Despite these rantings he had twice been granted audience of the King, who treated a great deal of impertinent probings as to his rejection of Catholicism with courtesy and kingliness and only with difficulty dismissed him from his presence. The cause of these audiences, to which Lord George as a duke's son had a certain right, was Lord North's refusal to accept that he, as Prime Minister, should present a petition from the Protestant Association.

The climax came on 2 June 1780. The president of the Protestant Association announced that he would present their petition to the House on that Friday so long as he was backed up by twenty thousand men, to assemble at St George's Fields (now Waterloo Station) at ten o'clock in the morning. It was a fine day and a huge multitude of what appeared to be mostly sober tradespeople crossed London Bridge and began the march to Whitehall, where they stopped singing and adopted, so far as possible, a restrained attitude of 'peaceable Deportment and Behaviour', as Lord George had wished. They were joined along the route by men of a rougher sort, who had been drinking, as well as by many fellow petitioners who had taken the quick route across Westminster Bridge. The approaches to Parliament were now filled with an excited crowd and the coaches of peers and commoners, especially peers, were mobbed as they approached. The great Earl of Mansfield, Lord Chief Justice, had all the windows of his coach smashed and his wig removed. Other peers were given like treatment;

Gight Castle viewed from the
north-east in 1851. The poet
Lord Byron was related
through his mother to the
Gordons of Gight.

Mrs Byron, the poet's mother,
by Thomas Stewardson.

General Patrick Gordon of
Auchleuchries (1635–99) served in
the armies of Poland and Sweden
before accepting service under
Tsar Peter the Great.

(*Right*) The General's nephew,
Admiral Thomas Gordon
(1662–1741) of 'the Russian
Service'.

Peter the Great, after a portrait by
Kneller.

William, 2nd Earl of Aberdeen (1679–1745) and (*right*) his eldest son, George, who became the 3rd Earl (1722–1801), by William Mosman, 1741.

Haddo House as it looks today.

George, Lord Haddo, son of the 3rd Earl of Aberdeen, by Pompeo Batoni in 1785 (the date on the portrait is believed to be incorrect).

General the Hon. William Gordon of Fyvie (1736–1813) portrayed in 1766 by Pompeo Batoni, and (*right*) his son William (1776–1847), the 'brat of Bell Black', by Beechey in 1817.

Adam Lindsay Gordon (1833–70), the popular Australian poet and great-great-grandson of the 2nd Earl of Aberdeen, by Sir Frank Madden.

Fyvie Castle with the Gordon Tower on the right.

(*Right*) Lord George Gordon (1751–93), who inspired the 1780 Gordon Riots in London.

George Hamilton Gordon, 6th Earl of Aberdeen, *alias* George H. Osborne, with the rifle he later sold to Melvin Othelar Randall.

The last known portrait of 'George H. Osborne', sent by Miss Cecilia Rook of Maine to Lady Aberdeen after George's death.

The library (*left*) in Main Street, Richmond, Maine, as it was in George's day.

The author's grandfather, John Campbell Gordon, who succeeded his brother, 'George Osborne', as 7th Earl of Aberdeen and was later created 1st Marquess of Aberdeen and Temair.

Johnny, 1st Marquess of Aberdeen and Temair (*left*) with Charles, 11th Marquess of Huntly.

Archie Gordon, 5th Marquess of Aberdeen and Temair (1913–84) with his godmother, Queen Mary.

members of the Commons were mostly better treated, but had to drive their coaches through a menacing crowd.

After the Commons had assembled, far too many men broke into the Lobby (one estimate said 60,000, which cannot be true) and defied all attempts to get them to leave. Several peers lost their pocket watches. Lord George darted in and out of the Lobby, eyes ablaze and in great excitement. Colonel William Gordon of Fyvie came up to him and said: 'My Lord George, do you intend to bring your rascally adherents into the House of Commons? If you do – the first man that enters, I will plunge my sword not into his, but into your body.' General James Murray M P, another close relation of Lord George, and Mr Henry Herbert (who became Earl of Carnarvon), likewise had their swords ready. Lord George in the House moved to have the petition taken into immediate consideration and after some debate the House divided, only six members registering their vote for the motion, with Lord George and Alderman Frederick Bull as tellers. Lord George then appeared in the Lobby, still full of fire, to announce what had happened. He had no doubt the King would 'send private directions to the minister to enforce the prayer of the petition, when he should be informed of the alarm the [Catholic Relief] bill complained of had given, though he assured them no relief was to be expected from the House'. The official record of parliamentary debates, from which this quotation is taken, goes on:

> The reverend gentleman who officiates as chaplain to the House attempted to urge upon the associators to part, and loudly told the noble Lord . . . that all the effusion of blood that should be spilt would be charged to his account. The associators . . . grew extremely riotous and much disorder ensued. At nine o'clock a large party of the foot guards and a troop of horse, with Justice Wright and Justice Addington, came down to the House, and peace and good order was soon after restored.

Another account implies that Justice Addington, after a cavalry charge had been a fiasco and caused many in the crowd to become helpless with laughter, persuaded the mob that if they would go away he would order the troops to march off. In the House Lord George was helpless in a different way. The firebrand had spluttered out and he seemed exhausted. He sat alone on a bench, his eyes now curtained in red hair, not in any way ablaze. A kind friend gave him a lift to his house in Welbeck Street. When the House met again on Tuesday 6 June the Attorney General was instructed by unanimous resolution to prosecute the persons found 'to have occasioned or aided and abetted the late disturbances'.

Even on the night of Friday 2 June rioting broke out; whilst Lord George Gordon had retired to bed at Welbeck Street. The first building to become a victim was the chapel of the Sardinian Ambassador in Lincoln's Inn Fields. After that Friday night the mob was loose on London for a week, Catholic chapels, the houses of the poor Irish and the opening of prisons being especially singled out. The house of Sir George Savile in Leicester Fields, whose bill had provoked the lobbyists and their riotous attendants, was mostly destroyed. By the time the troops arrived most of his furniture was ablaze outside and all they could do was to man broken windows.

A certain David Dundas, from the safety of Richmond, wrote to his brother James to tell him what was going on:

> On Monday night the Mob became more riotous and proceeded to pull down and burn the houses of the people who had given evidence against those who were apprehended for burning the Sardinian Ambassador's Chapel. . . . On Tuesday [6 June] they assaulted many Members going to both houses of Parliament and at night they began by bursting open Newgate, releasing all the Prisoners and burning to the Ground all that immense and Noble Building which has cost such an immense sum to erect and which was almost finished.

This was an extension to Newgate, a stylish building with niches for statues and the like.

> The house of a great Brewer in Queen's Street was totally demolished as was Lord Mansfield's noble house in Bloomsbury Square. A gentleman of my acquaintance was present during this scene of horror . . . a woman seeing a quantity of Linen thrown into the fire and being willing to avail herself of it, was carrying some of it off. She was detected, the Linen thrown into the fire again and herself stript naked and turned adrift, so that you see plunder was not their object. . . . All this time there was an evident concerted plan and destruction appeared their only object but on [Wednesday] night they made an attack upon the Bank which was protected by a pretty strong Guard and after considerable efforts they were beat off. . . . People hurry out of town as fast as possible, there was not a bed to be had at any Inn in Richmond last night. . . . Something more than a religious mob is here present and money must have been given to keep them together so long . . . Ld G. Gordon is damnably afraid – he endeavoured to wait on the King yesterday who would not see him.

Meanwhile Lord George had caused the Protestant Association to issue an appeal to its supporters to 'refrain from unconstitutional proceedings' and the president offered his services to North to restore law and order. In the Chamber of the House he even removed the Protestant symbol, a blue cockade, from his hat when challenged by another member with the impropriety and provocation of his wearing it.

In a second letter to brother James on 10 June Mr Dundas wrote:

> All is now quiet and peaceable and as there is now not less than 25,000 Soldiers in and about London it will probably continue so, at least while the Soldiers remain ... Ld Geo: Gordon after undergoing a long examination before the Privy Council last night was sent to the Tower under strong Guard.

He then reflects upon the puzzling aspects of the affair:

> In many instances you see them acting by a concerted plan and upon disinterested principles – in others only guided by the mistaken zeal of an ignorant enthusiastic rabble. . . . Their being kept so long together without any ostensible Leader, appears a thing not to be supported without the intervention of money, and many people are of opinion that the Court of France is at the Bottom of it. . . . Nothing can surpass the horrid appearance that London exhibited on Wednesday night even at this distance we were up almost all night looking at it, it appeared as if all London from one end to the other had been in flames. . . . I cannot help thinking that the more one looks forward the more disagreeable the prospect becomes.

The charge was constructive treason; the trial was delayed. Long before it took place, before the end of June 1780, there were rushed through at the Old Bailey a number of trials of malefactors – the real rioters, described in some quarters as Gordon's minions – and there were a number of hangings. The main case was put back and put back because the prosecutors were not ready. Lord George's initially harsh confinement in the Tower was gradually relaxed until he could see visitors without time limit. One of these was John Wesley, who was fooled by the now quiet madman into being shocked when he read the indictment. So were many others and the passage of time softened the opinion even of Horace Walpole, who had earlier exclaimed that all Gordons were, and always had been, mad. The trial at last came on in February 1781. Friends had put up enough money to hire two brilliant lawyers to defend Lord George, and the prosecution's first witness was slashed to bits. Others fared better, the chaplain to the House, the

Reverend Thomas Bowen, being unshaken in his account of the prisoner's provocative utterances to the lobbyists on 2 June, and the business of the wearing of the blue cockade at the sitting of 6 June was also sworn to by a fellow member. The Court did not rise then at a civilized hour and it was past midnight when Erskine, leading for the defence, addressed the jury. He spoke emotionally and at length. The Attorney General was brief and factual. Lord Mansfield's summing up was anything but friendly. It was past four in the morning. The jury took only half an hour to consider their verdict and returned at 5.15 a.m.: not guilty.

Nevertheless, Lord George's career was finished. An attempt to re-enter Parliament for the City of London later that year came to nothing and he unsuccessfully pestered everybody of consequence from the King downwards with letters. It is strange how eccentrics so often associate. At a parliamentary election in Aberdeenshire in 1786 Lord George and his friend 'Mad Jack' Byron cast their votes in favour of the Tory candidate. Captain Byron described himself as John Byron Gordon of Gight. Both votes were disallowed. In the same year he involved himself in close friendship with the sinister Count Cagliostro, who had been ordered to leave France after the scandal of the diamond necklace ordered bogusly from a Paris jeweller in the name of Marie Antoinette and then mysteriously stolen. In London Cagliostro and Lord George became inseparable. Gordon issued a notice in the *Public Advertiser* in defence of his friend in the face of the French Queen's malevolence, and this was considered grounds for libel. Gordon then, having for some time taken an interest in penal reform, which the quality thought should be left to the bourgeois John Howard and his sort, wrote a pamphlet which purported to be a petition from prisoners in Newgate begging him to take steps to prevent their being sent to Botany Bay. This was grounds for a charge of libelling the judiciary. He was indicted on both charges and fatally conducted his own defence, being now unable to afford expensive counsel. Of course he was found guilty, but the judge decided to adjourn the court and to pass sentence the following day. Gordon did not appear; the next day the house in Welbeck Street was deserted.

The court had not bothered to put him on restricted bail, so escape was both easy and attractive; almost a practical proposition, a gamble at odds even, with additional penalty not to be imposed unless the law was bent. He fled first to Protestant Holland and made his way to Amsterdam, where many Jews resided. He lodged there at the house of

Moses op den Berg, but his reputation had gone before him – there was always trouble wherever he appeared – and Protestant Holland wanted him not. He was bundled on to a boat bound for Harwich accompanied by Dutch militia who dumped him on the quay, on English soil again, without bothering to hand him over to the court. From now on his movements are hazy: there are conflicting stories, nearly all post-humous except for a few contemporary newspaper accounts. Somehow he made his way to Birmingham and there settled in the squalor and poverty of the small Jewish community. It is difficult, too, to disentangle when and where he first received instruction in Judaism. He had been noticeably attracted to this faith in London before his libel trial and had been noticed at a party refusing food forbidden to Jews. Dickens, in *Barnaby Rudge*, implies that his interest began as early as the 1780 Riots. Yet Rabbi Tevele Schiff sent him packing from the synagogue in Duke's Place, probably in 1787 before his trial for criminal libel. He had tried to infiltrate this synagogue in the neighbourhood of fashionable St James's in the West End of London. Though they may have felt flattered that this milord showed every sign of liking Jews, the merchants who worshipped there can have had no wish to add to their unpopularity by helping him to join their number. It is not a proselytizing religion, but in some less exalted part of the town he must have gained rabbinical help. By the time he arrived in Birmingham, where he lodged in the house of a woman who sold capers and anchovies, he was well advanced in his studies of Hebrew language and scripture. He underwent circumcision and preserved the evidence of this rite in a suitable box.

Dickens, long after the event, in chapter 37 of *Barnaby Rudge*, imagines a conversation at Welbeck Street between Lord George and his secretary Gashford.

> 'To say the truth, I have slept so soundly,' said Lord George, rubbing his eyes and looking round the room, 'that I don't remember quite – what place is this?'
>
> 'My lord,' cried Gashford with a smile.
>
> 'Oh,' returned his superior. 'Yes. You're not a Jew then?'
>
> 'A Jew,' exclaimed the pious secretary, recoiling.
>
> 'I dreamed that we were Jews, Gashford, you and I – both of us – Jews with long beards. . . .'
>
> 'Dreamed he was a Jew,' he [Gashford] said thoughtfully as he closed the bedroom door. 'He may come to that before he dies. It's like enough. . . .'

By 1783 he was writing ranting letters to emperors and kings as well as to Jews of Portuguese and German origin living in London, letters as long and dotty as his parliamentary speeches. Everybody, including Dickens, seems to have chosen a different date for his conversion. Some writers place it at the time of surreptitious visits to the Hambro synagogue in London from his hiding-place in Birmingham. More likely is an account which claims that he was received into the holy covenant of Abraham by Rabbi Jacob in 1787 at the synagogue in The Froggery, Birmingham. His lodging was near by in the house of the Jewess who sold anchovies. On 10 December 1787 the *Birmingham Gazette* referred to his residence at this house in Dudley Street and the smart Bow Street runner may have picked up this clue.

From then on, during his imprisonment at Newgate, a host of magazines and newspapers used his story as often as today's gossip writers write about each other, and cartoons, many of them not at all unkind by the standards of the day, were issued as prints. There were, too, verses, mostly long and bad. The final lines of one, though silly, show a certain skill:

> Doddle doodle do, my tale though strange is true
> And certainly Lord G. must be the jewel of a Jew.

It was in February 1788 that the Bow Street runner picked him up. This official noticed that in addition to the lank red hair a beard of darker hue straggled untrimmed from his chin.

He answered only to the name Israel bar Abraham George Gordon. Thin and badly dressed, he was brought to London for sentence. The consequence was five years' imprisonment, a £10,000 fine as security for fourteen years' good behaviour, and two sureties of £2,500 each. After a short time in the common felons' part of Newgate he was put in better quarters and eventually gave kosher dinner parties to visitors of astonishing diversity, in comfortable quarters. Namier and Brooke comment that 'this was probably the happiest period of his life'. No wonder. A portrayal of his serving maid, Polly Levi, who cooked kosher meals for him and his guests, shows a very pretty face of modesty and charm, wearing clothes that look absurdly fashionable. At the beginning of 1793 he appeared in court to pay up, his prison sentence having expired. Of course he could not raise £10,000 and argued that the fine should never have been imposed since everybody knew he did not possess so much money, and his two chosen sureties in the sum each of £2,500 were penniless Polish Jews. Rabbi Isaac Titterman of Ipswich, who often visited him at Newgate, could not help him with money. He was returned to prison, and survived the summer heat, when the violent jail fever was always at its worst. He caught it in October and died on 1 November 1793.

Lord George's American stepfather, by now General Staats Long Morris, appears to have played no part in this drama. Duchess Catherine having died in 1779, he remarried in 1780. His only recorded speech in the House of Commons was made in 1775 when he showed that the British were outnumbered two to one at Bunker Hill, the disastrous battle which was the point of controversy on a motion to stop hostilities. His position was delicate, since his family were prominent patriots, but he voted with the administration consistently, especially after the King had demanded of North that there should be a better attendance of placemen. At the general election of 1780 he was again returned for Elgin Burghs after an opposed election, but was defeated in 1784. With his new wife he spent much time abroad. Although he had acquired properties in America and later inherited his family's estates in New York and New Jersey he preferred to live in London. In 1797 he was appointed Governor of Quebec, and died there in 1800. As for that other general, William of Fyvie, the rest of his story is told in the following chapter.

Before turning to that tale there is another William to be mentioned. He is Lord William Gordon, Lord George's senior by seven years, and the second son of Duke Cosmo and Duchess Catherine. He was born in 1744 and by the time he was fifteen he was gazetted lieutenant in the 89th Foot, the regiment of his stepfather, Staats Long Morris. Handsome, dashing and fond of the fashionable life of London and Edinburgh, he was considered a most accomplished young nobleman, a reputation not difficult to accord to a person of moderate intellect who was a good-looking duke's son. He had also, behind the frivolity, the eccentricity of his family welded to his being. In 1769, aged twenty-five, he sensationally eloped with Lady Sarah Bunbury, wife of Sir Charles Bunbury and sister of the Duke of Richmond. Sir Charles Bunbury's surname is immortalized in *The Importance of being Earnest*, the name being suggested to Oscar Wilde for the non-existent character in the play by Ouida, who was a Bury St Edmunds girl. Bunbury is a Suffolk family and Sir Charles was MP for the county for forty-three years. The loving couple, William and Sarah, ran away to Scotland. Love lasted only a few months, when William, ostracized by the society he loved, cast her off. She had no Bunbury children, and she was returned in disgrace by Sir Charles to her brother the Duke of Richmond. In 1776 the cuckolded baronet divorced Sarah by Act of Parliament; he married a girl of no lineage and died childless. Surprisingly, Sarah made a successful second marriage of acceptable quality to a member of the Napier family.

William, meanwhile, shocked to the core at being shunned by society, chopped his hair close and conspicuously took to the road with a knapsack and a large dog. He vowed never to return to London where the Press had scurrilously lampooned him, and said he would walk to Rome. Where he went is uncertain, but he was on the Continent for three years before he returned without explanation to take up again the life of a man of fashion. His brother, the Duke of Gordon, was determined that he should settle on a serious life. He had resigned his commission in the army when he eloped with Lady Sarah, and his brother now wanted to put him in charge of the regiment he was hoping to raise. The King wrote in 1779 with a firm veto against the appointment of a man who had flouted the etiquette of his virtuous court: 'I can never think of giving Lord William Gordon the rank of lieutenant-colonel . . . not the smallest claim to military rank.' This flat refusal infuriated the Duke, already smarting from his cousin Fyvie having stolen a march on him in the matter of raising an Aberdeenshire regiment. To keep this angry nobleman quiet Lord North was authorized to procure for Lord William the place of Deputy Ranger of St James's and Green Parks, with which office went a very pretty lodge. In the end the King relented even over military rank. When the Duke was given the go-ahead to raise his Fencible corps with himself in command, William was allowed to be second-in-command.

Other ambitions of the Duke for his brother were now realized. The parliamentary seat of Elginshire was held by Arthur Duff. After long negotiations between Lord Fife and the Duke, Duff was moved out in 1779 and William moved in. He was completely out of sympathy with Lord George's incitement of the mob and greatly distressed by the aftermath. He visited his youngest brother in the Tower of London, probably with a sense of shame often felt by flippant persons having to take matters seriously, and, according to the chattering Horace Walpole's journal, 'seemed by his harassed and dishevelled appearance more of a gallowsbird than his brother'. He sufficiently distanced himself from the scandal to be re-elected for Elgin in 1780. If Walpole's observation was anything like accurate it must have been a temporary aberration from his usual style and appearance. In 1781 the *English Chronicle* wrote of him:

> He possesses that kind of ability with which nature has benevolently supplied the more impotent order of her beings: a quick perception in all the modes of applicable adulation, and an intuitive sagacity in discerning the most direct and effectual roads to preferment. He is a constant attender at St James's on every vacancy, and is polite enough to be on all occasions the *most obedient humble servant to command* to the premier and all his colleagues in Administration.

He needed to be a toady. Never rich, he was in debt and given to gambling on a scale that would shock richer and more prudent men. Luck turned in this same year, 1781. He landed a rich girl in marriage. She, heiress of Viscount Irvine, brought to an end his financial worries. Better still, a complicated plot to exclude Lord George from returning to Parliament – he again had his eye on Inverness-shire – involved the appointment of William to the sinecure of Vice-Admiral of Scotland. Consequent on his appointment to this office of profit he was required to resign his seat and seek re-election. The proposal was to remove him to Inverness-shire where the incumbent MP, Simon Fraser, had recently died, and so block any move to install Lord George. The King at first objected to the appointment as vice-admiral because it would 'give well grounded disgust to the peerage of Scotland, he not being one of them and certainly his private character not being much in his favour'. He yielded, however, before the spectre of Lord George and the appointment went ahead. Characteristically Lord William sat tight in Elgin, which accepted him without competition. He transferred to Inverness-shire in 1784, and by that time William Pitt had succeeded Lord North. Lord William was not disposed to annoy people in high places and followed the interest of the administration. For some reason he switched to Horsham in Sussex in 1792 and remained there for four years, not seeking re-election after 1796. His final appointment was as Receiver-General of the Duchy of Cornwall. That sounds all right as an office of profit. William had become a great survivor, living until 1823, only thirteen years before the death of his nephew the last Duke of Gordon.

6

The Brat of Bell Black

After the shattering events in London of 1780 William Gordon of Fyvie, Member of Parliament and Colonel, resumed his normal life, divided between Parliament, soldiering and making improvements to the Fyvie estate. In about 1777 he had initiated the building at Fyvie of the Gordon Tower. The castle, originally a royal fortalice guarding the priory founded in Fyvie parish in mediaeval times, had become by 1400 the property of the Preston family. Every succeeding family to own the estate added a tower to the castle; after the Prestons came the family of Meldrum, then the Seton Earls of Dunfermline, and now Gordon. Colonel William was not going to be the first owner not to build, so the Gordon Tower went up, adding a certain symmetry to a castle already large, and which had no need to become larger to accommodate a bachelor frequently absent. He could have married, being a man of substance and property, and was handsome if also a trifle pompous and vain, as revealed in his 1766 portrait at Fyvie by Pompeo Batoni, the fashionable Italian portraitist. He preferred, however, the embraces of a serving-maid at the castle, who bore him a son in 1776. Isobel Black and her son William were consigned to one of the miserable hovels that lined Fyvie village, the father removing himself to service with his regiment in Ireland. After the affair of the riots he plainly had no taste for Parliament and did not seek re-election in 1780. He devoted himself to extensive improvements to his estate, both practical and aesthetic.

A nineteenth-century memoir in the Fyvie parish magazine by 'Septuagenarian' recalls the writer's earliest memories and includes a reference to Isobel Black, disowned by her own family and, with her lover absent, spinning wool to try to provide for herself and her infant son. In time the boy was brought before his father, who, impressed by his intelligence and agreeable looks, decided to bring him up in the castle as a gentleman. This resulted in young William being sent to to school at Eton.

Lord Rockville and his family were frequent guests at Fyvie and when the bibulous judge died in 1792, Fyvie, soon to be advanced to the rank of Lieutenant-General, arranged for his brother's widow and children to stay at the castle for at least six months. Lord Rockville's income died with him, his savings having been blown in the failure of the Ayr Bank and the man entrusted with the sale of his spanking new house in Queen Street, Edinburgh, having absconded with the £4,000 that it fetched.

By this time young William was seventeen and finished with Eton. It must be hoped that his cousins were friendly and helpful towards his development as a gentleman. In those days many bastard siblings were accepted fully within the legitimate family, though in William's case his mother was unfortunately of stock very low in the social order.

As described in chapter 5, Fyvie's action in pre-empting his powerful cousin the Duke of Gordon by raising his Aberdeenshire regiment, and so making it more difficult for Duke Alexander to achieve royal approval for the raising of his Northern Fencibles, caused a rift between Fyvie's branch of the Gordon family and the ducal line. It must, too, have marred the raising in 1794 by Duke Alexander of the most famous, and surviving, regiment – the Gordon Highlanders. Alexander's duchess, the former Jane Maxwell, is credited with offering a kiss to every recruit. She was wild, very wild, having made herself notorious before her marriage by riding a pig, alongside her sister, down Edinburgh's High Street. In between numerous affairs she allowed her husband officially to beget upon her blowzy body two sons and five daughters, at least one of whom was not the Duke's child. The girls were all married off to suitable husbands, including the Dukes of Richmond, Manchester and Bedford. The eldest son, the 5th Duke, had no children and that, crudely, is the story of how the dukedom of Gordon became extinct and how the marquessate of Huntly passed to the last Duke's remote kinsman the Earl of Aboyne. Duke Alexander, like the 3rd Earl of Aberdeen, had studied at Leyden University, and took to himself a mistress or two, marrying after Duchess Jane's death in 1820 his current favourite, the douce Jane Christie, but there were no children of this liaison; consequently he could not legitimise his children, who included boys, by earlier mistresses. One of these, who rose in the Navy to become an admiral, retired to a modest dwelling in the little town of Huntly, where during the Calvinist minister's long sermons he habitually drew from his waistcoat pocket a small looking-glass in which he studied at length and with care his tongue.

Meanwhile, back at Fyvie in his comparatively demure demesne, despite the huge size of the castle, William, now General the Honourable William Gordon, continued his improvements, turning the bog, or moss, to the south of the castle into a lake. Originally important to its defence since a sluice in the river Ythan above the castle could be opened to flood the area, it now formed the key to the landscaping of the pleasure grounds or 'policies' as they are called in Scotland, studded with fine trees which concealed the curving road to the castle entrance, at whose back the river Ythan forms an elegant loop. His Gordon Tower incorporates a magnificent dining-room which, by some ingenuity of the architect or master mason, avoided interference with the Setons' great newel staircase, nine feet wide, enough to allow a man mounted on a horse to ride up it – or so the story goes. At a date unknown, with his son William now adult, Fyvie married the boy's mother and installed her in modest rooms high up in an unimportant part of the vast dwelling, whence she performed the duties of housekeeper, unpaid but kept in comfort and suitably fine clothing.

The prudent man also bought the small estate centred on Maryculter (pronounced Marycooter) House in case the busy children of Rockville should try to oust the young man from his inheritance of Fyvie. None of General Gordon's other brothers had procreated their species; just as well since they were a dubious lot with their wild ducal blood allied to the normally placid Haddo strain. One of them, Cosmo, killed an opponent in an illegal duel in Hyde Park. This was the culmination of a long quarrel with a fellow officer in the forerunner of the Scots Guards, the 3rd Foot Guards. During the War of Independence they were stationed at Springfield, Massachusetts, and in the boring circumstances of the muddle of battle, Lieutenant-Colonel Frederick Thomas accused his CO, Cosmo, of skulking. A message had gone astray. The first consequence of this was that Cosmo caused Thomas to appear before a court-martial in New York. Thomas was acquitted. The positions were then reversed, Thomas securing a court-martial with Cosmo as the accused. Cosmo was acquitted, but he continued to smart under the insult by his junior; hence the duel, which itself was a muddle since at the first firing neither man was hit. On the second advance to within eight yards of each other Cosmo was wounded in the thigh, as he had been at Springfield, and at a third firing Thomas fell dead. Cosmo ran away to the Continent rather than face a murder trial, became a great friend of our two busy old chatterboxes the Horaces Walpole and Mann, the latter being British Ambassador to Florence, and paid visits back to England, continuing thence to visit his brother at Fyvie. Like Byron's Gordon grandfather, he was buried at Bath Abbey in 1813.

General William's son William must have known Cosmo well, as he also must his aunt and near neighbour, Lady Henrietta Gordon of Hallhead and Esslemont, the ancestress of Adam Lindsay Gordon (see chapter 7). The mild man appears not to have been touched a bit by these weird ones, and grew up at Fyvie and Maryculter a scholarly man of righteous, sober and upright habit, outwardly at least. He had little time for the society in Aberdeenshire that he now was part of, and his peasant connexions equally despised him for his lily-white, soft ways. His portrait by Beechey is very revealing. He might have become a cleric; although the local quality often worshipped at Calvinist shrines it was not respectable for a gentleman to enter the ministry. The Episcopalian tendency, very strong in the north-east, might have been suitable, but his tastes lay elsewhere – this was long before the 'Episkies' became High and crazy (the two other principal moods of the Anglican Church later becoming known as Low and lazy, Broad and hazy). For William the younger there was an attraction of another kind. Within walking distance almost, certainly only a short ride away from Maryculter House, was the Roman Catholic Blair's College, where William often went for conversation with the fathers, more probably for intellectual refreshment than for religious instruction. His father's peers among the landowning lairds were nearly all boorish, drunken, unwashed and stupid. A wide gulf between mother and father, and a forcing-house of education and introspection, seem often to lead to a personality of distinction untraceable to the recognizable influence of either parent. Alone of all these Gordon contemporaries, he never held any military rank, despite his coming to adult estate at exactly the time of the Napoleonic wars. The quiet man did, so the story goes, come out of his shell so far as to sigh for the love of a neighbouring girl of high class. When the mother became aware that his intentions, and the girl's, were serious, she exploded: 'I would be honoured for any daughter of mine to be the daughter-in-law of General Gordon, but I be d—d if I will let my girl have marriage with the brat of Bell Black.' Charming: a good deal more withering than Lady Eglinton's 'Be sure to clip his wings', her witty comment upon the ambitious 'vews' of William's grandfather, the 2nd Earl of Aberdeen. The woman who uttered this vile remark about young William, and meant it, was probably herself of middling lineage by comparison with him, the grandson of a duke.

In due time the tired old General of Fyvie, who had lived such a full and normal life save for his funny marriage, died in 1816. His widow, going blind now according to one of the curses laid upon Fyvie – in this case referring to the condition that would come upon some member of the family if one of them started to open up the secret chamber at the base of one of the two early towers – kept to her upper rooms, dying there in 1823. The younger William was forty when his father died, fully legitimized according to Scots law and entitled without condition, as his father's only child, to be served heir of entail in the estate and castle of Fyvie, and unfettered inheritor of Maryculter, to whose house the General had added a substantial wing with crow-stepped gables, amounting to a whole new house, with a vast stone stables and cattle byre. In spite of the unassailable legal certainty of his inheritance the children of the tiddly Lord Rockville, his first cousins, descended upon him in the bullying manner of which greedy persons thwarted by so narrow a margin of great possessions are capable. They cajoled, whined and ultimately persuaded this mild son of a housemaid that they would not interfere further with his inheritance so long as he undertook never to marry; and to leave the properties to the senior amongst them living at his death. Why he accepted and fulfilled these terms is a mystery, but he did. Perhaps, like his revered papa, he was not the marrying sort. What we do know is that he frequently visited London, where he had rooms above a baker's shop in Queen Street, Mayfair: built, maybe, at about the same time as his uncle Rockville's elegant mansion in Queen Street, Edinburgh, but of modest size and very handy for visiting the whores of Shepherd Market, a few paces away.

From Fyvie he rode often into Aberdeen, where he cultivated the acquaintance of artists and the intellectually more interesting members of the University staff. He had shown from his Eton days an interest in astronomy, and installed at the castle equipment for gazing at the stars. He added many valuable books to the library in addition to fitting up his observatory, and the latter gained him the reputation amongst the villagers of being a sorcerer, a necromancer, midnight black. They knew also of his indulgences in visiting the reverend fathers at Blair's College, and of their visits to him. When he called at the school in Fyvie village the children at their lessons there wished they could sink into the earth floor, so frightened were they of the tittle they had overheard about him from their parents. He was indeed despised and rejected. His firmness of character is silently witnessed by his apparent indifference to the slights of the gentry and the fear of the peasantry that seemed to accompany his coming in and his going out. As regards his coming in, he showed a very different face to his watchful relations, who were regularly summoned for visits. Then they had to behave as he, as head of the family, wished and he probably took quiet delight in obliging them to attend the Kirk every Sunday while himself never entered the place. He also made sure that they knew what a fortune he was spending, continuing the improvements begun by his father and making this work a central feature of his life. In its later stages he gained the assistance of the Aberdeen artist James Giles, who loved landscape and painting animals from life, especially in the wild tracts round Braemar in Upper Deeside, so different from the treeless pastures of Buchan, where Fyvie and then Haddo were becoming gracious exceptions. Giles was introduced to William in 1822 by the carver and gilder John Hay. This was a year before Giles set off on a tour of France and then Italy, the source of some of his most arresting watercolour landscapes. It is not clear that he professionally worked for William on his return – there is no evidence through writings or invoices in the Fyvie charter room, but Giles knew that William spent in all £40,000 on improvements of every sort, and he was often at hand visiting his friend. In 1830 William introduced Giles to his cousin George, 4th Earl of Aberdeen, who had been planting, draining, improving and setting to rights the disastrous rental system of his grandfather Lord 'Skinflint', and Lord Aberdeen practically ate up Giles from then on, as Giles's personal diary reveals. He was obliged in 1847 to make-drawings of the interior of 'old' Balmoral Castle to show to the Queen, who was looking for a Highland home. Balmoral Castle in fact was new, built for a younger brother of Lord Aberdeen, who complained of Sir Robert Gordon's extravagance in doing so, on the huge tract of land he leased from the Duff family. On Sir Robert's death in October 1847 (from choking over a chicken bone at breakfast) the lease of Balmoral Castle estate reverted to Lord Aberdeen, to whom it was an embarrassment. With the help of Giles's three coloured interiors and with the Queen's doctor coming to sniff the air and test the soil and water, the Queen and her consort took a lease on the property, paying their first visit in the autumn of 1848. Giles charged the huge sum of 1,000 guineas for his work. He disliked this sort of commission, wanting only to draw and paint from nature, but it worked the trick. He could not, and did not wish to, refuse the Queen's later commissions to paint Balmoral's deer forest, Lochnagar, and a view of Windsor Forest. Poor Giles! He was ostentatiously devout, even in his personal journal, but occasionally breaks out in anguish at being summoned to visit the lonely Earl late in both their lives, being treated to antiquarian conversation ranging from ancient Greece to Byzantium for a couple of days, and then a great silence and gloom falling upon his host, the cause of which he could not even guess, though his sensitive self partly blamed his own inadequacy in failing to match the formidable torrent of his lordship's outpourings.

Let us not stray too far from 'the brat' of Fyvie, third of that ilk, the 2nd Earl William being the first, and at this point recite part of the memorandum he attached to his will. To dispose first of the monetary improvements: between 1816 and 1844 rents, other than for the Mains Farm, increased from £1,979 to £4,300. With the exception of a few apartments the furnishings at Fyvie when he inherited were dilapidated, the farm offices nearly ruinous and there were no suitable arrangements for a proprietor permanently resident. William renovated completely every apartment, step by step, and provided outside such necessities for a dwelling of this size as a larder, icehouse, laundry, brew house, poultry yard, kennels, porter's lodge, butler's quarters, bridges across the river Ythan, glasshouses, coach house and stables, as well as a threshing mill, grain loft and byre for the Mains Farm. Water from a distant spring was piped into the castle. How on earth had the General and – when children – his brothers and sister and his mother Countess Anne (who dwelt as much as possible at Edinburgh) survived without these basic elements of good living in the eighteenth century? It all shows how crude were Scotch standards of living, even at the level of a duke's daughter who became whilst young the widow of a rich earl. William then goes on to claim the whole credit for the draining of the moss, the ornamental parkscape within the policies:

> A new channel for the Ythan was made above and below, and through, the Castle grounds to an extent little short of three miles. I have planted upwards of 200 acres of unproductive land, enclosing it with stone dykes within the demesne; planted about three miles of hedges and the same extent of roads and drives. The garden has been enlarged and filled with all the most expensive flowers and fruit trees.

> Upon the estate generally liberal encouragement has been given to the tenants by draining, liming, building houses [normally the tenant's job]. The manse office, school and schoolhouse, vestry, churchyard walls have all been erected since I became proprietor.

He finishes by drawing attention again to the capital outlay and increase of farm rentals: 'My successor will reap the benefit in the great increase of his rent roll, and in the increased amenity, comfort and beauty of the place.' Had he known it he might have quoted in his own favour Sir Henry Wotton's great dictum laying down the three essentials of 'commoditie, firmeness and delight' in the judging of a house of quality. In 1839 he sold the greater part of the Maryculter estate, retaining the house and grounds beside the River Dee, and carrying off to Fyvie the housebell.

In the village there remained his reputation as both a friend of the Prince of Darkness and the receiver of visits from Roman Catholic priests and monks. Anything and anybody connected with Fyvie Castle were likely to add to the superstitions which have for so long attached to the place. It was covered with curses, still is, and one of them was considered the cause of his mother's developing blindness. There was another which declared that no eldest son born at Fyvie would live to inherit it, already disproved over and over, but doubtfully escaped by him. He was probably born in the hovel assigned to Bell Black. All these curses, including those visited upon the neighbouring Castle of Gight, were ascribed to Thomas the Rhymer, who had been captured by the Queen of the Fairies and taken by her for a residential course of seven years in her domain beneath and inside the Eildon Hills far away in the Scottish Border country. She taught him to let loose curses on all who refused him hospitality. If True Thomas ever existed, he was Thomas of Ercildoune or Earlston, and he flourished fully two centuries before the first Gordon of Gight was granted a charter of this barony around 1480 and another century before the building of the castle in 1580. The original fortalice of Fyvie, built to protect the priory, an offshoot of the great foundation of Arbroath, may just have existed during Thomas's lifetime, but its only inhabitants then were a garrison under some portable lieutenant who was neither proprietor, nor heir, nor able to pry into the recesses of a secret chamber which did not yet exist. In the late nineteenth century a clairvoyant was called in to guess what were the contents of the chamber that had no entrance, no window, below the charter room. The answer was mundane: 'I see nothing but dust and a few scraps of paper.' Nevertheless a nosey daughter of the house – Janet Ross after her marriage to a rich merchant of Alexandria, and who became an enemy of the writer Ouida by stealing one of her gentlemen in Italy — had persuaded her brother Sir Maurice Duff Gordon to start tracing downwards a staircase she had discovered at the head of and behind a safe in the charter room. Sir Maurice, who was a bit of a scamp, started work, finding men to do it with some difficulty, and quickly stopped when his wife developed a touch of pink-eye.

William in his time had no patience with this sort of nonsense, and having set up the observatory he compiled a complete and scholarly record of the parish of Fyvie. His lonely life ended in 1847. His will is more revealing than the sad memorandum above-quoted in which he seems to be justifying to his successors the accidental barrier to them of his existence, despite his canny way of keeping them both at bay and at his beck during his lifetime. He was buried alongside his parents in Fyvie kirkyard, in which long ago a stone inscription gave the bare information of the dates of the death and the ages of all three. He had no option but to leave the entailed property to the senior of his Rockville cousins: a man too old to bother to move from his comfortable home in Hampshire and who therefore appointed his son to take up the inheritance. Maryculter House went also to these Gordons, now Duff Gordon. One of the witnesses to William's will was Alexander Luckie, baker, of 23 Queen Street, Mayfair, and his first-named trustee was George, Earl of Aberdeen, his cousin. His housekeeper at Fyvie, Sarah Thomson, received an annuity of £25 a year, and £10 a year went to Ann Guild, similarly employed at Maryculter. Then follow annuities to tradesmen in Shepherd Market and Curzon Street; Joseph Grigg of Market Street, oilman and grocer, John Probull, butcher of Shepherd's Court, Curzon Street, each of £100 a year. Other legacies to his lawyers and the estate factors were to suffer abatement should prior claims show a shortfall in the ability of the estate to meet them in full. This did not apply to the two London legacies, and somehow in the memorandum the witness, his landlord the baker Mr Luckie at 23 Queen Street, and the two tradesmen legatees receive a friendly reference not as regards themselves so much as to the kindness the testator had received from the several members of their families, and the rewards he hopes they may receive in addition to the gifts he has bestowed upon them in his lifetime. We need probe no further into the yearnings of this unhappy and good man, who might very well, after the treatment he received from his relations in 1816, have married and had sons, or alternatively have so conducted his affairs that at his passing the entailed estates would be so indebted as to amount to no more than a handful of air, with in addition nothing but dust and a few scraps of paper. I know what I would have done in his place.

7

'If I Had to Live Again'

Life is mostly froth and bubble,
Two things stand like stone,
Kindness in another's trouble,
Courage in your own.

These homely lines, so much better known that their nineteenth-century author, hardly proclaim an immortal poet. Minor artists are often most remembered for work not their best, and artist Adam Lindsay Gordon undoubtedly was. When he attempted 'dramatic lyrics' and a heavy heroic style the consequence could be disastrous. The uneven quality in his work is of a piece with the particular character of the man. Never a great stayer at any occupation or place, subject to intense depths of melancholy, he yet had such pronounced likes and dislikes that he was no drifter who could not determine his course through life: on the contrary.

Before setting down a brief account of his doings in a life of only thirty-seven years, it is necessary to describe how in his immediate ancestry he was drenched in Gordon blood. Only a hundred years before Adam Lindsay Gordon's birth in 1833, his great-great-grand-father the 2nd Earl (William) of Aberdeen, married to Anne, daughter of the 2nd Duke of Gordon, had a daughter, Lady Henrietta Gordon. This turbulent ladyship, at a very young age, determined on marriage with an eminent lawyer more than twice as old as she. Until, that is, she met young Mr Robert Gordon of Hallhead. She then behaved more cautiously than her aunt Lady Betty, whom we have already met in chapter 4, but in a way more deserving of censure. Not wishing to be off with the old love before she knew she was acceptable to the new, she parried messages between third and fourth parties, and set up such a cat's cradle of tangled strings that her mother, Lady Aberdeen, and her formidable granny Henrietta, Duchess of Gordon, were put in a great worry. Eventually she landed Mr Gordon, who owned the estate of Esslemont, which his grandfather had purchased. Two of their grandchildren, first cousin to each other, were Harriet Gordon and Adam Durnford Gordon. They married, and were the parents of Adam Lindsay Gordon. I will not now dwell on this abundance of Gordon ancestors, nor on the conventional doubts about cousin marriage, and remark only that Harriet Gordon was six foot high and very thin, a physique emphasized by her clinging to long, limp dresses after the crinoline came in, and was of uncertain temper, being given to really awful rages.

Their son was born on 19 October 1833 on the island of Fayal in the Azores. Durnford had, on marriage, resigned his commission in the Indian Army, Harriet having refused to live in India. She had a fortune of £20,000 which would have been much larger had not slavery in the West Indian plantations been foolishly forbidden. She had been brought up very spoilt, with two governesses and the best of everything. Adam Durnford Gordon must have been disappointed to abandon a military career, but wisely yielded. Their residence in the Azores was for the sake of her health, mental rather than physical ailments dominating her behaviour. Soon the family settled at Cheltenham, where Captain Gordon, a man of scholarly tastes, taught Hindustani at the newly opened Cheltenham College. Here Lindsay at the age of eight became one of the first pupils. After a year this skylarking boy was 'sort of rusticated' as a contemporary expressed it in reminiscence. In 1848, not yet fifteen, he was admitted to the Royal Military Academy at Woolwich, where he made friends with his exact contemporary Charles George Gordon, later the martyr of Khartoum, described by another cadet as a 'sulky little devil'. Later the renowned General gave a friend a volume of Lindsay's poetry and wrote in it: 'he was a sort of cousin of mine'. Alas! after less than three years Captain Durnford Gordon was asked to withdraw from Woolwich the unruly boy so unamenable to discipline and already keeping a horse, which was against regulations as well as being beyond his means. So the only son of the soldier who had said, at the time of his marriage in 1831, that 'father, grandfather, six uncles and all their sons, twenty of us, have all been brought up for the army', left Woolwich without a commission.

Back at Cheltenham aged eighteen, Lindsay was readmitted to the College for a short while, and dodged the knife- and poker-throwing antics of his sweet mamma, who in between tempers was gracious and far too free-spending. He originally had four sisters, two older and two younger than he. The eldest and the youngest both died young, and he seems to have been on good, but not close, terms with the two survivors. He took up with the steeplechasing and boxing fraternity. A famous middleweight, Jem Edwards, known as the Earywig, coached him and boxed with him, and he went a few rounds with the even more famous prizefighter Tom Sayers. Boxing saloons and racing stables seem unlikely nurseries for a poet, but this life had a great influence on the best of his verse, mostly written in Australia. It was good training, too, for the life he was to lead there. These pastimes did not totally absorb his interest. His closest friend was Charley Walker over at Worcester, who was perfectly content never to cross a horse, and who best liked to read a book and smoke a pipe. Charley would listen patiently to tales of the horse-racing and boxing with which Lindsay tested his endurance. There were also long recitations of poetry – every poet's poetry – for which Lindsay had an uncanny gift of memory. He disliked team games and was not attracted to hunting, partly because he could not afford it; mainly because he liked only sport where you were entirely on your own for survival and success. A combination of grit and talent enabled him to match his skill as a rider and a boxer against proven professionals. Going about Cheltenham and Worcester in flashy clothes and behaving conspicuously was defiant, but it was not an affectation. The other side to that was his shyness with girls.

It was through Charley Walker that he met a girl called Jane Bridges living at her home in the village of Broughton Hackett near Worcester, and gradually he fell in love with her. Both these young people were too shy to do anything about their affection for one another. She recalled in old age the scene when he called on her to tell her he was going away and had come to say goodbye. She simply said: 'I am sorry you are going.' They looked straight at each other and she instinctively realized from his expression the depth of his feeling. He flushed crimson and said: 'One word from you and I will not go.' She asked him why he had not declared himself before; she pretended there was now another friend in her life and he replied: 'I will *hope*,' and kissed her hand. She then rushed off, hearing her father, who was waiting to take her out for a drive, thumping impatiently on the floor of his gig.

The cause of this distressing scene between swain and damsel, which was a necessary prelude to his departure for Australia, owed nothing to his shyness. He had broken into a stables, thrashed the ostler, taken a horse called Lallah Rookh and ridden it in a race. Past the post the owner and the law were waiting. His father somehow patched up the business, which cost him £30, but it ended in Lindsay being packed off to Australia. His mother was wrapped up in her own concerns. Of the two surviving daughters one was married, and Captain Gordon had let his wife go her own way – he had taken up the post at Cheltenham College so that she could use her money in her own extravagant fashion – and, mild man that he was, had corrected his son severely only when it was necessary. There was little of the fatal distancing between parent and offspring. The scenes between them, as Lindsay told them in letters to Charley Walker, were almost like rows between equals, though his accounts may have been bravado between boys. Originally it was his own idea to go to Australia, then he abandoned it for his interest in Jane Bridges. The Captain had been sniffy about the idea of an Australian venture, but after the temporary theft of the horse, and racing it without being weighed, 'the Governor' forced the issue and got Lindsay

the offer of an appointment as officer in (what should you think, Charley?) the Mounted Police in Australia, devilish good pay, a horse, three suits of regimentals yearly and lots of grub, for me, of course, and he wants me to take it. I think I shall, in fact it's no use mincing the matter, I know I *must*, but I must do something first to make my friends remember me, rob somebody or something equally notorious.

The army was ruled out because of his near-sightedness. One English friend wrote later: 'Pluck? ah! yes, he had pluck enough but he was fearfully short-sighted; why, he used to be knocked out of his saddle by obstacles he couldn't see.' There were many goodbyes, and nothing notorious was done.

The principal survival of his leavetakings was some lines written before his departure to a sister, probably the married one who was away from home; this poem at his age of twenty must be reckoned juvenilia. Here are a few verses:

> Across the trackless sea I go,
>   No matter when or where,
> And few my future lot will know,
>   And fewer still will care.
> My hopes are gone, my time is spent
>   I little heed their loss,
> And if I cannot feel content,
>   I cannot feel remorse.

My parents bid me cross the flood,
   My kindred frowned at me;
They say I have belied my blood,
   And stained my pedigree.
But I must turn from those who chide
   And laugh at those who frown;
I cannot quench my stubborn pride,
   Nor keep my spirits down.

I loved a girl not long ago,
   And, till my suit was told,
I thought her breast as fair as snow,
   'Twas very near as cold;
And yet I spoke, with feelings more
   Of recklessness than pain,
Those words I never spoke before,
   Nor never shall again.

Her cheek grew pale, in her dark eye
   I saw the tear-drop shine;
Her red lips faltered in reply,
   And then were pressed to mine.
A quick pulsation of the heart!
   A flutter of the breath!
A smothered sob – and thus we part
   To meet no more till death.

The 'Governor' paid most of his bills and he arrived at Adelaide in November 1853. There he found no possibility of a direct commission, and by the end of the month he was in the South Australian Mounted Police as an ordinary trooper posted to Mount Gambier near the border with Victoria. Of one man he arrested he wrote to Charley: 'He is a rough customer, a fighting man and as strong as a bullock, but men out here are not very scientific fighters and he is rather shy of me . . . most of these rough bushmen are so horrid strong and heavy that it requires all the efforts of superior science and determination to beat them.' He goes on to write of the improvement to a man's health in the bracing climate if he does not drink much, in contrast to the life he had led in England with his very pluck broken down and his strength shattered. And to Charley he continued:

To rightly learn the pugilistic art
Such as Jem Earywig can impart,
Refines the manners and takes off the rough,
Nor suffers one to be a blooming muff.

But after two years enough was enough, and he resigned from the police. His intention then was to be a drover, but he became a horse breaker instead, and soon began to win a few races, never on the flat, on his own horses. Steeplechasing in Australia was very different from the sport he knew in Gloucestershire; the ground harder, the jumps more solid, the going deliberately dangerous, and the racing not confined to the winter months.

In 1855 he met a Roman Catholic priest, Father Tenison Woods, in charge of a vast parish centred on Penola in South Australia, who rekindled his literary interests and freely lent him books, some of which received pretty rough treatment, because he was sharing a hut with another horse breaker, Billy Trainor. Tenison Woods came into his life when he needed somebody who might understand how fragile was his temperament. He had already been on the verge of melancholia, and had written to Charley Walker that 'a few months of total abstinence have restored health, strength, spirits and pluck to a wonderful extent and I am now *as good a man as ever I was*, and with hopes of being a still better one, and I mean to show some of the cocktails yet what stuff I'm made of'. He was just gone twenty-two. Much later Billy Trainor, a great supporter, recalled Father Woods saying that even then Gordon was subject to a restless sort of discontent which at times almost impelled him to the idea of putting an end to the weariness of life. 'This', Gordon explained, 'was a sort of melancholy through which much of the finest poetry owed its existence.' The priest told Trainor he was impressed by this conversation, and connected it with those sad and moody fits which grew upon him more and more. He often failed to hear half of what was said to him. Then there would be jottings on scraps of paper of the verse that had formed in his head. One of these poems was almost a premonition of suicide. These are the first three stanzas of 'De Te':

A burning glass of burnish'd brass,
  The calm sea caught the noontide rays,
And sunny slopes of golden grass
  And wastes of weed-flower seem to blaze.
Beyond the shining silver-greys,

Beyond the shades of denser bloom,
The skyline girt with glowing haze,
   The farthest, faintest forest gloom,
   And the everlasting hills that loom.

We heard the hound beneath the mound,
   We scared the swamp hawk hovering nigh –
We had not sought for that we found –
   He lay as dead men only lie,
With wan cheek whitening in the sky,
   Through the wild heath flowers, white and red.
The dumb brute that had seen him die,
   Close crouching, howl'd beside the head,
   Brute burial service o'er the dead.

The brow was rife with seams of strife –
   A lawless death made doubly plain
The ravage of a reckless life;
   The havoc of a hurricane
Of passions through that breadth of brain,
   Like headlong horses that had run
Riot, regardless of the rein –
   'Madman, he might have lived and done
   Better than most men,' whisper'd one.

This is not perhaps great poetry, but it beats out at the reader with life –
and death – and the feeling, which is the case in all his better poems, of
being brought out of first-hand experience.

The tall, slim man with the sloping shoulders was always neatly
dressed, carried with him the air of a gentleman, and astonished his
companions by his reading of Horace and Browning, anything, at night
by the feeble light of a pannikin lamp, so helpful to his defective eyes. In
fact Father Woods and Trainor were both impressed by his capacity to
read, nose on book, by a poor light. It was solely his temperament that
caused this struggle to overcome physical deprivation and intellectual
frustration. He was educated to a pitch that would have enabled him to
enjoy a softer life had his spirit demanded it. He must have felt cut off
from home, for with his roving life letters to him from home were
addressed at his request to a friend, and when his father sent him
money the friend took the money and destroyed the letters. Not hearing
from home, he gradually stopped writing to the 'Governor'. After his

father's death in 1857 the truth came out. Lindsay did not mind about the money, but was very bitter about the letters destroyed and those consequently not written by him.

Apart from frequent steeplechasing these years from 1855 to 1862 were years in the wilderness in every sense, saved by the intellectual stimulus of Tenison Wood's occasional company. He brooded over Jane Bridges – his letters to Charley Walker show that – but he was shy and awkward before women, and resented certain occasions when the lady of the house where he was engaged for horse breaking would not admit him to the visitors' bungalow, and expected him to be content to bed down in the workmen's hut. Then in 1862 there was a rapid elevation from this state. A bad fall – sometimes landing from a fence was like coming down on a macadamized road – confined him to bed for a long time at the little coastal town of Robe. There, lying in the hotel, he was nursed by the proprietor's niece, a Glasgow girl called Maggie Park. When he was recovered and preparing to take his leave he blurted: 'Well, girl' – he always called her 'girl' thereafter – 'I like your ways, you seem industrious and sensible. If you like I will take a cottage at Robe and we will get married next week, and you shall keep home for me.' At eighteen Mrs Gordon was slim, like her husband, but as short as he was long, and Lindsay trained her to be a tiptop horsewoman.

One of his most famous poems, 'How we beat the Favourite', from *Bush Ballads and Galloping Rhymes*, celebrates the Loamshire Hunt Cup. It was probably written at about this time, and recalls vividly his experiences in and around Cheltenham and Worcester. A few verses give its essence:

'Aye, squire,' said Stevens, 'they back him at evens,
    The race is all over, bar shouting, they say;
The Clown ought to beat her; Dick Neville is sweeter
    Than ever – he swears he can win all the way.

'A gentleman rider – well, I'm an outsider,
    But if he's a gent who the mischief's a jock?
You swells mostly blunder, Dick rides for the plunder,
    He rides, too, like thunder – he sits like a rock . . .'

Dark-brown with tan muzzle, just stripped for the tussle
    Stood Iseult, arching her neck to the curb,
A lean head and fiery, strong quarters and wiry,
    A loin rather light, but a shoulder superb.

Some parting injunction, bestowed with great unction,
  I tried to recall, but forgot like a dunce,
When Reginald Murray, full tilt on White Surrey,
  Came down in a hurry to start us at once.

She raced at the rasper, I felt my knees grasp her,
  I found my hands give to her strain on the bit;
She rose when the Clown did – our silks as we bounded
  Brush'd lightly, our stirrups clash'd loud as we lit.

A rise steeply sloping, a fence with stone coping –
  The last – we diverged round the base of the hill;
His path was the nearer, his leap was the clearer,
  I flogg'd up the straight and he led sitting still.

She came to his quarter, and on still I brought her,
  And up to his girth, to his breastplate she drew,
A short prayer from Neville just reach'd me, 'The Devil!'
  He mutter'd – lock'd level the hurdles we flew.

A hum of hoarse cheering, a dense crowd careering,
  All sights seen obscurely, all shouts vaguely heard;
'The green wins!' 'The crimson!' The multitude swims on,
  And figures are blended and features are blurr'd.

'The horse is her master!' 'The green forges past her!'
  'The Clown will outlast her!' 'The Clown wins!' 'The Clown!'
The white railing races with all the white faces,
  The chestnut outpaces, outstretches the brown.

On still past the gateway she strains in the straightway,
  Still struggles, 'The Clown by a short neck at most,'
He swerves, the green scourges, the stand rocks and surges,
  And flashes, and verges, and flits the white post.

Aye! so ends the tussle – I knew the tan muzzle
  Was first, though the ring-men were yelling 'Dead heat!'
A nose I could swear by, but Clarke said 'The mare by
  A short head.' And that's how the favourite was beat.

'All sights seen obscurely', indeed. In the last few months of his life he
frequently went to the Yorick Club in Melbourne, where a friend and

fellow poet, George Gordon McCrae, observed him closely. Writing to Douglas Sladen he said:

> He wore a not too long russet beard, with moustache a little lighter in tone run into one. Gordon's eyes, none too large, were of a steely-grey, and lighted up to blue as he became excited in conversation, his nose straight, long, thin and pointed, his lips (what one saw of them) thin and determined, his forehead deeply lined and the crowsfeet at the corner of his eyes, carried at times much merriment in them.
>
> He was very short-sighted, yet I never knew him to wear glasses. In reading, his book or paper was held up close against his face, his nose almost touching the page. Once I asked him how he managed in steeple-chasing. He replied: 'Well enough, but I see in a mist and never beyond the ears of the horse.'

This was the sort of man with whom the virtually uneducated Maggie Park was jerked into marriage so unceremoniously. This was the man, too, one of whose famous sayings was:

> Look before your leap, if you like, but if
> You mean leaping, don't look long,
> Or the weakest place will soon grow stiff,
> And the strongest doubly strong . . .

In recitation, McCrae wrote, for which a prodigious memory well suited him, 'there was a sort of chant or croon, and I think it must have been peculiar to himself. The time in it very well marked. Once one got used to it, one liked it.'

Eighteen months after his marriage he heard that his mother had died and had left him £7,000. In 1863 he had written to his uncle Robert Cumming Hamilton Gordon: 'You would like sheep farming extremely. I wish I had taken to it, it is the fastest way and the safest way of getting rich.' Alas! the land he had taken up in partnership near Cape Leeuwin in Western Australia turned out to be unsuitable for sheep, having 'poison plant' on it. He lost most of his flock of 5,000 sheep and a good deal of his money. Back in South Australia he accepted an offer to stand for Parliament, in the Victoria district in which Penola and Mount Gambier lie. He and John Riddoch, who later became a close friend in Melbourne, beat Judge Stow, then Attorney-General, by three votes and this had the effect of breaking up the ministry, just what their backers wanted. He took his seat in the Adelaide Parliament on 23 May 1865, and on 20 September won the Adelaide Grand National on Premier. He was a failure in Parliament. Way above the heads of the company, speaking with classical allusions and in a hesitant manner, very few understood him. Meanwhile steeplechasing as an amateur led him to race in Victoria at Ballarat, Melbourne and Coleraine. All this did nothing to enhance his depleted fortune. In November 1866 he resigned from Parliament. He went to Western Australia and spent several weeks camping out on his land there, returned to the cottage the couple rented at Glenelg near Adelaide, and then decided to return to Mount Gambier to live.

Meanwhile his verses were appearing in *The Australasian*, and in September a paper-bound volume of *Sea Spray and Smoke Drift* was published at his own expense. The very first four lines of the first poem in this collection, 'Podas Okus', seem to derive from the ballad about Nathaniel Gordon. It is known that he had read Sir Walter Scott's *The Minstrelsy of the Scottish Border* and would probably also have known Peter Buchan's *Ballads*, so was this a conscious or an unconscious echo?

> Am I waking? Was I sleeping?
> Dearest, are you watching yet?
> Traces on your cheeks of weeping
> Glitter, 'tis in vain you fret . . .

A few months later came a real shocker – 'Ashtaroth: A Dramatic Lyric'. Hardly a copy sold. It should never have been written, let alone published. It is so bad that even to call it pretentious is fulsome praise. Then he rented a livery stables at Ballarat which he could not afford as such businesses are always run on credit to customers, had a bad fall and whilst he was bedridden in their cottage at Lake Wendouree their ten-month-old daughter died.

There was a muddle over the business side of the stables. He had no head for it, nor had his partner, Harry Mount. He wrote in October 1868 to his great friend John Riddoch:

Mrs Gordon went away by the steamer *Penola* [from Melbourne]. I was glad for many reasons that she should go away for a time. I gave up the stables on the first of this month. I have had some money left to me . . . it is not much but it will set me straight. I heard from my uncle Hamilton Gordon and he wants me to go to England. It seems I am the next heir to an entailed estate in Scotland called Esslemont. It was thought a certainty but I fancy there is a flaw in the entail. [There was; the previous owner had broken the entail and left the property to his niece, his predecessor's daughter.] I do not think I shall go, even if I could get the estate; having no male heir, it would be of no use to me beyond my lifetime, and that is very uncertain. . . . The stables have been very badly managed and Mount, though a well meaning fellow, has a head worse, if possible, for business than mine. . . . Since that heavy fall of mine I have taken to drink. I don't get drunk but I drink a good deal more than I ought to, for I have a constant pain in my back and head. I get so awfully low spirited and miserable that if I had a strong sleeping-draught near me I am afraid I might take it. . . . When I lost the Ballarat Hunt Cup on Maude, I thoroughly gave in and refused to ride Cadger for the Selling Steeplechase, saying it was no use. Mrs Gordon said: 'Don't give in like that, old man; you've gone too far to back out now. It's only a small stake, but every shilling is of consequence to us now.' So I rode Cadger and won. Then Viking won the hurdle race. So I didn't do so badly. You have no idea how sick of horse racing and steeplechasing I am now; but when a man gets so deep in the mire, it is hard to draw back.

The Esslemont affair involved correspondence he barely understood, but an Edinburgh advocate's report gave him hopes too high, and the small legacy enabled him to pay off all current debts. After Maggie's departure he was very low spirited, could not sleep, smoked all night long and took 'a stiff nobbler' when it was time to get up. Somehow, he told Riddoch, he got through his work. He then stayed two months with Robert Power at Melbourne, and in January 1869 for a month with the Riddochs. Maggie rejoined him when they rented from a Mr Kelly a cottage at Brighton on the coast, at that time outside Melbourne. Then she had to leave him again on hearing news that her father in South Australia was dying. There was news in May 1870 of some favourable reviews in England of *Sea Spray and Smoke Drift*, and he was working hard that month, through gloom that was sometimes impenetrable, to get *Bush Ballads and Galloping Rhymes* through the press. The note of self-pity, as well as despair, was at last sounded in another letter to John Riddoch:

If I've been a great ass I have gone through as much trouble as I can bear. Indeed, had it not been for my wife I should have got out of my trouble somehow before this. I don't think the next world is worse than the present, and if I get a little more desperate I am sure my wife would be better without me. You, who are differently constituted altogether, cannot perhaps understand how a man who has been naturally reckless feels when he gets in a hole, especially if the man is naturally vain. . . . I find my head failing me sometimes, and cannot write sometimes when I want to do it. There is not much to be made with a pen, but I could have made some if I had not been worried so. I enclose you a letter of Kendall's. [This was Henry Kendall, another poet and critic with whom Lindsay had become friendly.] He is *reckoned* the best critic of poetry here, and he is certainly the best poet. A. C. Swinburne has sent him a most complimentary letter upon a work of his which went home – indeed, a sort of rhapsody. I have no great opinion of Kendall's judgment myself, but he certainly writes well.

Kendall had become a firm friend and was reputed the better poet. Then on 4 June 1870 came the news that the Esslemont entail *had* been effectively broken in favour of the niece of the last laird, who had died in 1864. It was not so much that those Aberdeenshire doors and their lucrative acres were closed to him, as that rents accumulated since 1864 would not now help him to provide for Maggie. The news pitched him to yet lower depths of despair, for on the strength of his expectations he had allowed Riddoch to lend him money.

The bad news at last braced him on 23 June into settling up the bill for the printing and other costs of *Bush Ballads and Galloping Rhymes*, published that very day. Kendall had written a generous review from the proofs, Lindsay took another friend for a celebratory drink, then he met Kendall for a drink, both of them pretty well broke. On the way home his head ached. He walked part of the way with Frank Madden,* and hinted strongly that he should kill himself. He spoke little to Maggie at their tea and was still gloomy when they went to bed. Their landlord Kelly noticed his ill temper. On 24 June 1870 he rose in the midwinter cold at daybreak, went quietly out, failed to greet some fishermen who saw him walking off into the scrub with the rifle issued to him when he joined the Brighton Artillery Corps, and shot himself.

Let these verses from 'The Sick Stockrider' in *Bush Ballads and Galloping Rhymes* be his epitaph:

> Hold hard, Ned! Lift me down once more, and lay me in the shade.
>   Old man, you've had your work cut out to guide
> Both horses, and to hold me in the saddle when I sway'd,
>   All through the hot, slow, sleepy, silent ride.
> The dawn at 'Moorabinda' was a mist wrack dull and dense,
>   The sunrise was a sullen, sluggish lamp;
> I was dozing by the gateway at Arbuthnot's bound'ry fence,
>   I was dreaming on the Limestone cattle camp.
> We crossed the creek at Carricksford, and sharply through the haze,
>   And suddenly the sun shot flaming forth;
> To southward lay 'Katâwa', with the sandpeaks all ablaze,
>   And the flush'd fields of Glen Lomond lay to north.

* The Hon. Sir Frank Madden, later Speaker of the Parliament of Victoria.

Now westward winds the bridle path that leads to Lindisfarm,
    And yonder looms the double-headed Bluff;
From the far side of the first hill, when the skies are clear and calm,
    You can see Sylvester's woolshed fair enough.
Five miles we used to call it from our homestead to the place
    Where the big tree spans the roadway like an arch;
'Twas here we ran the dingo down that gave us such a chase
    Eight years ago – or was it nine? – last March.

I've had my share of pastime, and I've done my share of toil,
    And life is short – the longest life a span;
I care not now to tarry for the corn or for the oil,
    Or for the wine that maketh glad the heart of man.
For good undone and gifts misspent and resolutions vain,
    'Tis somewhat late to trouble. This I know –
I should live the same life over, if I had to live again;
    And the chances are I go where most men go.

The deep blue skies wax dusky, and the tall green trees grow dim,
    The sward beneath me seems to heave and fall;
And sickly, smoky shadows through the sleepy sunlight swim,
    And on the very sun's face weave their pall.
Let me slumber in the hollow where the wattle blossoms wave,
    With never stone or rail to fence my bed;
Should the sturdy station children pull the bush flowers on my grave,
    I may chance to hear them romping overhead.

8

The Storm Petrel

The date of the first appearance of 'George H. Osborne' is established beyond any reasonable doubt. At the moment of his emergence he was a handsome young man in his mid twenties, six foot two inches tall, with an easy gait, brown hair, ruddy complexion and grey eyes; he had about him an air of aloof confidence, an outward nonchalance.

His first action was to walk into the reception hall of the Revere House Hotel in Boston, Massachusetts, and book a single room for the night of 22 May 1866. He signed the register, left some unimportant luggage, and walked out again into the street. From a discreet distance, Mr Bingham, part proprietor of Revere House, a first-class hotel, watched the young man. Surely he was familiar? Then Mr Bingham remembered that the young man had stayed several days at Revere House with two other English gentlemen only a few weeks earlier. Mr Bingham glanced idly at the register: '22 May – Geo. H. Osborne'. No indication whence he had come. The H in the signature was a little shaky; it might be an N. Perhaps his confidence and outward nonchalance had momentarily deserted the young man, but Mr Bingham was not concerned about that. Casually he turned back the register, and there was the entry for which he was looking: '27 April – Earl of Aberdeen, Earl of Gosford, Mr J. Grant Peterkin. Rooms 114, 115, 116'. They were all from St John, New Brunswick. Turning to the departures Mr Bingham noticed that the Earl of Aberdeen, whom Mr Osborne so closely resembled, had left Revere House two days before his companions, at 5.30 pm on 2 May, to travel by the Providence Line of Steamer and Rail to New York. Now, it appeared, he had returned alone. Even the handwriting of the two men was similar. Mr Bingham dismissed the matter from his mind, for there was no knowing the strange ways of travelling Englishmen.

The birth on 10 December 1841 of George Hamilton-Gordon, the firstborn child of Lord and Lady Haddo, took place in the Palace of Holyroodhouse, where Lady Haddo's brother-in-law and sister, the Marquess and Marchioness of Breadalbane, had the ancient privilege of occupying apartments from time to time. There was much competition amongst parents for their first son to be born there.

George was the eldest of what was to become an affectionate, close-knit family of three boys and three girls. In the year of his birth his grandfather, the 4th Earl of Aberdeen, became for the second time in his career Foreign Secretary, this time in Sir Robert Peel's new administration, whilst one of Aberdeen's brothers, the Member of Parliament for Aberdeenshire and a captain in the Royal Navy (later promoted to the rank of admiral), secured office at the Admiralty.

Lord and Lady Haddo lived unostentatiously, despite the fact that from the moment of their marriage at Taymouth Castle, Lord Breadalbane's residence, there was at their disposal – besides the numerous homes of their titled relations – the family seat of Haddo House in Aberdeenshire, and Argyll House, Lord Aberdeen's London residence (later replaced by the London Palladium). The first home of the Haddos was a modest dwelling at St Leonard's, on the outskirts of Windsor.

One day, walking in Windsor Forest, the Queen of the Belgians, consort of Queen Victoria's Uncle Leopold, remarked upon George's good looks, especially the rich brown curls reaching to his shoulders, and asked who he was. Having been told that he was the grandson of Lord Aberdeen, who also happened to be staying at Windsor Castle, she later described him to the Foreign Secretary as 'un petit Murillo'. Between the ages of two and three, however, George's curls were chopped off to discourage any signs of vanity that might develop from the appreciative attention of admirers.

After the Haddos had been living at St Leonard's for four years, Lord Aberdeen was made Ranger of Greenwich Park and with the honour received the Ranger's House at Blackheath. It was his wish that his eldest son should go to live in this imposing mansion. The move was made with reluctance, Greenwich Park and Blackheath being no substitute for the beauties of Windsor Forest, but nobody disobeyed the wishes of His Lordship (as Aberdeen was always called within the family), not even his several brothers and certainly not his sons.

Lord Haddo's religious leanings, unlike his father's, had rapidly deepened from association and by choice. He had been under the tutelage of an Anglican clergyman called Elliott in Brighton, and at the time of his mother's death in 1833 he was staying with Elliott's brother, who was also a clergyman. Later, the two brothers became Haddo's biographers. Their work was modestly entitled *A Memoir of Lord Haddo*, the Reverend H. V. Elliott having composed the material, which was edited after his death by his brother, the Reverend E. B. Elliott.

Lady Haddo shared her husband's evangelical interests. One day they hoped to build something to the glory of God and, in the meantime, they were anxious to help the poor, though their efforts in this direction were somewhat indiscriminate. As a consequence, a neighbour in St Leonard's complained that half the riff-raff of Windsor were knocking on his door to ask for alms. Later, according to the brothers Elliott, the Haddos learned to give help where it was really of use.

Lord Haddo had sole charge of the education of George and his next brother James after the age of six; until then their mother had instilled the rudiments of the three Rs. So close were George and his father that they were hardly ever apart until the boy was on the threshold of adult life and, save for one brief period, he had no other tutor until he was nearly fifteen.

Before George was ten, Haddo took him and James on what became for some years an annual trip in August by ship from Blackheath to Haddo House. There lessons were light, it being considered a time of holiday, but even so, amidst the fishing, walking, playing with boats, cutting bullrushes and flags, as Haddo wrote to his wife: 'Jem is writing his exercise at the same table with me; George is doing his Latin in the billiard room.' And later he wrote: 'I foresee what may be a future source of anxiety in George's extreme eagerness, which shows itself in his fishing, and in every other amusement of an exciting nature.' There was also a visit for a day or two to the marine villa which Lord Aberdeen had built in 1840 at Buchan Ness, high up on the easternmost promontory of Scotland which shelters the fishing village of Boddam, near Peterhead. There they could watch the surging of the sea and the comings and goings of the small herring fleet of Boddam. Lord Aberdeen was also at Haddo at this time and, after the children had gone, he wrote to his daughter-in-law: 'You may tell George that I look for his merry face every morning in the garden, at our usual meeting place before breakfast.' Much later George's mother commented on the mode of her sons' education:

> It is generally supposed that home education makes boys oversensitive, pampered, and afraid of what is called 'roughing it' in any way. But Haddo succeeded in imparting to his boys while young a love of outdoor exercise, and a hardy energetic spirit; with an absence, moreover, of all inclination to luxury and display. This was done more by example than by precept. His own constant self-denial, the extreme simplicity of his habits, and his contentment and enjoyment in the most natural and childlike pleasures, could not but influence them.

In the summer of 1853 Haddo began to show symptoms of an illness, and by the end of the year had alarmingly lost weight. Doctors who came and went were puzzled. Then the hydropathic cure at Malvern was recommended, and there by the following June he was installed under the care of the notorious Dr Gully, with twelve-year-old George in attendance. Haddo's normal weight had been twelve stone, his height almost six foot, but after nearly two months at Malvern he failed to turn the scales at eight stone, the minimum the machine measured. The following day Dr Gully admitted that his treatment had failed and declared that he considered recovery hopeless. The disease has been described by the biographers as a wasting atrophy, but it has recently been suggested that it was the onset of motor neurone disease.

Whilst his father was taking the cure at Malvern, George's doings were recounted in a letter home by Haddo: 'Dod [George's nickname] takes letters and goes errands. After breakfast we pretend to do lessons till twelve. At dinner Dod has his pound of chops and mashed potatoes.' Haddo himself lived on a diet of a little rice or macaroni with milk and water. 'I am sometimes rather tired by Dod, the exuberance of his spirits is somewhat out of place . . . but he really is a very pleasant companion and I feel rather jealous of Money [a clergyman] who is always taking him out for walks.' George's letters to his mother tell the same story; he did not seem distressed by his father's chair-bound condition.

The next move towards a restoration of Haddo's health was a visit to Egypt. In September 1854 George accompanied his parents from Southampton to Alexandria in an Egyptian frigate. Lord Aberdeen was by now Prime Minister and this handy vessel was placed at the family's disposal by the Egyptian Viceroy. An old quartermaster told George the name and use of everything on board and whetted his appetite for a life at sea by recounting him long yarns. In Egypt they visited Cairo and travelled up the Nile to Karnak, Thebes and Aswan. In Haddo's letters to his father, Lord Aberdeen, George is mentioned only once, when they reached the first cataract:

> The days are now furiously hot; but the mornings and evenings are delicious. *February 17th.* A very distressing accident has happened. The doctor and George went out riding yesterday, as they have frequently done before; and by mere accident passed the place where I was. I did not like the look of George's horse, and made them exchange. Imagine my distress to see the doctor in a few minutes carried back senseless; having been thrown, and nearly killed. I trust that no bone is broken. But he is unable to rise; and will not allow himself to be examined by the Duke of Brabant's doctor, who arrived last night in the superb white and gold steamer belonging to the Pasha.

Some time after the Haddos returned to Britain, George asked to be entered for the Royal Navy. His father made inquiries at the Admiralty, but at fifteen he was already past the age at which he could be enrolled. It must have been scant compensation for this disappointment that he was allowed on occasions to go out with the night herring fleet from Boddam.

Father and son remained in the relationship of dominie and pupil for another two years. When, in 1857, Lord Haddo's improved health allowed him to pay more attention to his duties in the House of Commons, where he had represented Aberdeenshire unopposed since 1854, George was sent to a private tutor's establishment. This was their first real separation, and the father suffered weeks of poor sleep because of the parting. It is likely that George reacted with more resilience. The knowledge he had gained from his father put him in no way behind the other boys at Mr Bradley's establishment at Southgate, to the north of London. Besides, Argyll House, the Ranger's House at Blackheath and the open delights of Aberdeenshire were not things of the past: they were still there to be enjoyed, when he could get away from Southgate. Whilst he was there he learned to play the cornet. He wrote to his mother about buying one: 'The music master will choose a superior cornet . . . there is no chance of ever wanting another as they will always improve in tone as they get older.'

For some obscure reason he visited a neighbouring lunatic asylum – possibly Colney Hatch – whilst at Southgate and was left alone by a careless warder in a room with a fire burning, when in came an inmate shouting that he was being badly treated by the warders, who would thus drive him mad, and that if George was one of the warders he would be quits with him yet. The youth sweated with fear, but kept calm and, when the unhappy lunatic picked up the poker by the fire, George advised him that this was the right thing to do since the fire indeed needed livening up with the poker. The madman's attention thus distracted, George made his escape and was in too much of a fright to do other than accept the warder's lame explanation that a closet door had been left open by mistake.

The resilience of the boy must have been fortified by the inner independence of spirit which was so marked a feature of his later career and which had manifested itself in an odd way a few years earlier. His youngest brother, Johnny, had a clear memory of the occasion, though he was little more than five years old at the time. The three brothers were presented to Queen Victoria at a private family audience by their grandfather at the time he became Prime Minister. George, then about twelve, found himself quite unable to bow to Her Majesty when his name was announced. He stood rigidly upright until his mother, standing beside him, pressed firmly downward and forwards upon the back of his head, so that its correct inclination was achieved. Was this a rigor of nerves, or was something deeper coming unexpectedly to the surface? The two younger boys had no trouble with their obeisance.

By the summer of 1859 Lord Haddo was again ailing, so he stayed at home in Blackheath when the rest of the family went to Haddo House, where old Lord Aberdeen, retired and weary, was feeling the pinch of his great age and his loneliness, alleviated only by the presence of his daughter-in-law and her children. In one of his letters to Haddo he made a singular gesture of appreciation for the presence of his eldest grandson. For Haddo another visit to Egypt was prescribed: he booked berths for his wife and himself to sail from Trieste in October, then changed his mind because of the reports of his father's decline. All through that winter and the spring of 1860 the two men grew more frail. However, Haddo's craving for warmth became so great and his father's condition so improved that at last he and his wife sailed from Southampton to Alexandria in the early days of June. This time George was left behind at Southgate. In October the evangelizing pair again sailed up the Nile, keeping a careful tally of the Bibles, Pentateuchs, testaments and tracts which were sold at a very cheap price to the Coptic Christians and others. This evangelism angered the Coptic Patriarch. On 14 December, four days after George's nineteenth birthday, when Haddo and his wife were busy dispensing testaments and tracts at Souhadi and Ekmin, Lord Aberdeen died at Argyll House in London. George was there, together with other members of the Gordon family.

It was some time before the missionary couple learned the news, and they did not return to England until the end of May. Meanwhile, George had written to his father in a letter firmly dated 30 February 1861: 'You will have heard from Alex [an uncle] that I was with poor grandpapa at the last. Arthur [another uncle] was ill and quite unfit for anything. [The valet] Jones's devotion and kindness was beyond all praise.' Then followed much advice about the shootings on the Cromar estate in western Aberdeenshire, about which George was very keen. The head keeper there was old and needed whisky with almost every step, and George suggested replacing him with the younger and more able McBean: 'This man having been always a slave will be delighted to be his own master . . . and will not want so much wages as Ross, whose chief occupation is now stuffing birds.' Also in this letter is his response to some suggestion by his father that part of the Cromar estates, not subject to the 2nd Earl's cumbersome entail, might be sold. He would not object, he said. Then, at the end, in a breathless, unpunctuated rush:

> You will no doubt have heard about the election from other sources . . . Arthur has not behaved well and there are proofs of great duplicity and hard heartedness caused by an insatiable craving ambition to get into Parliament. He has told a genuine story which is now in writing so the proofs are evident do not be persuaded by him until you see the copies of some of his letters and hear what his words were and then see what he wrote directly afterwards.

For a youth of nineteen much of this letter seems perceptive and mature. The handwriting is well formed, flowing and precise, but what is to be made of the last sentence? Perhaps it was due to the extreme eagerness in amusements of an exciting nature which had made his father anxious when he was a boy, or perhaps it reveals slightly hysterical meddling in adult affairs from which he had hitherto been so lovingly protected. Arthur Gordon, Haddo's youngest brother, was only twelve years older than George, had been MP for Beverley from 1854–57 and had for many years acted as Aberdeen's private secretary. Now that this task was done, what more natural than that he should seek re-entry into Parliament? Yet perhaps he had behaved badly or at least rashly, because when his interest was diverted by the offer of the governorship of New Brunswick, he quickly accepted and set sail for the New World to take up the appointment. George, meanwhile, modified his attitude towards his young uncle, for directly after his father's return from Egypt they discussed the possibility of a visit by George to Arthur. During 1861 he wrote to his father: 'I still would wish to go out to Arthur, but I am very much afraid this prospect of war [between Britain and the Federalist States] may make him not willing to receive one.' That war was averted, but the American Civil War was not, and the visit was postponed for two years.

Because the Ranger's House was no longer available to the Aberdeen family, the new Earl first wished to convert part of Argyll House into a Ragged School and, when this was shown to be impracticable, sold the house, and provided schooling for the children of the industrious poor of the neighbourhood at a house in Foubert's Place, Soho (still standing at the time of writing). He himself settled permanently at Haddo House.

George, meanwhile, at the beginning of 1861, was posted to a tutor at the vicarage of Aller, on the edge of the King's Sedge Moor in Somerset, an extraordinary choice, being low-lying and damp, for a youth who complained of his chest and his cough. Nevertheless, he seemed to flourish, he liked Mr Nicholson, the vicar who instructed him, and thought of going up to Oxford. Part of the summer was spent at Haddo and Boddam, and, on his return to Aller, he hankered for Scotland. He wrote to his father imploring his permission to reside at Haddo and complete his reading there. Possibly because of his disappointment over the visit to Canada, his wish was granted and he arrived home after Christmas 1861.

The year 1862 may well have shaped the course of events during the rest of George's life. It must be borne in mind that he was now Lord Haddo, eldest son and heir to his father, the 5th Earl of Aberdeen. So shy was he of this advance in rank that, in the first weeks after his grandfather's death in December 1860, he drew cash at his bank to pay London shopkeepers with whom he had an account, rather than bring himself to say that the transactions should now be put down to the account of Lord Haddo. Though he must soon have grown used to the new name, he never wanted to flaunt himself in society as the heir to great properties, nor did he show any taste for high position. Dispensing non-alcoholic beverages at local events on the family estates was about the limit of his social and seigneurial ambition. There can be no doubt that, in the first days of 1862, he went to visit his friends among the fishing community of Boddam, where there resided also a certain milliner named Jane Ogilvie.

The first months of 1862 saw the arrival at Haddo of a tutor and chaplain, the Reverend W. B. Alexander, an English Presbyterian divine, who henceforward was daily in George's company. Decisions had to be made and preparations put in hand for the celebration of his coming of age on 10 December. After much deliberation, it was decided that acts of piety and charity should prevail over fireworks and parties, and George's majority was eventually marked by the presentation by his father to each tenant, numbering nearly a thousand persons, of a copy of *The Pilgrim's Progress* specially bound and suitably inscribed, and the distribution of blankets to the poor on the estates. All this probably suited George very well with his lack of interest in conventional junketings, though he probably had to undergo presentations to himself from the tenantry. As for *The Pilgrim's Progress*, the book had been a favourite of his since childhood.

Another landmark was the decision that he should spend the session of 1862/3 at St Andrews University. This effectively removed him from home on the actual date of his twenty-first birthday. He was accompanied to St Andrews by the faithful Mr Alexander, who had become a sort of substitute for his father, who was either ill or attending to his parliamentary duties in the House of Lords. It seems extraordinary that a young man of such sober habit should need his private tutor beside him at the university. The only explanation is that watchfulness over him was considered necessary, for the reason that there was born at 11.15 am on 27 October 1862 to Jane Ogilvie, late of Boddam, a son at 14 Kincardine Street, Montrose. The event was witnessed by a relative of hers residing at another address in Montrose, and the birth certificate describes Charles Gordon Ogilvie as illegitimate. Even before the building of the Tay railway bridge, Montrose was at no great distance from St Andrews, and maybe a part of Mr Alexander's duties was to make sure that such journeys were not undertaken.

If the deduction that George was the father is correct, one can only marvel at the speed of the change in social attitudes to natural children by these sort of people in so short a time. William Gordon of Fyvie, the son of 'Bell' Black, was fully accepted within his cousin's family (see chapter 6), though admittedly he was legitimized according to Scots' law by his parents' later marriage, and there was constant traffic between the Gordons of Haddo, legal descendants of the 3rd Earl of Aberdeen, and his natural children, their cousins, at Ellon Castle. The same applies to their relations on the other side, the numerous illegitimate children of the 4th Duke of Gordon, so closely related to the 3rd Earl of Aberdeen. There is no direct written evidence in the Haddo family papers of the existence of Charles Gordon Ogilvie, who later dropped the name Ogilvie and called himself simply Charles Gordon.

By the autumn of 1863 everything was arranged for George's visit to his uncle in New Brunswick. Despite his father's increasing weakness as winter advanced, their last days before his departure were occupied in riding together about the estate. The invalid could happily spend hours on his pony in these cold months, when even walking downstairs was a trial. They parted. 'Perhaps it is better that he should go; for if he were always at home, and as much with me as now, it would be *too* pleasant.' They never saw each other again.

After delays *en route*, George embarked from Liverpool on 16 December in a ship bound for Portland, Maine, and thence by stage-coach to Fredericton, New Brunswick. He was pleased by the American scene, its atmosphere and the difference in the Yankees' mode of life delighted him. 'All the Yankees wear square toed boots and they are very comfortable – the boots I mean,' he scribbled in a letter dated from the stage-coach.

Having arrived at Governor Arthur's little court at Fredericton George wrote to his father:

> Everything is so much like home that there is nothing which seems worth writing about. While in the States everything was curious and noticeable and I am glad that I came by Portland. I was particularly struck by the beauty of the backwoods in Maine as seen from the stage at night – the huge tall pine trees towering up . . . [Had he been reading *Leaves of Grass*?]. I was at Bangor on Sunday, a pretty town built chiefly of red brick. I went to Episcopal Church in the morning, Presbyterian in the afternooon, and a Sunday school meeting in the evening.

Quite a schedule, even on a Lenten Sunday. He included a tiny pen drawing in this letter of the stage-coach mounted on a horse sleigh: a weird box-like structure with the driver at a low level in an open seat and the luggage and mail precariously cantilevered at the back, strapped to a sloping platform.

In Fredericton the woods were calling him. After all, he knew how to use a wood axe and could quickly learn more, and his cough eased in the dry cold of the open air.

Arthur Gordon was by no means the stuffy, conventional colonial governor, though he liked to be comfortable, and he encouraged George's plan to spend some time in a lumber camp.

George's descriptions of his life, terse and vivid, show relish in the roughness and are accompanied by little ink sketches. The food was mostly salt pork cooked in its grease with molasses thrown in; wonderful light, sweet bread they baked themselves, putting the dough in a large, lidded pot over the fire with ashes piled over the lid to maintain an even heat and strong tea with no milk or sugar. 'They certainly eat more than we do here.' He admired the Indians, too, uncontaminated by whisky, who circled about and mixed with the lumbermen. They acted as guides and huntsmen when George shot caribou. He wrote with pride to his mother that once he did not take his clothes off for three weeks and only once during that time washed his face and hands.

Arthur's description of a similar expedition he had made earlier, in the summer or autumn, also living rough, is contained in a long letter dated 21 January 1864 to a young protégé, George Allan, a talented engineer who had worked as a youth in the gardens at Haddo, and for whom Arthur had secured employment with Armstrong's of Newcastle. 'I travel about a good deal, visiting all the different towns and settlements, and making exploring expeditions into the forests and wildernesses. I was for five weeks this year together in the woods without ever being under a roof. The fishing on some of the wild rivers of the interior is something quite marvellous.' He then continues:

Even a camp life in winter though not so delightful as in summer has its charms for me – a proof that I am *acclimatizing*, for two years ago I should as soon have thought of sleeping standing on my head as of sleeping in the open air with the thermometer at 20° below zero. It has its discomforts certainly – the *smoke* which chokes, blinds and blackens you, for of course the fire has to be much larger and much closer to you than in summer; the *dirt* for of course you never take off your clothes from the time you start till your return; the insufficient shelter which a camp of boughs affords, and the impossibility of peeling the bark to make one as in summer; the rapidity with which everything freezes within a few feet of the fire. You cut your bread with an axe and then thaw the *chips* at the fire; you put down your fur glove for a minute or two and take it up again as stiff as a board. You hesitate to gobble up your food Yankee fashion and it becomes hard and frozen on your knee.

This sort of going native, in moderation of course, was a regular feature of Arthur's long career as a colonial governor in Trinidad, Mauritius, Fiji, New Zealand and Ceylon, and it earned him much criticism and rather less of praise, according to the nature of those who bore witness to it. The wish, rather than the realization, of shedding for a time his aristocratic skin he had discussed over a period of some years, before his departure for New Brunswick, with George Allan, when that young man was working his way steadily upwards from an apprenticeship with Armstrong's. The idea was that George Allan should pave the way for Arthur to spend a couple of months disguised as Oliver Grant, an artisan wearing corduroys, in the carpenters' shop of the armaments factory. He had set aside a room in Argyll House to get practice in carpentry. They must not, he said, see much of each other – Allan was in a different department – in case the young man let fall an inadvertent 'Sir' in front of workmates. This somewhat strange fantasy was never carried out.

On George's return to Fredericton from the lumber camp, his heart's desire came tumbling out in another odd, unpunctuated rush of words: 'I suppose I shall come back in the beginning of April when Arthur does th^o if he were not coming back I think I should not return for some years but I suppose I must come back with him. This is a good country for anybody who likes to work I can get £4.10.0 a month and my food now and £6.10.0 next year that is for going lumbering in the woods.' Perhaps the idea of not returning for some years was a means of escaping the responsibilities of paternity.

He still had his reservations about Arthur: 'I always take Buchan's side if Arthur abuses him. . . . Captain Moody is invaluable and without him Arthur could not get on.' And then one of those rushes: 'I have suddenly decided to go out into the woods again. . . . Not Arthur's fault if I do not come home with him he is very anxious I should but I know I shall never get another chance to see the Indians and the prairies.' That letter is dated 15 April, but the sick Earl had already died on 22 March.

The last letter his father received from George before he died was dated 29 February 1864, and it stayed by the 5th Earl's bed until the end. He was only forty-seven. For the second time within four years an Earl of Aberdeen had died whilst his eldest son was far away. The news must have reached Fredericton soon after 15 April, because, of course, George did return home, for he was now the 6th Earl of Aberdeen. In writing his sorrowful feelings and condolences to his mother, he concluded: 'I am giving the strongest proof of wishing to do what I ought by coming back. Inclination would lead me to retire from sight and be no more heard of.'

For the next two years, until he assumed the identity of George Osborne, his secret self must have been in turmoil, now of doubt, now of determination. He could never forget the impression made upon him by the lumbermen and the life they led, never forget everything curious and noticeable about the Yankees whom he had so briefly seen. Nor could he for long forget the sea. As a child toy boats had been his favourite playthings, and later real boats on the lake. The visits to Boddam were remembered with pleasure for the joy of being at sea. Ashore he was not for a moment allowed to forget that he was heir to very large estates entailed upon him, nor that he must take his seat in the House of Lords and carry out a variety of public duties in the tradition of his predecessors and relations. We cannot know to what extent he was obliged to forget Jane Ogilvie. That spring and summer he was able to enjoy the company of his family during the period of mourning and much enlivened it by constructing in miniature a Canadian lumber camp to amuse his brothers and sisters. He even tried on them the nearest equivalent he could obtain to the staple dish of pork and molasses, which they much enjoyed. Above all, there was practice with James on the 1,000-yard rifle range he had devised. They were both now crack shots, and with Jem he was closest of all. Both his younger brothers were now at St Andrews University – Johnny, the youngest, having been taken away by his father from Cheam School to go there at the tender age of fifteen. Their father had been wise, for the family loved being together.

But for George the future presented sizeable problems for a young man not yet twenty-three. His father's education of him had been admirable, but it had ill prepared him for all his responsibilities. It had not been soft, yet it had sheltered him completely and deliberately from the worldly economic knowledge needed by a rich man.

It was largely his parents' fault that he so lacked understanding. In a long, grumbling letter to his mother dated only 4 April, when he was at Bradley's, he moaned about having no regular allowance, only 'this paltry pittance which is the smallest at Bradley's' save for that of the Bradleys' horrible son, who lived at home. 'Please ask papa', he continued, 'to recall what was his allowance at the same age, and to remember that all things were dearer than ten years earlier.' He cited examples from collars to boots, and complained that all his clothes were in rags or shrunk, and 'I have no evening things and now I am expected to dress decently'. Tips, books, newspapers, visits to the Crystal Palace, stamps and subscriptions were all thrown in as part of the plea for an allowance befitting somebody (though he did not mention this point) who now had to endure life as Lord Haddo, and who would one day inherit great possessions.

Much later, his mother, as shrewd as she was pious, recorded that:

> He had never been accustomed to great expenditure, nor to hear large sums of money spoken of and had not turned his attention at all to business matters. When his father's settlements were read, the impression made by them on his mind was a very exaggerated one. He did not distinguish between burdens on an estate [raised to provide the younger children's bequests] and personal debt, and he told me that it distressed him, after having carefully avoided ever being in debt, to think that he must now live on borrowed money. This was in some degree cleared up to him, but from his having enquired how many years' rental would clear off the encumbrances on the property, he was told that about three years' rental income would be sufficient.

Three years – well, he would do it, but there were other things to be arranged first. He put in hand the building of the new kirk in Methlick, as he had promised his father he would, and on 25 July 1864 he went to the House of Lords to swear the oath of allegiance to Queen Victoria and to take his seat in that august assembly. All this greatly tried him. Used as he was to hearing about the whirligig of grandeur and statecraft from infancy, he had no taste for it himself. There is no record that he again visited the House of Lords. One of the last acts of Parliament before it was dissolved in the summer of 1865 was the enactment by royal assent of the Aberdeenshire Roads Bill. Not even that tempted him. By the time the new Parliament met in 1866, he was at Liverpool, about to leave Britain for ever.

Despite the opposing tensions within him, the thread never snapped. The youthful zest and powerful talents of George and James found an outlet in what some people regarded as a good deal more than youthful larks. James, especially, handled his guns and rifles with a dangerous ease. In the autumn of 1864 George was demonstrating to the family how the Canadians had taught him to use a broad-axe and also how not to; the latter demonstration was all too successful and he very badly cut his ankle. Lying in bed recovering, bored once the wound had started to heal, Jem and he devised pastimes. One day pistol shots rang out from his bedroom. People came running in alarm. There was Jem, standing at the far end of the room holding a book in his outstretched hand. George was potting at the book from his bed with a pistol. There were remonstrations: 'Suppose Dod were to miss?' 'Dod would never miss,' was the calm reply. But that game was stopped.

In April 1865 the family was on holiday at St Leonards-on-Sea in Sussex, having rented the house of relations. One night Dod and Jem rowed out in a hired skiff determined to reach Boulogne, and then row back again. During the hours of darkness they got safely in the lee of a barque under full sail, but later were nearly run down by a steamer which suddenly changed course. By daybreak they were told by a sailing barge that they were nearer Folkestone than Boulogne. This news invigorated rather than depressed the brothers and they pulled away in the right direction. Jem later became aware that Dod was going through the motions of rowing but was in fact fast asleep. This made Jem laugh so much that Dod woke up, abused his brother for such insolence and renewed his exertions. At last they arrived, found a café to gorge on omelettes and bread, and only then were they pounced on and taken to the customs house. Here they were properly grilled in the most hostile fashion, were ordered to fill in papers, and at last released, only to be told that they must row out to sea again early next morning with both wind and tide against them.

They had the sense, on the return journey, to take some food and drink with them, but they got caught in a dangerous sea and were taken aboard a cross-Channel packet thoroughly drenched, handed over to the coastguards at Folkestone and were eventually restored to the bosom of their family at St Leonards. Jem's comment was that fortunately their mother was not apt to give way to groundless fears.

Time was running out. Jem was due to go up to Trinity, Cambridge, and Dod must have been actively planning for the three years ahead of him. Perhaps the escapade was an exercise for the serious business of becoming a seaman.

Always in the background there was Mr Alexander, kept on in the family's service to assist Lady Aberdeen in her religious projects and to act as tutor and guide to her children. He showed years later the value of his always being by George's side, ready to give advice:

We frequently talked of the importance of his getting ready for his position in life. I recommended him very much to take a degree at one of the English universities, as he was all but ready for it, and he used to tell me that unless he knew men, unless he knew what it was to be a working man, he could not talk to working men. He took a very great interest in them, and he used to tell me that we could not talk to them because we had no experience of their habits and so on. I used to laugh at that idea. I told him that he had other work, and that his work was to get ready for his position, that he was bound to get ready for it. I did not know whether he was serious at that time, or whether he was only jesting, but suddenly I had reason to believe that he was serious.

These words were uttered before the Committee for Privileges of the House of Lords in 1872.

During those two years when George was so troubled by the notions of which Mr Alexander had no understanding, one of his greatest pleasures was the rifle-shooting competitions in which he and Jem took part. Twice they were selected for the Scottish Eight to compete at Wimbledon, the forerunner of Bisley. Twice the Scottish Eight won the Elcho Trophy. The drawback to the shooting competitions was the dinners. Never much of a drinker, not even in such congenial company, these parties spoilt the fun for George. He vowed that on his return, when the three years were over, he would give up the shooting competitions so as to avoid the dinners. He told his mother as much, she wrote later, but would not alarm her by saying how long he meant to be away. He did say something of it to a cousin, Helen Scott, and also in confidence to an old friend – possibly Mr Alexander. He told his mother he would leave her with perfect comfort, because having his brother Jem, she had everything, and that Jem would be all she could possibly want.

He visited the family lawyer, George Auldjo Jamieson in Edinburgh, and caused him to draw up a trust disposition and settlement in case of his death, which he signed in London on 27 February 1865. The trustees were all within the closest range of the family and the disposition dealt only with his personal property, not the entailed estates.

So he laid his plans. The first move was to arrange another visit to Arthur Gordon, now married, in New Brunswick. The Earl of Gosford and James Grant Peterkin, contemporaries and friends from the rifle-shooting competitions, would accompany him. George determined to go in a sailing vessel, claiming that this was on doctor's advice. Mr Peterkin wished to go by Cunard steamer and Lord Gosford booked in an Inman ship. George hoped for a passage to St John from Glasgow, but had to go to Liverpool, where the *Pomona* was due to sail in January 1866.

Suddenly he turned up in Edinburgh to see Mr Jamieson – perhaps an impulsive dash to make some provision for a mother and her son. The eminent lawyer was a bit put out, but did not reveal anything of the transaction between them. It was only to sign routine papers, he said.

There were further delays:

Liverpool. 28 January

Dear Mama,

You will be surprised that I am not off and in fact so am I but we waited for a fair wind and yesterday the Capt. got drunk and *luckily* lost the keys of the cabin where the chronometers are kept so that the owner with the old brown coat found him out and dismissed him. . . . I have a nice large cabin all to myself but it is rather dark there is a nice fire close to the door so that I won't be cold, only we take some gunpowder as cargo so much care must be used and it is a good thing to get rid of a drunken Captain. . . .

River Mersey. 12 February

You will no doubt be surprised to get this so soon, but the fact is that such fearful gales have prevailed of late from N.W. that it has been impossible to get to sea. You may be glad to hear this because if the same hurricanes have prevailed with you you must have been very uneasy. Of course I am very sorry I attempted to go in a sailing ship but it can't be helped now and there is no chance of getting there for a very long time.

Fredericton. 8 April

I hope you will not be getting very anxious because of my long voyage. I was very glad to get your letter saying that you would not be anxious till the end of April as I am in hopes you may get this before that time. [She did; it was sent by Governor's Bag – London postmark April 23.] I had a delightful voyage out, fine warm weather and little wind. We were down south as far as 45°N. for some weeks so you can guess how hot it was. No words can tell how much good I got from the voyage in health tho' the food was very bad and very little of it at that. I like Mrs Arthur very much she is quite pretty and young. . . . I had some nice surgical jobs to do in the 'Pomona' as 4 men fell from aloft. [He had studied 'surgery' – first aid most likely – at St Andrews.] One had his thigh broken (simple fracture) another his collar bone and another 3 or 4 ribs. We had no materials but I made splints out of a board; and his leg is now joined and quite straight and as long as the other one. I am feeling pretty ill today owing to the change of food and too much of it. We were 45 days at sea and 3 weeks in the river. I was pretty sorry when we got to St John. We had some nice men in the ship – we used to read aloud on Sundays the Bible and bits out of a Roman Catholic prayer book. The Captain never had service or anything he was a Welshman. . . .

> By Governor's Bag
> London. 6 May
>
> I have just come back from a place called Grand Falls where we went for duck and geese shooting. We had a very nice time but got very few ducks. I got nothing at all, perhaps because I did not shoot at anything. I am going this week to Boston and elsewhere with Gosford and Peterkin but expect to return here shortly so any necessary letters had better be sent here . . .

There were two related reasons why he was 'pretty sorry' to arrive at St John. First, he had carefully avoided revealing the name of the ship in which he had sailed from Liverpool and had booked his passage in the name of 'Mr Gordon'. It may reasonably be supposed that his mother was not only anxious for his safety on the voyage but also, knowing something of his plans, worried that he might slip off into the wilds from the point of disembarkation and not visit his uncle at Fredericton. Accordingly she asked one of their naval relations to find out the name of George's ship and, when this had been done, she posted the information to the Governor of New Brunswick. As a result, directly the *Pomona* had put into St John's River, a launch was seen approaching from the shore and an ADC of Arthur's, resplendent in uniform, came on board and boomed at the captain, asking him if he had Lord Aberdeen aboard. The captain replied that he did not do much in the line of carrying lords, that he only had one passenger, and he was a good enough young fellow up forrard working the windlass. George confessed his identity, collected his things from his cabin, said goodbye to his crewmates (for he had been working among them while the man with the broken leg was laid up), gave them each a small present of money and departed with the ADC, suppressing as best he could the anger he felt.

The second cause of his pique was well summed up later by the words of Lady Aberdeen:

> He was excessively annoyed at my having allowed enquiry to be made at Liverpool as to the name of the vessel in which he sailed, and its becoming known who he was before he left the ship. There was a paragraph in the New Brunswick newspapers headed 'A Nobleman before the Mast' (which was not true on this occasion as he went as a cabin passenger, but often assisted

in the working of the ship) and the idea of his project, which he had concealed from all his friends except his brothers being thus rudely revealed, vexed him very much and in one of his letters he says he cannot bear the thought of returning to England if his name is to be in the newspapers and all he does spied out.

Despite his liking for Arthur's wife Rachael – a daughter of Sir John Shaw-Lefevre, the senior official of the House of Lords known as the Clerk of the Parliaments, who had probably helped him in his induction to the House of Lords – George seems at Fredericton to have been reserved and unsociable. 'I got nothing at all, perhaps because I did not shoot at anything.' For a first-class marksman fond of sport this sounds precious like the sulks. Arthur's entry in his laconic personal journal is equally reserved: 'Easter Tuesday. April 3. Aberdeen came.'

Then, as we know, George went to Boston with Gosford and Peterkin and also to New York, where they all stayed at the Fifth Avenue Hotel. Then George told his companions he was going first to Niagara, and afterwards back to Arthur at Fredericton.

George then cast off the travelling nobleman and put on the robe of George H. Osborne. After his first encounter with the world in Revere House Hotel, Mr Osborne felt full of life. It is improbable that he spent time strolling on the Boston Common, fond of walks though he was; more likely he went the rounds of the shipping offices and ships' masters seeking an engagement. He later returned to Revere House and changed his booking to a double-bedded room. It was too late for the companion whom he accommodated to register that night, but he did so next morning. The entry read: '23rd May. E. A. Whitman. New York.' Mr Bingham duly noticed this. Mr Whitman, if that were his real name, disappeared from George Osborne's story as completely as he unexpectedly entered it, but the very name is a strong evocation of that other Whitman, which in turn evokes some lines from the 'Song of the Broad-Axe' that seem to capture at least part of George's restless spirit:

The beauty of all adventurous and daring persons,
The beauty of wood-boys and wood-men with their clear untrimm'd faces,
The beauty of independence, departure, actions that rely on themselves.

George had now determined entirely to rely upon himself.

It is not known for certain why George assumed the name Osborne. He was widely read and may have taken it from *Vanity Fair*. If so, it was an odd choice; he had little in common with Thackeray's 'regular Don

Giovanni, by Jove!' There is, however, a more likely explanation. George Alexander Osborne, composer and pianist, was born in Ireland in 1806 and, after completing his studies in Paris, divided his time between France and London, where he settled in 1843. In Paris he had become friendly with Berlioz, who admired his playing of Chopin, whom Osborne also knew. So it was not hard for him to establish a fashionable connexion in London. Amongst much else, he wrote a number of songs including, possibly, a setting of Longfellow's poem 'The Rainy Day'. George, 6th Earl of Aberdeen, procured a copy of some song settings of G. A. Osborne and seems to have taken it with him to America and to have written on it in his own hand. There can be little doubt that George Alexander Osborne was the inspiration for that signature in the Revere House Hotel register. George H. Osborne carried the song sheet with him everywhere, and this fact later assumed unexpected importance in establishing the single identity of the two men.

At this point George's movements become difficult to trace. He wrote in a letter to his mother addressed from Revere House on 1 June 1866 that he had been to New York, to Beecher's Church, and then: 'I have still got a cough so I start tomorrow for Buenos Ayres so if you don't hear from me for some time you need not wonder.' He wrote a similar letter to Arthur. However, he did not go to Buenos Aires nor anywhere near it; nor did he sail at that time to Cárdenas in Cuba, another false trail unwittingly laid by him. In the end practically all his movements aboard ship and ashore became known due to a thorough inquiry held after his death – the reasons for which will become apparent if we now jump forward more than four years from the date of that letter ostensibly sent from Revere House on 1 June 1866.

One day early in August 1870 James Erastus Green, formerly of Richmond, Maine, received the following letter from Captain James H. Kent of the schooner *Hera*:

Melbourne. 10 June 1870

Dear Sir,

Finding no address but yours, I take the liberty to address you, hoping you will inform his friends of the sad news. Mr G. H. Osborne of Richmond shipped on board my vessel in Boston, Jan. 14 and left said port on the 21st for Melbourne. On the morning of the 27th, while seeing the mainsail lowered, was knocked overboard. All means was taken to rescue him, but could not, being a very heavy sea at the time. The 'Hera' will probably return by way of China. His friends will please address me at Chatham, Mass.

George's last letter to reach his mother was dated April 1869 from Molino, Florida, and in it he gratefully acknowledged seeing in that improbable place an old copy of the *Boston Herald* in which she had put an advertisement saying that she was alive and well. In fact there were two advertisements in personal columns in the American press over a period of several months. The first, which appeared in January 1869, stated: 'Dod, I am well but we are in affliction, and I long for you that we may comfort one another. There is a long letter for "Dod" at the Post Office.'

When it became apparent that this was money wasted, a second message was substituted: 'METHLICK, July 12th, 1869 – I have been seriously ill; getting better but very weak, come if you possibly can immediately, for you are more needed than you can think. M.A.' This one was headed not 'Dod' but 'Haddo'.

These advertisements were in response to fears about her which he had expressed in his letters. On his trips about the States and at sea he never seems to have picked up any of the mail that was sent to him, for he never in his letters acknowledged receiving any, yet there is inferential evidence that he did get some. Not that it matters. The pain was with her, not him, and there were now special reasons why she badly wanted him back. Her anxiety about him had intensified to agony, for his beloved Jem was dead. Dod, in his turn, was determined to play out George Osborne a little longer; for a start, deep friendships had been formed and besides, although the three years were up now and over, there were reasons of personal pride in achievement which prevented an early return home. A certain voyage must be accomplished. Nevertheless, had the news of Jem's death been made known in those advertisements, Dod might have returned home.

In Scotland in autumn 1869, Lady Aberdeen wrote to Mr Alexander, who was by this time minister at the English Presbyterian church in Birkenhead. Would he, she asked, throw up his living for a while and go to America to find George? It would be difficult. In his few letters home George had never once mentioned the name of a ship in which he had sailed – only places he had visited and written from. Neither had he given the name of any man, only initials and occasional descriptions. (George seems not to have written a single letter to the daily companion of his student years, although Mr Alexander wrote several to him.)

The diligent minister took up the challenge at once on generous terms and sailed from Liverpool in November 1869. He arrived in New York by the end of the month and put in hand a number of inquiries both there and in Boston, travelling several times between the two cities. It is most likely that Mr Osborne and Mr Alexander were at least once in one of these places at the same time, but Mr Alexander did not know that it was George H. Osborne he was looking for, and George, had he become suspicious that his doings were being spied out, had become good at not being found. Mr Alexander, of course, spied out nothing and set off for Molino, Florida, where George's last letter had been posted, and then to Pensacola on the gulf coast of Florida. He made the acquaintance of the mayor of Pensacola, Mr Cobb, whom he described as 'a godly, intelligent and penetrating man', confided his mission and showed him photographs. Mr Cobb said: 'How strange; I know him.' At the end of 1868 a young man called Wood had come to his office with a sea captain, who had asked Mr Cobb if he could give the young man clerical work. Mr Cobb sent them up to Molino, a small town where a sawmill might offer a suitable job. The young man had said his chest was weak and he wanted to spend a year in Florida for his health. This is the first revelation in the documents that George had adopted the name of Wood, a most appropriate choice for a potential employee of a sawmill.

Mr Alexander then busied himself inquiring on the river between Pensacola and Molino, and on the new railroad under construction for somebody of that name. He went to Molino and called on the sawmill manager there, but he knew nothing. The foreman was in the forest, but the watchman declared that a young Englishman named Wood had been in Molino, had stayed in his house for one night, and had left the next day. He at once picked out George as Wood when shown photographs: 'That's Wood, only he was fairer than that makes him.'

In a book-length letter to Lady Aberdeen, Mr Alexander launched into a meditation on whether his absence from his pastoral work in Birkenhead was good or bad for his flock, concluded that it was good, that the work he was doing needed to be done for Christ. 'I repeat therefore that to find the wanderer as I shall call him is well worth any search and many many months' delay. He must be got alike for your ladyship's sake and for his own. So that though I am cast down about the disappointment I am not greatly discouraged. Wait in Jehovah!! He is faithful and He will do it.'

The common identity of Wood, Osborne and Aberdeen cannot be doubted. On 13 April 1870 it became apparent to those at home who were busy trying to trace George's whereabouts that a certain Captain Otis of the brigantine *Normanby*, sailing from Boston, had put in at a port on the coast of Belgium. It was guessed, rightly, that he had taken George as a passenger to Florida. It was arranged that Captain Otis should be visited by William Alexander Baillie-Hamilton, George's first cousin who was three years his junior. Photographs were shown to Otis, but he was not able to identify George or Wood with absolute certainty. 'I tell you what, though,' he said, 'there is something of you that reminds me of him far more than this photograph.' When Baillie-Hamilton first came into the room, the image of Wood had at once sprung to the Captain's mind. He then described George in detail, including a 'rather peculiar sort of slouch', characteristic of his posture. Baillie-Hamilton concludes his account somewhat brusquely, complaining of his close relation 'going about the world under half a dozen aliases'.

In May 1870 Mr Alexander at last left Pensacola for New Orleans, where some spirit prompted him to make for Galveston in Texas. He now behaved more like a professional sleuth, and somehow worked through the customs' lists of sailings to and from Boston in February and March 1867. He saw also a missionary for seamen and enlisted the help of the British Consul. The missionary promised to write to him should he unearth the name of any 'very nice' captain at the date indicated in certain of George's letters to Jem and to his mother. Mr Alexander arrived in Boston on 21 May to find a letter giving the name of Captain Wilbur of the *Abbe E. Campbell*.

When he went to call on Captain Wilbur, who was living ashore at that period, he became aware for the first time that George was using the name of Osborne. The photographs and the descriptions tallied. Wilbur knew a small ship George had skippered. This led Mr Alexander to Richmond, Maine, where he was told that George had sailed in January in the *Hera* bound for Melbourne. He thereupon visited the Boston firm of H. W. Peabody, which had chartered the *Hera* from her owners, Nickerson & Co., and he found them helpful and informative. All this was before the arrival of Captain Kent's letter from Melbourne. Mr Alexander telegraphed Lady Aberdeen and returned to New York, where Mr Dabney, the banker representing the family, advised him to stay and await news from Peabody's. The impetuous man of God agreed to do so. Thus the chain of communication, which had started with Captain Wilbur, extended through Peabody's to Sewell Small of Richmond and James Erastus Green, George's principal friend in Maine. It was a good thing that Mr Alexander took Mr Dabney's advice, instead of dashing off to Australia as he had wanted, for it was thus that he heard of the news from Captain Kent in his letter to Mr Green. At last, therefore, the cable on 30 August 1870, followed by a letter, followed by himself, conveyed the sad news to Haddo House.

By coincidence Arthur Gordon was staying at Haddo House when the news arrived. He had long left New Brunswick and gone, via New York, to be governor of Trinidad. Whilst in New York in the autumn of 1866 he may have seen George. An entry in his journal simply records: 'Oct. 21. Sunday New York a nasty town. George came.' There may have been other Georges. In August 1870 Arthur was home on leave, soon to take up a new appointment in Mauritius. Returning one day from a walk with a young relation, a descendant of the 3rd Earl's Ellon Castle brood also called Arthur Gordon, he 'heard the news which had arrived – George was dead – washed overboard on the 27th of January'.

'What a close to what a strange story!' wrote Arthur in his journal.

I shall not soon forget that evening – the empty places of Mary and his sisters at dinner and the hush on everything – I went to see Mary at once, calm and composed and thinking of others, but heartbroken.

On Tuesday 30th Johnny, who had been sent for, returned. The day was a strange one. Lindsay [husband of George's sister Harriet] unpleasant. On Wednesday the Jamiesons [he was the family lawyer] came and on Thursday morning Admiral Hamilton [a relation of Mary Aberdeen]. On that day we had our meetings and resolved at once to recognise Johnny as Lord Aberdeen, though in my mind some doubt lingered. The next day Alex [a brother of Arthur] and Lord Jerviswoode [Mary Aberdeen's brother] came and also Mr Alexander whom we cross-examined. By Mary's desire I wrote an article for the Banffshire and other papers.

The article in the *Banffshire Journal* is unremarkable, but is neatly and concisely turned.

Arthur and his family then left to spend a couple of days at the marine villa at Buchan Ness, where they were joined by the same young relation who had been at Haddo and who was a kind of permanent ADC to Arthur. 'After our return to Haddo we spent a quiet but very pleasant month. It was in many ways very enjoyable. I went once to Edinburgh with Johnny which was *not* enjoyable but was useful . . .

how lovely the valley looked above Gight and what nice walks I had with Johnny or alone. Unhappily Johnny has no taste in aesthetic appreciation.' Then Arthur, his wife and baby went on their way to stay elsewhere; eventually he took off for his new appointment in Mauritius.

The resolution at once to recognize Johnny shows a touch of pompous self-importance, despite the fact that he was the only survivor of the three brothers (Jem's unhappy fate will be told later). Arthur knew perfectly well that for Johnny there lay ahead a long and complicated web of legal and constitutional processes before he could establish himself either as a peer or as the rightful inheritor of the entailed estates. Suppose George had married in America, and had left surviving male issue? Mr Alexander had naturally not been able to prove that, nor prove that he was really dead, but it would have to be done. And what about Miss Ogilvie's son Charles? It is from part of those processes, depositions by shipmates and others sworn in Boston and elsewhere, the hearings before the Committee for Privileges of the House of Lords, as well as from George's letters and from Mr Alexander's travels, that we learn in some detail what Mr Osborne had been up to during the years since George, 6th Earl of Aberdeen, had left the Fifth Avenue Hotel in New York.

Before turning to that story, two questions must be asked. How much did Arthur know? Why, during his long stay as governor of Trinidad, did he apparently do nothing to find out where George was, when ships were passing continually in and out of Trinidad through the narrows of Bocas de Dragón? Mary Aberdeen must have written asking him to make inquiries through the official and other resources at his disposal, but there is no evidence that he did so – rather the contrary. Even when Seaman George did put in to Trinidad there is no reference to a visit on that date in Arthur's journal; only a later entry, recording news of the tragic end of Jem in February 1868, reveals that George had been in Trinidad in December 1867 and had called on him. Whether he or anybody else ever knew about the illegitimate Charles Gordon Ogilvie is not established.

Arthur can be largely exonerated for not giving as great attention as he might have to the whole curious business. He had tried his best whilst in New Brunswick, and had made considerable inquiries. It is clear from his journal, too, that being governor of Trinidad was no rest cure. There were many difficulties in the handling of a strangely mixed population – Spanish, French, Negro, Indian and English – with largely separate and jealous communities. Above all, there were peculiar personal difficulties with Captain and Mrs Moody on his staff, and most particularly with that young relation also called Arthur Gordon. This young man, to whom Arthur was greatly attached, and who had been with him first in New Brunswick, often became sulky and silent or at best monosyllabic, sometimes went off on expeditions for several days, came back no better tempered, and even stopped attending Holy Communion. He had his twenty-first birthday in Trinidad, almost rejected a signet ring Arthur gave him, and seemed to exhibit the usual symptoms of tiresomeness and frustration of his years. On occasions Arthur's usually laconic diary suddenly bursts into agonizing over this boy. He even prays to God in the journal that these unbearable trials may be taken from him, or that he should suffer rather than the young man's sins go uncured. Thus Arthur may be excused if he did not bend his energies to the arduous pursuit of the feckless sailor, and Mary Aberdeen's worries were thousands of miles away, to Arthur quite out of sight. He had never shirked *his* responsibilities, nor sown any wild oats; his devoted service to 'His Lordship', as his father was universally known amongst the family, had made any such thing out of the question for him.

At the time of the Boston hearings at the end of 1870 into George's life and death in the USA, a long article about the aberrant 6th Earl of Aberdeen appeared in one of the Boston newspapers signed D.M. This writer, however indirectly, seems positively inspired by the viewpoint of the former governor of New Brunswick. Although D.M. is understandably inaccurate in some of his facts and sometimes takes to fancy, passages of his article throw light, however distant and distorted, on the degree of knowledge Arthur had of his nephew's life and attitudes, what he thought of him and what he did to try to dissuade him:

In the spring of 1866 he visited his uncle at Fredericton, N.B., but was quite restless during the visit, apparently disliking company and the deference paid to his rank. His uncle . . . used every means within his power to induce the young Earl to give up his roving life and return to Scotland, but in vain.

The Earl was next heard of from Boston. He wrote to his uncle early in June 1866 from the Revere House, that he intended to sail the next day for Buenos Ayres, which caused him great uneasiness, for there were matters in the county of Aberdeenshire in which he was interested that could not be adjusted without his presence. This had been represented to him before he left Fredericton; but he seemed utterly indifferent to any business at home, intent only on becoming a sailor.

His uncle employed agents in Boston to find him, and furnished a specimen of his writing as a guide by which to trace him at any of the hotels. . . .

After a careful search it was ascertained that he had not sailed for Buenos Ayres, but had shipped before the mast on board the barque *James M. Churchill*, of St Andrews, N.B., commanded by Capt. Hutchinson, on the 28th May, 1866, bound for Cárdenas, Cuba. F. W. Grantham Esq., the British Vice-Consul at Boston, observed the ceremony, recognized him by the description, and asked him, when the shipping articles were before him, if that was his signature, and if he knew the nature of the agreement he had signed. 'O, yes, Sir', he replied in an easy off hand style, and stepped aside for others to come forward and answer to their name. Mr Grantham has forgotten the name he signed, but feels confident it was the young Earl who stood before him. Subsequent inquiries show that he left the Revere House on the 26th May, two days before he signed articles. As the vessel did not sail for several days after she cleared, the fact that he wrote to his uncle in June is explained. His uncle supposed that at this time he assumed the name of Adams or Anderson to correspond with the letter 'A' marked on some of his clothing. [George did not, in fact sail in the *James M. Churchill*, probably for fear that Mr Grantham would uncover his new identity.]

It is supposed in opposition to this surmise that he had some friend in Boston, to whom he entrusted all his fine clothing, and that when he went to sea there was nothing in his possession by which he could be known. Sailors sometimes are in the habit of turning the inside of a shipmate's chest out when he is at the wheel. . . .

What could have induced his lordship, at 24 years of age, in defiance of the earnest entreaties of his family, to take up such a mode of life? A man of great natural abilities which had received the most careful culture, a personal reputation without even an insinuation of immorality, and with ample means to support his rank – what infatuation could have possessed him? In some of the correspondence before us it is stated that he was very much in love with a seafaring life, but we doubt it. . . .

We have heard that a fickle fair one was the only cause which drove him to change the current of his life. It is said that he was beloved in return, but she suddenly changed her mind and insulted him. It is this, we have heard, which induced him to sink his rank, and to alienate himself from the society in which he had been born and educated; and this view is confirmed by the fact that he did not wish to hear from his family, and took particular pains to conceal where he intended to go. Many letters had been sent to him addressed to the care of agents here and in New York who were instructed to find him, but as he could not be found, the letters were returned. . . .

* * *

Palmas. July 25th, 1866

How anxious you must be by my long enforced silence. I hope you got my letter stating that I was going on a voyage to try and drive off the nasty and dangerous cough which when I last wrote appeared a fixture, if so you will be glad to hear that there is now not a vestige of it and by the goodness of God I never enjoyed such perfect health in my life. How it will be when I return to the cool New England climate I know not but I believe that by passing this winter in a southern clime and thereby avoiding a cough my lungs will recover themselves and I may with safety return in the spring so much better and I trust wiser as to compensate you for the anxiety you must have felt during this time. . . . I am going to give this letter to the Captain of a Boston ship who will I trust post it but I fear it will be some time before you get it. [An Edinburgh postmark on the cover is dated 13 October.] It is long long since I have been able to get a letter from you and I am indeed anxious to hear how all are and how you are yourself in particular. It will be a long time before I can get any of your letters which are some now at Fredericton and others at 5th Avenue Hotel, New York. I feel persuaded that all is well and I expect to be back in New York or Boston about October when I will of course get letters and write you again. . . . This is a splendid place on the coast of Africa. It is pretty hot during the summer and I believe temperate in winter. The natives speak Spanish and are the most obliging, civil, hardworking and honest people I ever saw; food, lodging and clothing are cheap as dirt and wine is cheaper than beer. . . . I saw the most magnificent sight in passing far famed Teneriffe at sunset. The bold, ragged volcanic rocks lighted here and there by the setting sun with a glorious background of sky: high up a veil of fleecy clouds and all aglow far above this the famed peak of Teneriffe. It was a grand sight and one that called up in my mind solemn thoughts and good resolves, and especially vivid and pleasing reminiscences of dear Papa. I promise to give you the earliest information about myself.

George's relations might have liked better clean, plain prose and a clear statement of intent in this characteristic letter to his mother.

Boston. Oct 21. '66

. . . I am back again here in old Boston at last and to my great surprise I find that Arthur has left New Brunswick and I know not where he is gone; this is rather embarrassing to me as owing to the enormous expense of everything in New York and elsewhere I had spent about all my money before I went to the coast of Africa, so now I'm in considerable of a fix. Of course I have not heard from you because I suppose he has got your letters . . . I have no doubt it was owing to your prayers that we arrived here safe from the West Indies

148

before these fearful gales in which the 'Evening Star' was lost. The 'Evening Star' calamity was an exact repetition of the loss of the 'London' last fall so as I know you have read the account of that you know all about this. You will be glad to hear that I really think that my lungs are permanently cured by the long spell of warm weather and sea air, yet I think it would be foolish to risk a return to England at this season. No , much as I should enjoy once more to taste the sweet pleasures of family life I cannot yet leave this land of freedom and common sense, at least I cannot leave the protection of its glorious flag . . .

Excuses for putting off the day of his return were forming clearly in his mind; they were to be repeated and reinforced in his letters as time went by. Not that George was leading a cushy life; far from it. Arthur and his bride grumbled and groaned at the discomfort of the various sea voyages that took them from New Brunswick to Trinidad, although occupying the best staterooms, so what must it have been like for a nobleman now really before the mast? Discomfort seems not to have bothered George at all, and even accidents are casually referred to, though sometimes in gruesome detail. The first trip to the Canaries made him feel so alive that nothing else mattered. In a letter from Boston which reached his mother just before Christmas 1866, written nearly two months after the voyage was over, the style sparkles with deft impressions:

I never told you of my adventures on the African voyage, or about loading salt in the West Indies or about the mysterious man, or about the wounded cook turned sailor or the amorous mate or the mate in fits calling for his mother, or about the cook drunk, a Frenchman crying, the 2nd mate bullying, or about the Capt. drunk, the mate ¾ drunk, the 2nd mate green and the ship running on George's shoal and being saved by the undersigned who was not drunk – about the talking parrot overboard, 'saved, saved saved', about the honest soldier – about the happy island, the Arcadia of the Atlantic, about the French cook – good times now for the shell backs, plenty to eat and good at that. Or 'a shark, a shark!' pork the hook – he is caught, haul him aboard – frantic terror of the parrot – he tries to commit suicide – the shark is killed – shark steaks for breakfast – or about the undersigned sick with the cholera – he gets well – he gets his toe crushed. He knocks off at 5.30 p.m. – he turns to again at 6 a.m. next day. Spanish Pilots – or about the undersigned painting yards – *tired* and hot lets bucket fall – covers clean white boat with paint – sputters Captain over with paint. Captain swears – mate runs – undersigned tries to look serious – gets soap and hot water – and cleans boat – no more painting for undersigned – just what he wanted.

Homeward bound, provoking calms – gale of wind, the shoal of dolphins – of whales, of porpoises. Nantucket shoal, thick fog – and a half five. All hands 'bout ship – turn out here – no clothes on – work hard – get ship about. Fog horn! Blowing the fog horn all night and all day – pleasant sound – sore lips. Boston – pilot boat. Pilot long coat nice man – said undersigned good helmsman. Old Boston again. Home at last. Runners and pipes – man the boat. Undersigned stroke oar – take Captain ashore. Cook drunk no supper – cook drunk no breakfast – cook drunk no dinner. 2nd Mate drunk. Captain ashore – undersigned steals bread and sugar. Alongside the wharf – sleep ashore – pay day Savings Bank. Mysterious man drunk etc. etc. etc. Mysterious man disappears mysteriously. I have lost my cheque book and I mean to leave here in a day or two . . .

Late in 1870 Mr Henry Stone Smith, an Edinburgh advocate, was retained by the family solicitors to go to America as Commissioner charged with the collection of necessary evidence in the form of sworn dispositions to establish beyond doubt that George had not been, like the ridiculous parrot, 'saved, saved, saved', when he was swept overboard on his fatal last voyage; to corroborate so far as possible the course of his wanderings as described in his letters; above all to demonstrate – prove is too strong a word – that he did not marry and therefore had no legitimate male issue. Great care was taken, then, to find people whose testimony would be uncontaminated by any hint of scandal and believable to the Sheriff of Chancery in Edinburgh, and later to the Committee for Privileges of the House of Lords, so that Johnny's claims to succeed to the estate and to the peerage titles could be upheld.

As regards the voyage to the Canaries it was pretty hopeless to search for drunken captains, amorous mates, French cooks and the like, but the very man was sought, and gave his testimony last of all the witnesses, in New York on 24 April 1871. He was the 'honest soldier' so sparingly referred to in George's vivid, darting letter; a veteran sergeant of the Civil War, William Randolph Hawkins.

He sailed as a seaman from Boston in June 1866 in the brig *R. Wylie*, bound for Palmas. 'Captain Crosscup was master,' he testified.

A person of the name of George Osborne joined the ship as a seaman. Osborne and I were in the same watch, we became very intimate. I had myself enjoyed a good education, and I soon found that he was much my superior in that. But we took to each other. When Osborne joined the ship he was not dressed like a sailor, and I was surprised to find he had shipped as

one. His hands were tender, and they soon got blistered. Mine were then in a
similar state, and we joked about it. . . . He told me Osborne was an
assumed name, and that his real name was Gordon. But he said I must not
mention it on board the ship. He told me he was a Scotchman. But though I
touched him once or twice on the subject of his own history he seemed not to
like to speak of it . . .

Hawkins expanded on many of the details of George's account of the
trip – splashing the paint, catching the shark, the parrot (though the
sergeant could not remember whether it had been rescued), the
drinking, the loading at Turk's Island of a cargo of salt, and rowing the
captain ashore. 'I pulled the forrard and he the stroke oar. He was a
very good oar.' Commissioner Smith knew his stuff, for it was well
known that George and Jem had both been good oarsmen.

The honest soldier recalled that he had stayed in Boston for about
three weeks. He and George had seen each other every day, he said,
though they had not shared lodgings; George had been minded to stay
in Boston to perfect his navigation. Hawkins described how they had
walked together on the Boston Common one day before they parted for
ever, and had sat by a fountain, where an extraordinary conversation
took place:

He asked me if I would like to go to Scotland. I said I would, if I were to go as
a gentleman and not as a seaman. 'Well,' he said, 'if someone would furnish
you with means, would you go?' I replied, 'Yes.' 'Then,' says he, 'if I were to
do it, would you go?' I believe I declined. I did not see how he was to do it,
because he had only the same wages as myself. But he seemed to be speaking
seriously enough for all that, and if I had accepted I believe now he would
have done it. Osborne and I went down to see a missionary ship, the *Morning
Star*, in which he wanted to go. . . .

Sergeant Hawkins was able to give Mr Smith a photograph of
George. This was useful, because Mr Smith had brought with him a
number of photographs of George taken in Scotland and also a few of
contemporaries and relations, including members of the multi-
tudinous, closely related Polwarth Scott and Baillie-Hamilton families,
and got all the witnesses to identify him. To find an American friend
able to produce even a tin-type of George was vital additional
corroboration. Sergeant Hawkins's final words, which were echoed by
most of the witnesses, were that George was an unmarried man.

George had written home expressing his keenness, after his successful experience as a seaman, to join the missionaries in their beautiful little vessel, the *Morning Star*, due to sail for Honolulu and the Friendly Islands. She was built by the Sunday Schools in New England with the children contributing, he said, and would take out a load of coal and some missionaries. 'I am going tomorrow to see M— B— of the missionary ship. Pacific is a splendid climate and I have always wanted to see and taste breadfruit. What I made on the last trip is about half spent so of course I must soon be off again unless I go to the woods, which of course I should love to do but am afraid of my lungs.'

His next letter six weeks later, still at Boston, praises the city and the fine Indian summer which got him into December without any sore throats.

> I am deeply engaged in teaching navigation at present; it is a most interesting study, far superior to any I have yet come across. Jem would make a splendid navigator – I think much of him. . . . The missionaries went back on me for the sake of a Kanaka [Canadian]. I wish I could have gone with them. I think anyone who has not been round the Cape or Horn is small potatoes. I am small potatoes but I hope to go in a day or two. A man here wanted me to go to Gloucester and set up a navigation school – he pay expenses and me teach I get half the profits. I have not settled yet for I would rather go a deep sea voyage.

So that was it; carrying coal and missionaries would get him round the Horn on the east-west route. The *Morning Star* was built for the American Board of Commissioners for Foreign Missions. Alpheus Hardy, a member of the board, had the duty of engaging the crew. George applied to him for the post of first officer. The master already appointed, Hiram Bingham, was a missionary rather than a professional mariner, so the insurers stipulated a first officer of experience. Mr Hardy took to Osborne, much regretted not being able to place him in the berth, and the young man seemed much disappointed at not getting it. The *Morning Star* sailed, leaving behind the small potato determined to put right his deficiencies by sprouting the eyes of an experienced navigator.

George was lodging at the time in Boston in the house of Mrs Adaline Pearson, whose young son Frank, riding master in Draper and Hall's Riding School, recalled later how George had studied navigation at the Boston Nautical College in Tremont Street and also worked at it at home. Frank Pearson thought George had also been teaching somebody navigation. He did not mix with other lodgers in the house. Frank, being then recently married, had often talked with him about marriage. George had said there was time enough yet. Frank Pearson had apparently been greatly surprised by George's skill at sewing, which shows that he had already become a professional seaman.

On 4 February 1867 George gained his mate's certificate, being marked only one point short of the maximum for proficiency. A year later he got his master's certificate, the examination being the merest formality according to Thomas Ellison, secretary to the American Shipmasters' Association.

During his intensive studies George did allow himself one brief dalliance, in January 1867, by submitting for once to the lure of steam in the company of an American naval officer, Captain Eldridge, who had also introduced him to the Nautical College. They travelled as passengers in one of the luxurious steamships which plied between Boston and New York, stopping overnight at Newport, Rhode Island.

How far ahead [George wrote to his mother] of any English boats they are. They average from 1600 to 2000 tons register or larger than a P. & O. steamer. They can go 22 to 24 miles an hour. The saloon is the whole length of the boat, probably larger than any ballroom you ever saw and certainly much more gorgeously and elegantly fitted and decorated. The roof of the saloon which is about 20 ft. high is arched, moulded something like that of a cathedral and supported by massive corinthian pillars; it is lighted by numerous bronze chandeliers burning nothing but gas. All the state rooms of which there are about 100 are lighted also by gas. The saloon has lots of armchairs and lounges scattered about and is carpeted with the softest and most beautiful productions of Brussels. In the middle is a sort of screen wihh a plate glass window at one end of it, and here may be seen the polished engines. You may wonder how the smoke stacks do not interfere with the saloon but this is managed by having a large framework built out beyond the side of the boat on which are placed in the open air the boilers on each side, each with its own smoke stack. There is a ladies' saloon on the main deck and below this again is the sleeping saloon containing many hundred berths with a semi-circular rod carrying a curtain round them so that by drawing the curtain the occupant has a little private tent of his own. The charge for all this elegance, comfort and speed is only 5 dollars between Boston and New York. The Yanks know how to do the handsome thing. . . . England is certainly very small potatoes as compared with this country. The more I see of it the more I am disgusted with the old world institutions. . . . I have been trying hard to find out where Arthur is but without success, however I must get to him as he has no doubt many letters and also many valuable things I left with him. I am now going to start for the West Indies to seek for him. I suppose I shall go to Havannah first and then to Trinidad. I have just got a cough for the first time this winter. We have had the biggest snowstorm on record in Boston. It was a wonderful sight . . .

That letter was sent from Brooklyn in January 1867. Even steam and a popular floating equivalent of the glorious vulgarities to come later of the millionaires' cottages at Newport were good enough sticks with which to beat the English donkey. George admitted, even so, that this extraordinary vessel and its like were shy of putting out in hard weather. One of them had been lost recently, and the boat George travelled in only got out of Newport at the third attempt. In his next letter home, this time to Jem, his dislike of English institutions comes fairly pouring out. This letter and another to his mother gave Mr Alexander the leading clues in his quest for George, without a single name of a ship or of a person ever being mentioned.

Houston, Texas, March 15th, 1867

My dear Jem,

. . . I started out from New York in order to get to Arthur and recover the bulk of my property letters etc. which I believe he has got. I came here because I thought this was pretty near to Trinidad. I find now I can't get to Trinidad from here so I propose shortly to go to New Orleans. I had no money to get anywhere and as my clothes were all worn out during my voyages I could not think of any means to get some decent clothes and then I recollected as if by inspiration the name of a banker in New York who gave me money. Now I am here I think of going up the country to see what it is like. The people here are the most villainous cut-throat looking heathens I ever beheld but this is a grand country to settle in; healthy enough inland though here and along the bayous ⅔ of the people are attacked by yellow fever and ½ die. . . . I have now come to the conclusion that no one has completed their education till they have been 2 or 3 voyages at sea or one deep water voyage. I should like to go deep water once. A captain was anxious for me to go with him, he thinks very much of me [this was an invitation from Eldridge] but I fear he is going across the pond and is moreover one of your 'pocket book oh's'. . . . I despise people who think they have seen the world because they have made a trip on a Cunard or P. & O. boat. What better are they and how much wiser for their travels? No, let them get behind the scenes and their eyes will be opened, then they will make good resolutions for the future, then they will begin a little to know themselves, then they will understand what makes a man and a brother. I get sea sick and nauseated at the very thought of returning to the abominable bloodsucker of England. . . . You ought certainly to come to America for a short period just to see what a noble country it is and what lies are told by so called travellers about it. One of the commonest is that Yankees are always asking strangers questions. Now this is a *lie*, they don't, they never speak to a stranger unless introduced. I have travelled all over New England and never been asked a question as to where I was going or why etc. . . .

I don't like the Southerners as far as I have seen; any of your miserable rebel sympathisers in England ought to come here and see these murderous villains and see their towns dependant on Northern industry and Northern manufactures for everything. They ought to have been in New Orleans at the time of the riot last summer and then let them talk about the chivalry of the South. I don't want anything to do with them. Give me the New England States to live in and New Englanders for friends. I ask no more. . . . I have never seen an approach to a double of you or of Mama. I know there cannot be her double in the world. She has not an equal. I wish to see her again as soon as possible; I hope to do so this summer, I hope to come across the pond. I shall let Arthur and things rip. It is too much trouble to go there besides I don't know how to get there except by coming to England first. I have not fired a shot for a year. I hear the Scotch won at Wimbledon. I wish you were out here, we might have a real good time, if I thought you would come I would meet you anywhere. I was with a very nice captain last, he is a very good man. I got much comfort and good in that vessel. There is no better or happier place in the world than a *good* small *American* vessel. A person has few or no temptations to contend with. If you want to come to America you should go with him. He will be in Liverpool this June. No lime-juicers for me. I hope never to set foot in a juicer again. This Captain is [name left blank in original]. He is a Baptist and a teetotaller. My best love to dear Mama, I think of her only she is always in my thoughts. . . .

The 'very nice captain', John Palmer Wilbur, was eventually identified and from this slender clue the whole truth came out. George's next letter, to his mother, was sent from New Orleans on 8 April 1867:

I have been afflicted with dreadful thoughts lately that something might happen to you. The very thought of such a thing has made me wretched as I feel it might be partly owing to me, and you know that besides you there is nothing in the world that I care for. I almost feel that if anything should happen to you it would kill me. I hope you got my last letter from Galveston, Texas. It is very hard writing without hearing from you. I came here with the design of getting to Trinidad but find no chance, or as we say here *no* sight. How under the sun Arthur got there is to me a mystery unless in a balloon. Nobody here [in America] seems to have heard of such a place and as to getting there the only feasible plan was to charter a steamer and search the West Indies for it. I need not say I have rejected this plan with scorn. I now go to Havana. I mean to return to New York and thence probably across so please when you write, direct to the Post Office there. How I would like to know that you are well. I trust you are. . . . I have never had any self respect since I found means to get that money in New York. I have never had any pleasure in life since, I despise myself for my foolish weakness. I shall never hold up my head.

All George had done, at a time when he was very short of money and suitable clothes, was to go to the bankers Duncan, Sherman & Co., who had obliged with cash when he was in New York with Gosford and Peterkin before he became Mr Osborne, and present two cheques for £100 each on his account with the Royal Bank of Scotland, which they had honoured. Not a great sin, though admittedly a breach of the undertaking he had given himself, and it would hardly have made much inroad into the family's wealth, since the annual rent roll of the Aberdeen estates was at that time about £36,000 on the entailed properties alone, and the burden on the estate at the time of his succeeding to it in 1864 had been only £80,000, which because of his frugality was being quickly reduced. The letter went on to declaim about the prejudiced nature of English writing about the American scene, and concluded, as it began, with dreadful forebodings and expressions of affection.

Meanwhile George was in the Gulf of Mexico. In New York in February he had met Captain Wilbur, who took him as a passenger in his brig *William Mallory* to Galveston. Of course, in heavy weather he helped take in sail and the like. The two men had many conversations and the captain was impressed by his knowledge of nautical astronomy.

Here was a young man of superior education, as Sergeant Hawkins had found, 'posted up' in everything, as young Frank Pearson later described, a man who gave Captain Wilbur much information about the stars which was new to him, a man who had the resources of the Tremont Street Nautical College at his disposal, and the free public libraries of Boston, which he much admired. This was the man who wrote of his urgent need to get to Trinidad and to Arthur to collect his mail and his belongings, and who yet had no better idea than to try to get there via Galveston or New Orleans. (Geography was not George's best suit, excellent astronomer and navigator though he may have been. Before he left home Fernando Po came into the news in a way that interested him; in a surviving letter he cheerfully writes that he has no notion of where in the world it is.) Surely at least one of his seagoing acquaintances could have told him better than the need of balloons and of going via England to get to Trinidad? Most likely, as George said in his letter to Jem, 'let Arthur and things rip' must have been nearer the truth, because nothing should have been easier for him than to find out that the sea route from the USA to Trinidad was via the Danish West Indian island of St Thomas. There, passengers had to change ship, a nuisance to the fussy and the lofty, as Arthur and Rachael Gordon always complained, especially as they had to submit to an elaborate exchange of courtesies with the Danish governor. But this would present no difficulty to a seaman, determined to reach his objective, who could always jump ship. That George knew that Arthur was in Trinidad at all is something; he never acknowledged receiving the information from home, never acknowledged receipt of any of the letters sent to him. Yet somehow he found out and could easily have found out more if he had really tried. Perhaps he was understandably wary that his incognito would be given away a second time. This was a risk and yet, as we shall soon see, when at last he made his landfall where the calypso comes from, he had no hesitation in visiting Arthur and collecting his possessions.

At Galveston he stayed two or three days aboard the *William Mallory*, then went by boat up river to Houston. From Houston he made his way to Mobile, Alabama, where he engaged as second mate in a barque carrying old iron and machinery to Cuba. When his right hand was crushed in some machinery he had to leave the barque before she sailed and have the wound dressed in Mobile. He then went to New Orleans, where his hand again needed attention.

In New Orleans in April 1867 he met Sewell Small, a fisherman and seaman approaching forty and at a loose end just then. Small, coming from Richmond, Maine, was a Down-Easter, the name given by other New Englanders to any citizen of that state, which by an historical chance had never had the status of a separate New England colony, and became a State of the Union only in 1920 when its governance from Massachusetts was relinquished. Hence its inhabitants and its condition as a part of civilization were rather doubted by the swanky Bostonians, known amongst seafarers as 'Cape Codders'.

Small and Osborne at once became friends and soon engaged together in the schooner *Arthur Burton*, a ship crewed entirely by a friendly company of Down-Easters. 'It was a matter', George wrote of this impulsive act, 'of half an hour.'

In a few days they sailed for Vera Cruz in Mexico, carrying a general cargo including corn. Small noticed that Osborne did not work like a man who had been used to it. His hands seemed soft and his legs tottered a little when carrying sacks of corn, but he never gave in. The weather was hot, and it so happened that the whole of Mexico was on the boil. George only later became aware of what was going on. Just five days after George wrote to his mother on the 10th of May the Emperor Maximilian of Mexico, after only three years of shaky dominion, surrendered at Querétaro to the Republicans and, because of his uncompromising declaration about the Republican leader Juárez and his supporters, was shot there on 19 June 1867.

> May 10th. Vera Cruz, Mexico.
> I have got here on my way north and I am sorry to say I have been taken in, for owing to the war and other causes it is impossible to get away so soon as I expected so I am afraid it will be some time before you hear from me. Soon after I last wrote I went aboard a vessel going straight to Boston [not true] but I got three fingers of my right hand a good deal crushed by a piece of iron and therefore could not go and could not write. I came back from Ala. to New Orleans and there I made another attempt to get north but feeling still a touch of my cough I thought I would come down here to a warm climate. Well I am here and it is hot enough but the worst is I fear we cannot get away for more than a month and then I find we are going down the coast so that nobody knows when we may be loaded and ready to go home. Vera Cruz is being besieged by liberals and we can see the shot and shell falling in and around the city – they are only waiting for ammunition to make a general attack. I am in excellent health now – cough quite gone and don't mind the heat all. I ought to have written from New Orleans but it was quite a sudden thing – half an hour and I had agreed to come and got my things on board. . . . I expect to have some trouble to get this letter posted – I don't trust much to Mexican and Spanish mails. Of one thing I can assure you that except in being away from you I am much better where I am than at home. . . .

This letter was only a curtain-raiser to the alarming experiences which he recounted only when he was safely back in the North. According to Sewell Small, when she was eventually able to set sail from Vera Cruz the *Arthur Burton* went south to Frontera, some six miles up the Tabasco River. Four of the crew were berthed in the forecastle, but the heat and mosquitoes in these cramped quarters were too much for them. Small walked the deck. 'George (I mean Osborne) went up into the foretop and remained there until the next morning, when I saw that he had tied himself in. He was asleep, with his legs hanging down, when I holloaed him to awake him.' From Frontera the *Arthur Burton* sailed to Chiltepec, west along the coast towards Vera Cruz. Here they took on mahogany to complete the cargo.

> I remember [said Sewell Small] leaving the ship with George one morning about three or four o'clock to bring off a raft of timber, and we did not get back to the ship until about twelve o'clock. When we left we had expected to be back about nine o'clock to breakfast, but there was a heavy surf on the beach and we had to take the timber through it, one log at a time, and make up the raft outside the bar. We were quite exhausted by the time we got to the ship, having had nothing to eat all day.

It gave George a headache, he wrote in a later letter, but after some tea he was soon all right. Thence they beat up against headwinds along the Campeche banks and cut across to Key West, where they stopped only to take on water and provisions, having been reduced to eating beans, and finally arrived in New York early in August. It was a good ship's company, 'Down-Easters' who counted George one of themselves. Most days they read the Bible to each other; George was a great hand at reading it aloud, said Small. From New York George told his mother more of his experiences:

> On this howling coast where sandflies, horseflies and mosquitoes abound and where at night can be heard the savage roar of the tigers and wild animals which inhabit the impervious tropical jungle which lines the coast and comes quite down to the beach, we remained until the glorious 4th July when we up anchor and away for New York, but for many days we beat up against headwinds along the Campeche banks knowing nothing of the tragic scenes which were being enacted not far to the leeward of us. . . . We arrived here day before yesterday; I went to the Post Office expecting letters from you but great has been my disappointment at finding none. This leads me to fear that you never received my letter from Vera Cruz. You may be surprised to hear that I was the whole time exposed to the vertical rays of the sun without any shade and never had an hour's sickness and could with the therm at 98° in the shade eat three hearty meals a day. . . . I am now with a very good man; it is good for me to be here; he is the same I went to Galveston with but I must leave him today. I hope that you will get this letter and that it will cheer your heart, it tells you of my undiminished love though I have not heard of or from you for more than a year . . .

Boston. 28 August 1867

I take the opportunity of writing now as I am just on the point of starting for Baltimore, Md. . . . I dare not come across just now for I am afraid of the cold foggy weather of an English autumn. I may state that Baltimore is pretty healthy. Yellow fever is raging in Galveston, also in New Orleans. I have just seen a wretched picture of Vera Cruz in the London Illustrated News and I was concerned to see it states the place to be very unhealthy from May to October, for if by chance you did not get my letter from Vera Cruz telling of my good health and happiness you must have been very uneasy about me and this thought that your hair is turning grey on my account fills me with anguish when I think of it, though of course I did all I could paying for and posting the letter with my own hands, but then how can anyone trust a Spaniard or a Mexican? Quite likely he kept the money for drinking absinthe with, and hove the letter away. One day in Vera Cruz I saw 7 large boxes of people who had died of the vomits; they were being put in boats and taken away out of the city to an island for burial. The liberals prevented any one going out of the city on the shore side. The stench of them in the broiling sun was such that I could not stand it and had to lie down inside an old boiler; as soon as I was able I went up through the gates into the city and took a huge drink of pure gin about ¾ of a tumbler. This restored me and prevented me getting sick I am pretty sure. What would a t-totaller say to this, was I justified in drinking spirits to save my life probably? . . . One day a cannon ball came and struck a tailor's shop about 6 ft. from the ground. I immediately went and stuck my head in the hole until the cannonading ceased. I thought it unlikely that a second shot would come just to that same spot, but while I was there 7 people were killed in the same square.

Another day we were in a boat alongside the mole which is not high and smooth as represented in the picture but low rugged and ruinous with a lot of little cranes all along it. We heard a shot come whipping right over our heads and saw it strike the water right under the nose of a man who was washing his face. It wetted him all over and you should have seen him get up and get. We had a truly good crew and were just like brothers; never heard an angry word during all the three months and ten days. They are scattered on the face of this continent now. We used to read the Testament every other morning after breakfast, before we went to bed and a spell after supper too.

In Frontera way down the coast we were up a river teeming with tropical life and vegetation and were actually tied to a large mango tree whose luscious green and gold fruit came tumbling down on our decks at every puff of wind. We also had a fruit resembling a custard apple but much larger, looking exactly like a green horse chestnut but as big as a water melon and covered with bluntish prickles, inside it is white like a horse chestnut with brown seeds but so delicious no words can describe it; it is like cotton saturated with some delicious fluid somewhat tart and yet sweet and juicy and very wholesome. I do not know what its name is. Limes also grow wild and hence it is easy to have plenty of lemonade. Rum is very cheap a sort called Blanco costing 3 dollars for four gallons. We drank but little but rubbed it over our bodies . . .

There was then much coming and going, sometimes with Sewell Small, sometimes not, between Boston, New York, Baltimore and Philadelphia. The excuses for not coming across 'the pond' were renewed; in a letter home from Locust Point, Baltimore, dated 18 September 1867 he wrote: 'You will be glad to hear that I am very well indeed. I hardly like to come across just now as I know I am consumptive and the English climate might settle my hash after my having been so much in hot latitudes of late. I do love hot weather, none of your half and half but a regular Jamaica. That's what's the matter . . .' In his next letter dated 4 November from Philadelphia he refers to a touch of cold weather 'and accordingly I have taken ship for Jamaica which is very healthy at this season and well worth a visit'.

This was less than frank of George, though understandable, because, as Sewell Small testified, what really happened was rather different. They shipped together in Boston as able seamen on board the schooner *Zeyla*, bound for Philadelphia on 22 October 1867. At Philadelphia Captain Crowell left the ship. The mate, Howes, took command, Small became mate and chose George to be the man on his watch. They left Philadelphia on 8 November bound not for Jamaica, but for Trinidad. The proof of this is clear. Small kept a rough scroll book, from which George wrote up the log, he being the better penman. 'He used to write a good many entries in the rough-book as well . . . you will find George's writing on almost every page . . . I have the rough book still, which I now produce and hand over,' he testified at Commissioner Harry Smith's hearings.

The reason for George deceiving his mother about his real destination is clear enough. He was not going to risk for the second time an ADC of Arthur's bouncing up from a launch and booming out for Lord Aberdeen. This time he was going to take Arthur by stealth. His next letter to his mother, dated Sunday 8 December, two days before his birthday, was from Port of Spain:

161

It is some time since I wrote to you but I have been a good while getting here. Arthur is very well he sends his love. I forget if I told you I was coming here, it was quite accidental my coming. [It was no such thing.] This is a very warm climate, at this time hotter than summer in New York. There is abundance of every kind of fruit, the oranges in particular are delicious, 2½d. a dozen. The natives are very independent and apparently extremely intelligent and well educated; the laws appear to be excellent and well and promptly enforced; the police are numerous and apparently efficient; they wear during the day a London policeman's helmet and at night a soldier's forage cap, a truly sensible and thoroughly British piece of wisdom. In America the police wear a wide brimmed Panama hat in summer. Further comment is unnecessary. I will say this for England that the more I see of other countries the more convinced do I become that England is the most stupid, jug-headed, stick-in-the-mud of them all. I do not know if you will get this letter as I have no stamp and being Sunday I cannot get one. Tomorrow morning I leave for parts unknown. [This was not true; he saw Arthur again, but only from a distance two days later on his birthday, 10 December. Small had sent George and another seaman to row Captain Howes ashore on that day. They left Trinidad on 12 December.] Last Sunday I went to the Wesleyan Church in the morning where a mulatto preached; in the evening to the Baptist Church where a nice old man officiated; he was a Scotch-man and preached a very good plain earnest sermon just such as Smith of Ellon would. Talking of Ellon there is a nigger woman here keeps a small grocery store. She is the image of Mrs Boyle face, figure, style and everything and so black that charcoal makes a white mark on her. A nut for Johnny to crack. The mosquitoes here are a speckled black and white like a guinea hen. The island is very mountainous on the north side. The entrance from the W. reminded me of the Souters of Cromarty Firth [this was the Bocas de Dragón or Dragon's Mouth, the straits separating Trinidad and Venezuela]. Arthur is not going to Church this morning but he goes in the evening to the English church. I am going to the Baptist again.

In Arthur's journal there is no mention, at that time, of George: several days before and after 8 December are quite blank. That George met Arthur is mentioned again in passing in his next letter home dated 10 February and posted in New York on 18 February 1868. George's chief interest in getting to Arthur was to retrieve his rifle and his Colt's revolver, and possibly a certain song sheet. Small testified that George came to their home port after this voyage with both weapons. The rifle became of prime importance in the inquest proceedings.

New York, 10th February, 1868

I have done wrong in not writing to you much sooner for when I had time I was too lazy and lately I have been so busy that when it came night I was only too glad to go to bed and had no energy to write more especially as I have to do it standing. When I wrote last I promised you a longer letter but unfortunately my journal from which I meant to cull materials was totally destroyed during a very severe gale of wind which we experienced in the Gulf Stream on New Year's Day and the following three days. [Small said George had thrown his journal overboard because the sea-water had spoiled it.]

But for this misfortune I could have told you of a wonderful and very brilliant meteor which I observed on a certain night about 4 a.m.; of seeing two corposants or St Elmo's fires (thunderbolts) accompanied by the heaviest rain and the darkest darkness ever known by me, and this on the very day of the great St Thomas earthquake which you probably have not heard of yet; of my going out on the main boom to cast off the reef casing and of the boom tackle getting adrift, of the general consternation; the old man [Captain Howes] kept shouting to me to hold on; very needless advice under the circumstances our boom was 76 feet long [according to Small about 60 feet], imagine that swinging back and forth and bringing up short by the sheets at every roll, and you can guess what a jerk it gave me at every spring. I quietly shouted 'round in on your sheet and catch a turn' wherein I differed from Mrs Glasse who says first catch your hare. I said first round in, then catch a turn; they did so, and little by little the boom was steadied. I could have told you about starting from the ballast ground about 4 a.m. on the 10th December 1867 and rowing the old man to Port Spain. I saw Arthur on this day. I had a nice day and got back to ballast ground about 6 p.m. I could have told you of the Gulf Stream in winter, of trying to cross it, of a fearful gale in the Gulf lasting 4 days, of never having a dry stitch all that time, of doing all we could to save the vessel which was loaded with salt so deep that the deck was only 5 inches above the water, consequently the sea broke over it like a half tide rock. We had no regular sleep during these 4 days. The old man was awful scared and said if ever he got safe to land he would never go to sea again. I said so too. I could have told of the unsophisticated bookseller of Old Point Comfort and the divinity student; of beating up the Chesapeake against a N.W. gale; of the intense cold so that the sea as it broke over us froze solid and all our decks, rigging etc. were coated with ice. At last we could stand it no longer and anchored. Next morning, we were two hours slashing hot water on the windlass before we could start it. I got both feet frozen during this awful weather. Of course it felt worse on account of our only being days from hot weather.

I came round from Baltimore here in a brig we had some awful cold

163

weather. I could write more but I have a great deal to attend to and am very sleepy so goodbye. I will try and write from the West Indies where I am going to try and cure my regular winter cough which notwithstanding the fearful ordeal is no worse than usual. I trust you are well . . .

'I have a great deal to attend to and am very sleepy' . . . if he had only known he would have attended to a great deal else, rather than delayed posting the letter for eight days, for on 12 February Jem was found shot in his lodgings in Trinity Street, Cambridge, so getting this letter from George must have been anguish for Mary Aberdeen. She had just lost her second son, and here was her eldest cheerfully explaining how his life had been precariously balanced on a long boom. His letter bore no address; her earlier letters to him had been returned and all means of communicating with him seemed gone. It was then that she had the idea of placing an advertisement in one of the New York or Boston papers. 'Jem would be all she could possibly want,' she had quoted him as saying before he went away. Now that there was no more Jem, surely he would drop everything and come? But he did not know; he never knew.

The verdict of accidental death was the only one possible. As Henry Foster Baxter, of Trinity Street, surgeon, stated at the inquest in Cambridge:

> I was called in to see the deceased at a little after six yesterday evening. He was lying on the floor of a bedroom at Mr Clark's, his head towards the bed and his feet towards the fireplace. He was insensible and pulseless. He made two or three gasps and shortly after died. His head was lying in a pool of blood. On examining the head I found there was an opening on the left side just above the ear, and another opening on the top of his head on the right. It seemed as if a bullet had passed through. The opening on the left side was smaller than that on the right, and from this I infer that the bullet entered on the left side.

Mr Clark's servant Emma Groom said that James's own rifle had not been unpacked – this was another, new gun which the deceased took out of its case on the Saturday and put together. Both the rifles were in the bedroom.

Edmund Charles Russell Ross of 20 Duke Street, St James's stated:

> I have shot with Mr Gordon in rifle matches and in practice. I have not the slightest hesitation in saying that he was one of the most careless men in handling his rifle I ever met. I have frequently warned him of the danger he

incurred. I may state he was in the habit of experimenting with the rifle. . . .
Some of his experiments in this way were extremely hazardous. I have
known him to file the mechanism of the lock of his rifle as to render it very
dangerous. The weapon produced is a Whitworth rifle. It has a very fine pull
off. I can understand that this rifle would explode on a slight jar. . . . I have
seen Mr Gordon, as a feat of strength, hold out at arm's length, a loaded
rifle, with the muzzle towards his head.

Joseph Ritchings testified: 'I am marker at the University rifle
ground. I knew Mr Gordon very well. He was a very careless man with
his rifle. I have seen him put his foot on the hammer of his loaded rifle,
and so "full-cock" it with the muzzle towards him. The rifle produced
has a very light pull; it would hardly stand at full-cock; it would
certainly not pull a pound weight.'

James's had been a stronger, more handsome face than George's,
crowned with a mop of fair hair, and for him popularity and renown
came easily. He was a rowing Blue, and was captain of the University
shooting eight.

In April 1868 Sewell Small, now in Boston, received a letter from
George in which he said he wanted them to be together again. He had
made a voyage to Barbados and found the climate there second only to
that of the Canaries. Small confirmed this engagement: George had
been first mate of a brig, name forgotten, sailing to Barbados with a
cargo of mules and horses. Before Small could answer the letter George
arrived in Boston. They shipped together as seamen in a schooner
bound for Philadelphia, but were soon back in Boston. After a few days
they went to Richmond, Maine, where George lodged with Sewell and
his wife Lizzie: this became his home. They bought a boat which
needed fitting out and fished together. As Small recalled:

After that he bought a boat for himself. He knocked off the fishing business
about the month of August, and employed himself in the business of
shipping ice. This is not a regular kind of business, as it depends on ships
coming in to load, and when George was not at that he would employ
himself at rigging ships. In August I told him I was thinking of leaving
Richmond for Boston, and he went to board with James and Ella Green . . .
George was a tall man, with light hair and sandy whiskers. He was a good-
looking, intelligent-looking man. He never told me of what country he was a
native, although I often asked him. He would just put me off. He was very
careful about his letters. He never let anybody see what he wrote or what he
received. He was a great hand at drawing. He could draw almost any kind of
a picture. He used often to draw pictures for my children as well as others,

and he did draw them very well. He was very fond of children. He made a great pet of my little girl Abbie, who is in her seventh year. George was an unmarried man. He often spoke of himself as such. I used to joke him about getting married and he would say he would marry when he found the right one. To the best of my belief George was, in every respect, a man of high moral character.

After his examination by Commissioner Harry Smith, Small said to the Reverend W. B. Alexander that he 'would rather be in a rough sea than go through hours being examined'.

In October 1868 George joined the schooner *Walton*, lying at Bath about ten miles down the Kennebec River from Richmond, as mate, and when she arrived at New York he was made master by her owners T. J. Southard and Sons, shipbuilders of Richmond. He wrote to the twenty-six-year-old James Erastus Green, who appears to have been a son-in-law of Sewell Small, to tell him this, and to ask him to join him as mate, as he thought his mate was thinking of leaving. This invitation was repeated in a letter of 29 April 1869 to Green from Pensacola, Florida, where he spent some time, whilst the *Walton* was laid up for the winter. It was not until June 1869, however, that the arrangement came about and Green then came on board as mate at New Haven, Connecticut. They stayed together until they had a disagreement with the owners, whereupon they left the *Walton* and returned to Richmond.

Their departure was due to the written complaint of the senior owner, Mr T. J. Southard, that their running of the vessel was insufficiently 'equinomical': the confrontation between George and Southard was the only occasion when George was reported by anybody who knew him to have given way to temper. Southard notoriously baited his employees and suppliers and normally George refused to rise. 'See the fellow,' Southard complained on one occasion, 'I do my best to anger him and he holds silence, or shrugs and turns away.' This time, however, George at last flared up. 'Mr Southard,' he said, 'I could buy you up over and over. It is not your money I need; it is the work I like to do. But never again with you, nor with anyone of your kind.' Southard, noticed a relation of his named Springer, was for once left speechless, while onlookers smirked their satisfaction at his unaccustomed discomfiture.

George had written home in May 1868 from Philadelphia, and then nothing survives, perhaps nothing was written, until December, when he wrote from New York:

I have just returned from many wanderings and from such a situation that I could not write to you any sooner. I have many times prayed that you may be well and happy. I must come and see you soon though it is so long since I heard that a sort of vague dread fills my mind and I seem rather to go on in doubt than to learn what would kill me or drive me to worse. I mean were I to return and not find you. How many times has this thought come to me in the dark and cheerless night watches; but I have to drive it from me as too dreadful to think of. I wonder where you are now and what you are doing – something good and a blessing to all around you. Not many weeks ago I thought my last hour was come. I was in a small vessel, deep loaded and very leaky. A furious gale came on right on shore, the water gained on us, we could not keep her free – as morning dawned the gale increased in violence, to windward there was nothing but rain and wind and the ever rising white capped billows, to leeward was the low quicksands with roaring breakers on to which we were slowly but surely drifting. We carried an awful press of sail but the poor water-logged schooner lay over on her beam ends and made two miles to leeward for every one ahead; we were toiling at the pumps and throwing overboard our deck load but already there was 5 foot water in the hold, and nothing could have saved us but a miracle or a change of wind. At 10 a.m. God in His mercy sent a sudden change of wind all in a moment right off shore with perfect floods of rain which beat down the sea and in half an hour the wind moderated: after toiling 17 hours we got a suck on the pumps and took heart of grace and eat a little food. Next day we made the harbour of New York, where I am now: tomorrow we start for a coast famed for its tales of piracy, wrecking and murder; the coast of Florida, but those times are past now and it is only dangerous on account of its numerous shoals and sunken rocks. Give my love to all dear ones and believe in the never dying love of your affect. son George.

Upon being shown this letter the family lawyer, George Auldjo Jamieson, could not resist making the comment that George was 'sharp'.

Then came George's last letter, posted in Pensacola:

Molino, Fla. 24 Apr 1869

You cannot imagine how pleased I was here in the swamps of Fla. to find an old *Boston Herald* in which was your advertisement stating that you were well and that there was a letter for me in the New York P.O. Of course being here I could not go there after it but it did my heart good to know that you are well and happy. Do not fret for me for though I should like to see you now I must defer it a little longer. You may see me before you expect it. At present I am prevented by circumstances beyond my control from going or doing just what I might wish.

Lest you may think that I am hard up or otherwise unfortunately situated I may mention that thousands of dollars are entrusted to me and pass through my hands every few months, also more than a few lives and much property are dependant on my capability. The secret of all this is I have been for two years and am a rigid teetotaller. Time presses and I can only conclude with assurances of my undiminished and never to be quenched love for you . . .

He was indeed sharp: he spent only a day and a night at Molino. He was also devious. When the good weather was coming on, there were always pressing reasons for not 'crossing the pond'; in the autumn the prospect of the fogs of old England made it undesirable for his health. Mr Alexander had views about his 'thinking himself not well. I believe this is in the main an idea for him. However there is little reality in it.' In fact, he merely suffered from hay fever. In earlier years he had admitted that this, bad enough, was all that was the matter, and referred to it in a letter to his mother from Rossie Priory at Inchtyre in Scotland.

Back in Richmond towards the end of 1869 there was no longer room for George in the Green household; an elder of the church named Partridge occupied his room. So he lodged near by with Mrs Loomis, whose husband was a farmer who had retired to Richmond. He continued to see James and Ella Green almost every day. 'It is the custom in Richmond', said Green later, 'for friends, both male and female, to call each other by their Christian names. All his friends called Osborne George.'

At the Boston hearings James Green produced two tin-types of George, but he was not willing to part with them as he had no other portrait of his friend. George, he said, drew beautifully, and was very fond of music. He used 'very often to play on a piano in my house'. He played and sang amongst other tunes, a setting to music of Longfellow's 'The Rainy Day'. He was very good to children, recalled Green, and he also used to go rifle shooting with twenty-one-year-old Melvin Randall, a carriage maker in his father's business, to whom George sold his rifle before leaving Richmond for the last time. This rifle became important evidence of identity, because it bore the mark on the rib of the gunsmith 'Alex. Henry, 12 South St Andrew Street, Edinburgh'. It was marked 'Patent No. 655' also on this rib, and on the trigger guard No. 1145. A slug mould was marked 1378 A H. George at first was reluctant to sell it. It was, after all, valuable enough to him to justify a voyage all the way to Trinidad. It had a waterproof cover on it labelled 'Mackintosh &

Co.'. Young Randall later did a smart deal with the family's representatives because he got them not only to pay him the $25 for which he had quite legally bought it but also the promise of a new rifle from the same maker made to his specification in return for handing over George's rifle. The last time he and George shot together was on Christmas Day 1869. George also had a Colt's revolver and James Green recalled how on the *Walton*, he would throw a corked bottle overboard and break it with a single shot. He could also snuff out a candle from 5 or 6 yards.

> George used to complain sometimes of delicacy in his chest. He stooped a little in walking, and he 'favoured' his left leg a little as if it were weak from an old injury. I remember the great toe of his left foot was flattened as if it had been crushed. On board ship the sailors were attached to him, though he kept up strict discipline. He was an unmarried man. I have heard my wife joking with him about getting married and he would say he was not old enough to marry yet.

Soon after Christmas George went to Boston to look for a berth. He returned to Richmond and after a few days a telegram arrived from Captain Kent asking him to join the *Hera* as first mate. The pay offered and accepted was $40 a month. She was a three-masted schooner due to leave for Melbourne, and then to ply the China trade for some years. Ella Green was making him some summer clothes (he used to do his own repairs), but they were not yet ready, so he asked for them to be sent on to Boston. He then left Richmond by rail for Boston. At the posthumous hearings James Green still had the letter acknowledging their receipt, but he was not willing to hand it over to Commissioner Harry Smith for it was the only letter from his friend that he had kept. It was the last Green heard of George, until he received Captain Kent's letter from Melbourne the following August.

Meanwhile George was busy loading the schooner and, in the course of this, he became the object of particular curiosity to a bright, twenty-two-year-old shipping clerk employed by Messrs. Henry W. Peabody & Co., who had chartered the *Hera*. One of the partners in Peabody's was Francis Augustus Sargent, a member of that prominent Boston family to which the painter Sargent also belonged. The duty of Peabody's clerk, Andrew Charles John Blanckenberg, was to measure the cargo as it came aboard, so he saw George all day every day:

When I first met him he seemed to be shy and modest. I was very favourably impressed with him and we became more intimate than I generally do with people in his apparent position. He told me he had met the captain of the *Hera* accidentally. He had been on the wharf, and he joined the captain and asked him if he had a mate. The captain said no . . . . He said he hailed from Maine, and when he told me he came from Richmond I said the captain came from Cape Cod, and it wasn't often a 'Down-Easter' sailed with a 'Cape Codder'. A 'down-easter' means, according to Boston usage, a native of Maine, although out of the New England states every New Englander is called a 'down-easter'. There is a kind of rivalry in ships between them . . . . He expressed regret that he was going with the *Hera*, because he thought he might have got a larger vessel, having been a captain formerly. But he said he had given his word to the captain and he would not go back from it. Mates are not in my experience generally so scrupulous and will often load a vessel and at the last moment decline to sail with her, and draw their pay for their services in loading. I know that Osborne possessed a captain's certificate. The packet containing it came to our office and I took it down to him, and he showed it to me. He had previously spoken to me about the certificate, and had asked me to forward it to our agents in Melbourne if it did not arrive before the *Hera* sailed. He seemed very anxious about it as he thought it might be useful to him in getting another ship. I remember that on the day he left I told him I was going to attend the funeral of an intimate friend, and he showed great sympathy. He spoke very solemnly of the suddenness with which death sometimes comes upon us, and the little we do in preparation for it. He seemed to feel very deeply what he said. I remember this conversation came back to my mind very vividly when I first heard of his own death so soon after. . . . The last time I saw him I was on the wharf at Boston, and he was on the deck of the *Hera*, which was then in the act of leaving. He waved his hand to me as a token of adieu.

That was on 21 January 1870. Blanckenberg was the last person on land to see George. That wave must have concealed a certain elation. Although the *Hera* was only of 387 tons registered, she was a new ship built with a special view to the China trade. George was on his way to being no longer a small potato. Just before he left the ship outside the Boston Light, the pilot, John Henry Jeffrey, who was accompanied by young Captain Kent's father, Nickerson Kent, shook hands with George: 'Goodbye, Mr Mate!'

The second mate was Charles Franklin Smith, who had known George when he had the *Walton*. There were four seamen – Frank Pratt, William Scott, Richard Haydon, George A. Sumner – and a coloured cook-cum-steward, Robert A. Lee. A total complement of eight. The weather was very bad. Smith had the midnight to 4 a.m. watch, George from 4 to 8 a.m. The clearest account of the trip came from Scott, whose father farmed *The Ponds* at Pathhead near Edinburgh. The accident happened on the night of the 27th, at about the time of the changing of the watch. George had come up on deck; they were lowering the mainsail.

> Osborne and I were side by side, hauling on the same rope. I was between him and the sea. The ship gave a heavy roll, and the downhaul got slack, then with another roll the downhaul got taut. Osborne and I were both caught in the bight of the downhaul. The first shock came on him because he was nearer the sail than I. I had time to lay myself down, and the rope passed over me, while Osborne was dragged across me and into the sea. I saw him fall into the sea, but there was nothing I could do to prevent it. It was the work of a second. I saw him come to the surface. It was not a dark night. I threw him a rope as soon as I possibly could. I heard him call out to launch the boat, and call the captain. We threw him planks and ropes, but he did not succeed in laying hold. He would have to be very close to them to see them. The boat was cast loose as quickly as we could, but by the time the boat was loose it was too late. I don't think any men could have gone in the boat without great danger to life. Some of the Boston men volunteered to go in her. Frank Pratt was one, I remember. But the captain thought it was not right to risk their lives. I thought so too, and I think so still. I heard what I believed to be Osborne's last cry before the boat was ready. We never heard or saw him again.

Directly he heard the cry 'man overboard', Captain Kent rushed on deck:

> Everything that my experience could suggest as possible was done to save him. The boat was cleared away, but it was impossible to launch it in time to do any good. She is a very heavy boat. If it had been time to launch her, I doubt if she could have lived or cleared the vessel. The waves were very high. When I saw it was too late I knew it was my duty not to launch the boat. The danger of losing all her crew would have been very great. I saw Osborne struggling in the water. I am quite sure he must have drowned. We wore ship, and lay to till daylight, but we saw nothing of Osborne. There were no vessels in sight. The water was very cold, and even a good swimmer must have perished very soon.

One conspicuous example of seafarers' luck is contained in a letter from Henry Peabody & Co. to the New York bankers Dabney, Morgan

& Co. This letter states that 'a few weeks after the loss of Mr Osborne, chief officer, Captain Kent was knocked overboard by the main sheet but was washed on deck again by the sea'. The luckless Chief Officer Osborne was, however, without doubt at the bottom of the Atlantic.

The *Hera*'s log, hitherto kept by George, gave the ship's position as Latitude 40° 10′ North, Longitude 58° 14′ West. The nearest landfall is Sable Island, that curious sandspit island 120 miles off the coast of Nova Scotia, the inhabitants of which are wild horses escaped from wrecks and a bird called the Ipswich sparrow. So much for sable, and for ermine, too.

At the end of the hearings in Edinburgh the clerk of session to the Sheriff of Chancery wondered how many among them could undergo such a microscopic examination during four wandering years in their twenties and emerge without stain upon their character or morals. The clerk did not know about Jane Ogilvie and her son, the inquiries having been limited to America. In fact it seems impossible to ascertain who amongst the intimate circle of family and attendant lawyers did know. George's cousin and brother-in-law, Lord Polwarth, must have known, for on 1 September 1870, two days after Mr Alexander's news of George's death had been received at Haddo House, Walter Polwarth wrote to George's youngest brother and successor, Johnny:

> *Privately* I would say to you, do not on any account suffer any mystery, any concealment of facts. Some people are fond of doing so imagining it prevents surmises of a disagreeable nature. It is a great mistake and only creates worse. From all I have heard I believe the sad fact clearly established but it will be right to make further inquiry as far as that can be done.
>
> *You* know I daresay that some people like to fancy he must have been married. It would not have been wrong, but I do not believe anything of the kind and I sincerely hope none of your advisers will allow such thoughts to weigh with them a moment.

Even so, the unkindness of charitable Victorian society is not part of this story, and it seems fitting that a tribute should come from one of his Down-Easter friends. In acknowledging the gift of $500 from the Aberdeen family James Erastus Green wrote in appreciation of his friend George Osborne: 'Words are inadequate to express my thanks, while I deeply regret the occasion for them, for the friendship of the last was far more to me than silver, or gold. Mrs Green and myself wishes to be kindly remembered to the friends of him whom we have loved.'

Directly the news had arrived at the end of August 1870, it spread to relevant members of the family and, with the brisk certainty of that age, the meeting was held at Haddo referred to in Arthur Gordon's journal at which Johnny was recognized as the new Lord Aberdeen. Shortly after this, Arthur Gordon was reluctantly appointed Governor of Mauritius and was therefore no longer so closely involved in family affairs.

Meanwhile, it was arranged for Mr M'Laren of Tods, Murray & Jamieson to go to the USA with Mr Alexander to winkle out suitable witnesses as to George's actual death and, just as necessary, that he had behaved himself to the point of remaining unmarried and therefore without any legitimate male heir. Before the end of November 1870, Commissioner Harry Smith in America began to take sworn statements from upwards of two dozen witnesses. Evidence of identity was achieved by comparing photographs and the handwriting of George H. Osborne and George, 6th Earl of Aberdeen; by reason of the rifle bought by Melvin Othelar Randall; the boot last made for Osborne in Richmond by George Bradley Randlette; and, most strange of all, the song sheet of Longfellow's poem 'The Rainy Day'. Amongst the witnesses was a fourteen-year-old girl called Blanche Ellen Call:

> I live in Richmond with my father, who is a barber there. I knew George H. Osborne most of the time he lived in Richmond. I have two sisters. George used to tell us stories and repeat poetry to us. He gave me a copy of some verses on 'The Rainy Day' written out by him, which I gave in October last [it was now 6 December] to the Rev. Mr Alexander of Scotland.

Among the 'productions' put in as part of the hearings in Edinburgh was 'No. 69. Sheets of music, containing "The Rainy Day", etc.' In the hearings before the Committee for Privileges of the House of Lords the same production No. 69 was described as 'three sheets of music, containing two songs, the first entitled "The Rainy Day" '. No mention was made of Longfellow, nor of George Alexander Osborne. At no point during the whole story, publicly or privately stated, does there seem to have been in anybody's mind the suspicion that George's alias derived directly from the Irish composer's real name. Why else should he have bothered to take it with such other key documents as his master's certificate on his final voyage to Australia, except as a sort of passport to his new identity? Mr Bingham of the Revere House Hotel thought the shaky H might be an N, but a shaky H can also easily be read as an A.

As soon as the obsequies, the inquests and the claims were done with,

Mary Aberdeen set about honouring her dead son. Modest gifts of money were made to the Smalls and the Greens, to Sergeant Hawkins and to Captain Eldridge, whose purchase of a farm in New Jersey had been a failure owing to the poverty of the land. He wrote: 'I feel you must have been inspired to aid me.' He had 'loved George for his kind, Christian spirit. His name will be perpetuated in my little son.' Photographs of George were freely sent out, and in one or two cases reciprocated by pictures of him, mostly tin-types, taken in America. The receipt of these gifts and objects was widely acknowledged with the now familiar fanfares of praise for the character of their subject. Captain Wilbur, in particular, was lyrical about 'one whose features are ever fresh in my mind. I shall never forget . . . my strange friend.' He was one of the few friends to have visited Haddo, and he treasured also this memory.

In Aberdeenshire George's memory is quietly perpetuated in the rebuilt little kirk of Bartholchapel, a township on the Haddo estate, where carved in stone above the entrance porch is a familiar passage from Psalm 93, verses 4 and 5, mercifully rendered in the Authorized Version:

> The Lord on high is mightier than
> the noise of many waters
> Yea than the mighty waves of the sea.
> Thy testimonies are very sure
> Holiness becometh thine House
> O Lord for ever.

In the USA there were two major ways of keeping alive the memory of George Osborne, both of them to do with books. The Isaac Umberhine Memorial Library at Richmond was familiar ground to George, and he read there and borrowed very often when ashore. Mary Aberdeen suggested an 'Aberdeen shelf' and offered the amateur librarian, William C. Stuart, £35 ($190.57) for the purchase of suitable books to the tune of £30, leaving £5 for Mr Stuart's personal use. This good man preferred to spend all the money on books, and wrote acknowledging the gift on 21 March 1874: 'In the selection of books we shall endeavour to be governed by the taste of the late earl, as we are able to gather it from the character of the books which he took from the library.' There was not much more on which to base the choice, because it had not been his habit to speak more than necessary to the girl in charge of lending books. Down-Easters have the reputation of saying only two words where five would be nicer.

No serious proof of any female attachment by George comes into the whole story presented at the legal hearings. There have, nevertheless, persistently been tales circulating in Richmond and its neighbourhood of two girls between whom and George there was mutual attraction at one time or another. The more believable account is of his friendship with a girl called Cecilia or Amelia Rook, a resident of Parker's Head near Bath, not very far from Richmond. From there she sent Lady Aberdeen a tiny photograph of George, wearing a fringe of beard. Stories have persisted to this day of trysts with Miss Rook at Parker's Head and of wistful waves between ship and shore as George sailed by about his business. It must be added that these stories are embedded in accounts that howl with inaccuracy.

The account of the other lady needs more cautious attention, because, apart from a few particulars about his courtship of Jennie Swan, the rest of the story is pure invention. It appeared in *The American Weekly* of 9 December 1951 and recounts a totally false story of George's first arrival in Richmond. The journalist who tells this tale must have been fooled by the teller, who was the seventy-year-old son of Melvin Othelar Randall, also called Melvin. He spun a tale of make-believe as to how George first came to Richmond, walking through the snow from New Brunswick in 1866 and meeting Melvin Randall senior. The son Melvin proudly brandished his father's rifle at the writer of the article, who manages a number of inaccuracies even over that story. He also relates how at a barn dance George met Jennie Swan, how she was fascinated by him but was puzzled by his fine manners. In due course they stopped denying that they planned to marry, and she wore his large gold ring bearing the Latin inscription *Fortuna sequatur*. He told her that this was the family motto and meant 'Let fortune follow'. Even after the romance cooled she continued to wear the ring. It is only over this one point, of the family's motto and its meaning, that the story sticks to proven fact. If indeed George had hitherto possessed such a ring, what a lucky or clever girl was Miss Swan, with the whole of Richmond knowing that she wore it, not to be pounced upon by Mr M'Laren and obliged even temporarily to yield up the ring as evidence of identity. Or did Mr M'Laren deliberately ignore this lead, thus sparing Commissioner Smith from having to take a sworn statement from Jennie, who would certainly have represented a sensational aspect of the case?

Lady Aberdeen's agent in the provision of books was a well-to-do widow of Boston, Mrs Walter Baker. They had met in England some years earlier, and Eleanor Baker in one letter bemoans that she once narrowly missed meeting George's brother James, who had to excuse himself from attending a luncheon given by a friend at Trinity College, Cambridge, in her honour, because of the need to engage at 'his sport'. This must have been either rowing or rifle-shooting practice. George she had never met, but she enthusiastically joined in the negotiations to preserve his memory. As regards the provision of the books, Mr Stuart, or somebody, made a great mistake in their choice, for included amongst them were three 'objectionable books'. These were Huxley's *Critiques and Addresses* and *Lay Sermons, Addresses and Reviews*, and Matthew Arnold's *Literature and Dogma*. There was much correspondence about them, generally referred to as the '3 Huxleys', between Mary Aberdeen who was determined on their removal, Eleanor Baker who acted as her willing agent, and the unfortunate Mr Stuart, who in the end solved the problem by removing the books to another part of the library. So it was the mother's choice of books rather than the commemorated son's that was placed in the library with, pasted in the end-paper of each, a handsome bookplate referring in Gothic type, to George, 6th Earl of Aberdeen, but not mentioning the honorary Down-Easter and citizen of Richmond, George H. Osborne. There were 110 volumes in all purchased with Mary Aberdeen's donation. In addition to the bookplate, the Aberdeen case had a suitably inscribed tablet over it.

Mrs Baker visited Richmond for the first time in October 1872 and wrote – she was almost as lengthy a correspondent as Mr Alexander – to Mary Aberdeen how impressed she was by the neat appearance of the village, and described the building in which the library was then housed, on the second floor (English first floor) of a building at the end of Main Street. She met several of his friends, one of whom said 'he was with us but not of us', and proceeded to call on Mrs Loomis, whom she found loud-voiced and with much self-presentation. Mrs Baker admitted she had taken Mrs Loomis unawares, and it may be presumed that the wife of the retired farmer Ariel Loomis was quite thrown out by the sudden apparition of this grand lady from Boston. Eleanor Baker talked also with the proprietor of the Temperance Hotel, where George often spent his evenings in conversation. The hotelier, Harrison Springer, enjoyed these talks but, like so many other friends, found George's aloof dignity a complete defence against any probing of his background. Mrs Loomis characterized George as 'a very grave man'.

The other means of remembering George through books was on a larger scale. The American Seamen's Friends' Society was first organized in May 1828 and incorporated in April 1833. Mary Aberdeen heard of it through Eleanor Baker, who told her that the Seamen's Temperance Home in Boston, with which George had had connexions, was one of the centres from which boxed ships' libraries were issued on loan to American merchantmen voyaging world-wide. Mrs Baker also mentioned that the home, 'unfortunately for the owners', was not burned down in the big Boston fire of 1872. It had destroyed her home by Fort Hill and Washington Square, but spared the hostel, which badly needed rebuilding. The secretary of the ASFS, Mr Hall, writing from the headquarters of the Society at 80 Wall Street, New York on 3 December 1873, outlines the scheme in response to an offer from Mary Aberdeen to make a substantial donation towards the provision of additional libraries. Her offer of £300 secured one hundred libraries, to be numbered 5000 to 5099, and included an allowance for repairs and replacements. The books, as at Richmond, were of an improving nature, this time at the Society's insistence, because they were convinced from experience, as Mr Hall wrote, that when they are at sea sailors are at their 'most impressible, and a good book at that time very often accomplishes a most useful purpose'. By chance library No. 5001, inscribed with the name of George H. Osborne and with Captain Wilbur's description 'A good young man and a Christian', was borrowed for the ship *Undaunted* – master Captain S. B. Dinsmere, twenty-five crew, bound from Boston for San Francisco. Fifteen of the first twenty 'Aberdeen' libraries went to Boston for shipment via the Seamen's Temperance Hostel there, at last rebuilt on a new site, adjoining a Seamen's Chapel. Captain Dinsmere wrote to Mr Hall that 'he recognized the name George Osborne, an esteemed acquaintance and three times shipmate'.

In April 1874 the Reverend Dr J. E. Rockwell, pastor of the Edgewater Presbyterian Church, Staten Island, who took an interest in the ASFS (the present-day seamen's hostel is located on Staten Island), agreed to bring a specimen boxed library to Scotland when he came across as one of a delegation to the General Assembly of the Presbyterian Church of Scotland. He was unable in London to meet Lady Aberdeen for luncheon to hand over this gift to Haddo House, but it was conveyed to her in Scotland, and on the back of Dr Rockwell's letter to her is her draft reply:

I have received by the hands of the Rev Dr Rockwell the specimen library
. . . how can I sufficiently thank you for the touching words in which the
inauguration of the memorial libraries have been recorded . . . filled me with
gratitude for their appreciation of my dear son's character. I shall preserve
this proof of kindly feeling as long as I live, and shall leave it to the son whom
God has been pleased to spare to me, by whom it will be ever valued.

Mary Aberdeen lived until 1900, and the compartmented box is
mentioned in her specific bequests to Johnny. It does not appear to
have survived at Haddo the eighty-odd years since her death, but then
after Johnny married she did not live at Haddo, and may well have
taken it away with her, never to be returned by her executors. How
agreeable it would be to find out that a box still exists, perhaps in some
American maritime museum. The only physical object of like kind
examined by this author is Melvin Othelar Randall's rifle, now
belonging to his granddaughter. The handling of this antique weapon
was emotionally shaking, as well as rewarding.

In 1874 Sergeant William Randolph Hawkins was living at a
National Soldiers' Home near Augusta, Maine, and wrote to Lady
Aberdeen another version of his strange conversation with George
beside the fountain at Boston after the voyage to the Canaries. In this
account he wrote:

After a little while he said he would take me to Scotland with him, if I would
consent to go, and find some means for me, adding that he was getting tired
of going to sea and wished for quiet and repose. I deeply regret that I
declined to accompany him, for I am confident if I had consented he would
have gone at once, and would now be adorning the station which nature and
birth so well fitted him for. Does your ladyship blame me for refusing to
go?. . . . Poor George, my kind, loving friend, to be cut off in his youthful
prime while I, long past the meridian of life, alone, friendless in the world,
am left, for what purpose God alone knows.

Poor George still lies covered by several hundred fathoms of his
favourite element, below the grey, cold surface of the Atlantic Ocean.
They never, completely, spied out all he did; there still remain,
probably always will, those elements of doubt of which Arthur Gordon
and Walter Polwarth wrote.

9

From Inheritance to Insolvency

It was not until May 1872 that John Campbell Gordon, the Storm Petrel's youngest and only surviving brother, could legally take up his inheritance as 7th Earl of Aberdeen, and become owner as heir of entail of all the land and the big house. After the news of the death by drowning of George, the 6th Earl, it had been necessary to prove that fact to the satisfaction of the Sheriff of Chancery in Edinburgh, and the Committee for Privileges of the House of Lords. Lengthy hearings before both these Courts had also to show that George was unmarried and therefore had no legitimate heir. All this palaver – which made John impatient and anxious to be on his way – included establishing his claim to the United Kingdom Viscountcy of Gordon, created in 1814. This enabled his grandfather and all his male successors to sit in the House of Lords without the bother of canvassing to secure election by their fellow Scottish peers as a representative peer of Scotland.*

Johnny now became, at the age of twenty-five, heir of entail of some 75,000 acres in Aberdeenshire, the owner of Haddo House and its valuable contents, and with salmon fishing rights in the river Dee, where it enters the limits of the City of Aberdeen, as well as netting rights at the mouth of the river. Unlike his eldest brother, who inherited all this at twenty-three, he had no intention of running away. His brother's action had, however, had the effect that Johnny entered his inheritance, after more than two years' 'frozen' income accumulating, without any bond or burden on the estate. George had foregone more than enough income for this to have been paid off even before his death. Their mother Mary was well enough provided for, and the settlement George had drawn up in 1865 was proved in September, 1870, at £118,728, plus $600 in American banks, just within the threshold of

*This requirement was extinguished by the Peerages Act of 1963. Since then all Scotch peers and peeresses in their own right qualify to sit in the Lords.

£120,000 above which some estate duty was payable. The legatees were all close family; no mention of Jane Ogilvie, nor of Charles Gordon Ogilvie. Johnny waived his share of his brother's will so that it was divided equally between his three sisters, who had also had respectable legacies from the 5th Earl. The father's legacies to his five younger children, ironically, were the chief cause of George's fright at the indebtedness of *his* inheritance, because a bond had to be raised on the estate to provide them. Johnny's generosity was the first of the many actions by which he relieved himself of a considerably comfortable fortune.

The total cost of pursuing his claim to the titles and the estates was £2,485 7s. 6d., mostly in lawyers' fees. It is not clear whether this included disbursements to the Reverend W. B. Alexander: probably not. It is uncharacteristic of Johnny, though it conforms to a long future history of not having much 'sense of money', that he complained to the official family guide Mr Jamieson about the fee of 1,000 guineas that had been paid to Commissioner Harry Smith. Mr Jamieson replied sharply that Harry Smith had 'done a good job in avoiding the sensational aspects of George Osborne's case becoming too prominent' and that he deserved his fee. In the American press there have been printed stories down the generations which echo some invented assertion that the family spent half a million dollars on the trail of George and his associations; this is not so. Whether or not Jennie Swan and Amelia or Cecilia Rook were the 'sensational' aspects of the case, their names were certainly suppressed in all the inquiries of which evidence came to light.

The Parliamentary Reform Act of 1867 created out of the old Aberdeenshire constituency two seats, West and East Aberdeenshire. Proposals were well advanced for James – brother 'Jem' – to enter the lists for East Aberdeenshire, but his death in February 1868 from a self-inflicted rifle shot (see Chapter 8) put an end to this, and in any case Parliament and the Queen had not yet finally assented to the new arrangements. They did not come into force until the summer of 1868. Still, candidates had to be selected. Early in 1870, after George was dead, but long before the news was known, an opportunity to fill the East Aberdeenshire seat came Johnny's way. He gladly accepted the overtures made, and had no difficulty in taking the advice that he must conduct an election as a Tory, only not too much so. It was only after marriage to a Liberal zealot that he took to his knees before the awesome Mr Gladstone.

On 7 November 1877 John Campbell Gordon, 7th Earl of Aberdeen, married Ishbel Marjoribanks, a daughter of Lord Tweedmouth, himself a man of considerable fortune at that time and given to ungovernable rages which greatly frightened his children and his wife, formerly Isabel Hogg. The wedding of Johnny and Ishbel took place in London. The Liberal light had not yet come upon Johnny with blinding force, for the Conservative Arthur Balfour was his best man. The young couple spent the first leg of their honeymoon at a house lent by relations – Halstead Place – between Orpington and Sevenoaks. They were settling down to tea on the afternoon of 9 November when Ishbel's German maid burst distraught into the room and in German blurted excitedly that the jewels were missing. Ishbel had brought not only her expensive wedding presents but treasured ornaments lavished upon her in her maiden days. It was supposed to have been the work of the notorious cat burglar Charles Peace, but more than one pair of hands, more than one brain, had planned this outrage. How could insurance money, if any, and replacements by a doting husband and father (when he was not ill-humoured he was over-indulgent of his daughters) compensate for the calamity of the loss of ornaments like a locket which had been a christening present, valuable necklaces and the like? This must have made a bit of a hole in Johnny's purse, bottomless though it seemed at the time. When they could help detectives and insurance agents no more, they proceeded to Egypt, and there they adopted, and had baptized, four little boys brought to a slave market near Aswan. Mercifully these children were left at a missionary school, and were not brought home to the rigours of British living. Meanwhile the crafty dragomen extracted from the innocent pair what pickings they could.

At last the time came, in 1878, for Ishbel to be brought to Haddo House. Despite the month of June it was cold, blowing from the north-east. 'Why have you brought me to this horrible house?' she told me in her widowhood she had exclaimed to her beloved. Let me, however, stick to 'where the money went', the theme of this aspect of the story of 'We Twa' as they called themselves in their autobiography. The dinner for the Haddo estate tenants, 950 of them, was the culmination of celebrations both there and on the West Aberdeenshire estates centred on the Howe of Cromar, all of which cost a total of £7,500. By way of reply the tenants' gift to Ishbel was a pearl and diamond trellis-work necklace, with earrings and bracelet to match.

Johnny before marriage had already put in hand the building of the chapel adjoining the house, designed by George Street, architect of the

London Law Courts, the Guards' Chapel later bombed and now replaced, and much else of high Victorian Gothic pretension. Now it was Ishbel's turn, with his money, to set about the 'horrible house', with so many north-facing windows and corridors. The north wing, against which abutted the chapel, still smelt of the stables it had been in origin, and there was no cosy family wing for the young, their parents and attendant nurses, governesses and maids. The principal rooms were remodelled in the Adam revival manner by a fashionable firm. The result, where it is not damaged by later careless generations and their friends, is a *tour de force* of pastiche Robert Adam, a style Ishbel had known from childhood in her father's homes. The exterior architecture was 'improved' by the addition of huge bay windows with vast plate-glass panes, and the domestic wing, destroyed by fire in 1930 and not rebuilt, echoed more modestly this super-boarding-house style. They positively liked these vulgar additions, and took the Adamesque interiors for granted. It must be said that what in 1880 was considered advanced plumbing and gas lighting was also generously installed. The total cost is not known – it is impossible to break down some figures to represent what survives today – but no expense was spared on this expansive refurbishing. At the same time, during one year £2,000 was to be spent on estate cottages, £2,000 for charities, and a further £6,000 to cover all other outgoings.

Johnny's next major attempt to get rid of his money was a dead failure. He had always been passionately fond of railways, had been allowed to drive a steam train from Aberdeen to Ellon in his bachelor days, and developed a special manner of blowing the whistle which was a recognition signal as he approached Ellon station when he knew family would be waiting there. He could imitate this whistle most realistically using throat and cupped hands. He could also imitate the cuckoo's call by much the same means. I often heard him do the cuckoo in his old age, and nearly managed it myself. His interest went beyond these larks on the footplate and the like, and extended to a serious proposal to build a railway across the Haddo estate, leaving the existing line at Udny and proceeding via Tarves to Methlick. Ten miles of single-line track and a large number of bridges over and under roads would have cost £70,000 in 1878. The necessary Private Bill passed its second reading in Parliament, but then difficulties arose. The directors of the Great North of Scotland Railway, who had tolerated his driving their passenger trains, raised objections to 'a young nobleman who had no fear of the iron horse' meddling in their vested interest. They insisted that Lord Aberdeen should make good any deficiency in the railway not paying its way, which, despite a strong element of enthusiasm by tenants and others on the route, would certainly have been the outcome. The impetuous, high-minded and friendly young man therefore abandoned the project. The route was surveyed in detail, and maps of the proposed line still exist amongst the family papers.

This project was conceived at a time of severe agricultural depression due to a combination of bad harvests and cheap imports of foodstuffs both for us and for our farm animals. Johnny diverted part of the notional £70,000 not spent on the railway to a remission of rents for a half year – including tenantries in West Aberdeenshire and others not affected by the railway idea – which cost between £20,000 and £25,000, in actual cash, without in any way reducing necessary expenditure on capital works and repairs due by the landlord. Some tenants thought the rents too high anyhow, and when a revaluation was offered to all who liked to ask for it, the saintly man found himself committed to an 11½ per cent reduction in rental for the remaining period of the leases affected. Even when those leases ran out, renewal did not produce the increases expected. They had, however, secured something more than cupboard love from the majority of tenants.

Meanwhile Johnny had bought for £43,500 the Westminster lease of the house in Grosvenor Square he already rented, and proceeded to rebuild that, from necessity in the main; though perhaps a galleried ballroom at the very back of the house was not strictly in accordance with the couple's firm adherence to the severities of the Church of Scotland. Indeed, at the instigation of the Earl of Rosebery, Johnny was appointed Lord High Commissioner of the Church of Scotland in 1881, at the age of thirty-four. Instead of limiting his attentions to the honorifics of this office Johnny and Ishbel positively flung out and, in addition to exceeding the £2,000 allowance by £1,000 in each of the first two years, insisted on drawing in Free Church members to official parties of the established Kirk, for which they were much criticized but which they and their friends justified as being in the spirit of Johnny's grandfather the 4th Earl, who had tried so hard to prevent the breaches which led to the relentless secessions of the earlier part of the century, which still caused bitter conflict in the 1880s. The High Commissioner tried retrenchment in his third year: result, a net saving of £25. In the fourth year he tried to decline the offer to be reconfirmed in office, but the revered Mr Gladstone persuaded him, merely suggesting that their 'free and large current of entertainments' might be stemmed a trifle. As yet Johnny knew nothing of overdrafts, but the earnest intention with which they set out to save from income never looked like producing a farthing. Expenditure was always in excess of income.

Sales of land began as early as 1884. Some outlying portions of the Cromar estate, all within the Dee catchment area, but stopping short of the royal river itself, were the first to go. Where once Johnny's grandfather had sported his otter hunt by the burns feeding Loch Kinord, bloodily depicted by Landseer in a huge, horrifying canvas now in the Laing Art Gallery at Newcastle, there is land desirable for those wishing to have a mansion on Deeside. As the perceptive author, the eponymous itinerant fishwife of *The Christian Watt Papers*, writes: 'After Royalty came, Deeside was ruined. The rich came and built huge palaces to try to outshine Easter Balmoral. After the sport was properly organised we [the fishwives selling herrings and other dried fish] were officially banned.' The smoked haddock and dried herring trade was chiefly for the crofting folk scattered in the glens, and the villages in and above Braemar, Ballater and Aboyne. In addition people like 'Lady Janet Farquharson at Invercauld always took an order . . . the Duchess of Leeds in Dalmohr House always bought a big order'.

Some of the land Johnny sold adjoins that of another branch of the Gordon family, the Earls of Aboyne, who inherited the marquessate of Huntly when the dukedom of Gordon became extinct. Part of the boundary between the two estates runs along Bloody Burn. Charles Gordon, who succeeded as 11th Marquess of Huntly in 1863, was born in March 1847, five months before Johnny, and throughout their long lives various circumstances of propinquity paired them in others' eyes, though it would be idle to assume from this that they were close friends who had similar tastes and aims in life, except as regards the responsibilities and privileges of two noblemen in the grip of Aberdeenshire society, and an equal capacity for ridding themselves of their inheritance. Charles was in rank by far the senior of the two, being premier marquess of Scotland and enjoying the undisputed soubriquet of 'Cock o' the North'. *His* financial misfortunes began before he was born, though he in no way helped himself to recover from a disadvantageous start, despite marrying two rich wives.

His grandfather, 5th Earl of Aboyne, remotely descended from the Marquesses of Huntly before they became Dukes of Gordon, inherited considerable estates, mostly consisting of poor hill land and moorland, in 1794. He found that the best land had been drained and enclosed and improved, and he continued the process himself. All his inherited estates were heavily entailed, but he added other land by purchase in other counties. In 1825 he lost many thousands of pounds when a notoriously crooked banker, Fauntleroy, failed. The Aboyne estates were as a result put in trust: in fact sequestrated. The trustees sold the recently acquired estates and all the marketable timber on the entailed estates, so that when Charles's father inherited in 1854, all claims were soon paid off. Charles succeeded in 1863 and, on reaching his majority in 1868, he came into possession of a diminished inheritance of only 90,000 acres, worth comparatively little in rents, and found himself legally and morally bound to provide portions for eleven younger brothers and sisters. Two more, one of either sex, did not survive babyhood.

'Here', he wrote, 'was an estate of 90,000 acres, easily accessible [because of the Deeside railway to Ballater], with the finest opportunities for sport.' All this was strictly entailed. To obtain capital to rebuild farmhouses, and to improve Aboyne above the condition in which he found it, with only six stone and slated houses, he had to insure himself, an expensive business: a high risk, I reckon most insurance brokers would say. By 1882 two bills relieving the worst horrors of the laws of entail in Scotland were enacted, and the Cock o' the North was obliged to take full advantage by massive sales. He could not help himself to the whole proceeds, however, as he was childless and therefore had to pay each of his three brothers then still living, the Lords Douglas, Esmé and Granville Gordon, their share of the value of the formerly entailed property he sold. That led to more sales.

Charles was probably a shameless spendthrift from the time of achieving his majority. A grandson of Lord Granville told me that he tried to borrow back Granville's portion when it was his sole source of subsistence. The reason for this was principally Charles's compulsion to gamble, which reached such absurd depths as putting money on a favourite house-fly that it would be the first among flies to climb to the top of the wall of a room. An exceptionally handsome man of great charm, he appears to have escaped any sort of formal censure for behaviour that would have landed an ordinary mortal in the dock. It is said that he once pinched somebody's gold pocket watch and walked down Bond Street swinging it on its chain proclaiming his criminality to anybody who would listen. Nobody paid attention. This was daredevilry rather than robbery, but I feel sure he kept the watch, if neither the law nor its rightful owner contested his possession of it. He was outwardly an exceptionally stupid man, yet his two books of memoirs reveal the residue of a classical education, partly genuine and, I suspect, partly due to the promptings of somebody on his publisher's staff with a well tended acquaintance with Latin.

Charles's first wife's father, Sir William Cunliffe-Brooks, who had a passion for water, took on the vast Glentanar Estate as well as Aboyne Castle, and built Glentanar House on top of a spring, which wells up into a discreet granite fountain and trough in the bowels of the house. All this was later sold to the head of the Coats cotton family from Paisley, Lord Glentanar, who maintained the whole estate in magnificent order. Lord Huntly's principal occupations, apart from betting on house-flies, were racing and, one may suspect, the gaming-table, and it can be confidently stated that he was a born loser, finishing up with no land in Scotland and a meagre hold, in thrall to his second, American, wife Isabella, in Grosvenor Square and at Orton Longueville near Peterborough. In reality, if not in the eyes of the law, he was bankrupt. Charles and Isabella will be met again later in Johnny's story.

In addition to his being Lord High Commissioner of the Church of Scotland for five expensive years from 1881 to 1885, the 7th Earl was appointed Lord-Lieutenant of Aberdeenshire in 1880, and remained the Sovereign's representative in the County of Aberdeen until his death in 1934. I remember as a youth of seventeen being present at a luncheon party at his House of Cromar, with the Vice-Lieutenant and all the Deputy Lieutenants, to celebrate his fiftieth anniversary in the position. What a dull lot they all were; or so it seemed to a frisky boy wanting more lively entertainment. This post, too, carried expense with it. Nevertheless, in 1883, the year of my father's birth, the estate covered 62,422 acres worth £44,112 a year. These calculations are pretty meaningless, because they do not show the heavy annual expenditure on maintenance, but for what the figures are worth, there they are in black and, in due course, red.

Then, in February 1886, he was appointed Lord-Lieutenant and Viceroy of Ireland. This was always a political appointment – Gladstone had just come to power for the third time – and it carried a modest salary and entertainment allowance. There was grave trouble in the west of Ireland because the seed potato had not been supplied through bureaucratic bungling, and there were other causes of acute hunger. John Morley, the Irish Secretary in the Liberal Government, claims to have tried to rush through the necessary grants of money, but wrote that 'the Treasury took fright, and the Prime Minister too saw grave objections'. The newly appointed Viceroy offered the necessary £1,500 from his own resources, which was agreed on condition that his name did not appear. The Anglo-Irish Tory gentry, whose vicious swipes at the Aberdeens were to resound for many years to come, never knew about this gift, and the knowledge would only have fanned their fury.

At first the appointment was horrifying to the young couple. Gladstone summoned Aberdeen and virtually ordered him to accept or refuse the offer at once. He accepted without being able to consult the formidable Ishbel, who had left London to spend the day with Lady Rosebery at Mentmore. She wrote at once to the well-known divine Dr Henry Drummond: 'Don't you think I ought to be very much offended at not being consulted, I who have registered a solemn vow never to set foot in Ireland?' Yet her mother was an Ulsterwoman with O'Neill blood. Henry Drummond, whom Johnny met first and who enormously impressed him – he must have been magnetic even more than he was pious – became such an overpoweringly close friend that one wonders, with his somewhat untouchable beauty, what were her real feelings towards him. At least his influence released the young pair from the harshest aspects of the Calvinistic distaste for fun and laughter, and stopped them being, in Ishbel's own words, 'such a goody-goody couple'.

Ireland was then, as now, a burning issue, in domestic politics *the* burning issue, and the Aberdeens, like the Government, were committed to Home Rule. Neither was afraid of controversy, nor of standing their ground, but this sort of fighting politics was to them alien and odious. Nevertheless, in the end Ireland was to provide the most worthy outlet for her social, improving energies, and the spending of his money. This first viceroyalty lasted for only a few months, as had its Tory predecessor under Salisbury, and it fell on the rejection by the Commons of the Home Rule Bill. One fortunate outcome was that the Aberdeens had the right to take away from Viceregal Lodge the vast quantities of fine Irish linen it had also been their right to have supplied. Some of this, coroneted, numbered as to quantity and dated 1886, is still in use by the family. Two napkins are large enough to cover my humble eating-table. The Tory gentry made great play of this; vicious, scandalmongering ninnies many of them. Most Irish peers and peeresses stayed away from Dublin Castle levées when the Liberals were in power, except for agreeable grandees like the Marquess of Sligo. There were, of course, a number of exceptions who delighted to retail news of the goings-on. Ishbel's mother wrote: 'The Duchess of Marlborough says she never saw a jig danced in Ireland, much less at the Castle – very *infra dig*. – she is quite awfully jealous at your success.' They also gave a ball for servants of the vice-regal court and their friends, an innovation that raised many eyebrows. After the initial shock, Johnny and Ishbel fell in love with Ireland for the rest of their lives. They learnt to shrug off hostility from Conservatives, Irish gentry, powerful North Americans and smart Londoners to all their doings, both in and away from Ireland. Was it not better to do what they did than to sit on your acres and attend ceremonial occasions in funny clothes from time to time? They did that as well, of course, but in their case it was only one layer of deep seams of action.

After those hectic months of proconsular balancing on an Irish wire, they embarked on a world-wide visit, to India first, at Rosebery's suggestion, then to Ceylon, where they stayed with the Governor, that now familiar Sir Arthur Gordon. His personal journal is quite scathing. '1887, March 9. Took the Aberdeens to Peradeniya [the world-famous botanic gardens at Kandy] before breakfast, and took them down to Colombo by special train at 2.15, arriving just in time to take them on board their steamer. They were in their usual self-important fidget and fuss and I think never looked at anything either on the way down or at Peradeniya. Dined at Club.' Two days before he had taken them to his elegant bungalow at Nuwara Eliya for one night. 'Ishbel appeared as the Queen of Erin,' says the waspish diary.

Poor Arthur! Those of us who remember the Aberdeens must agree that they could and did get into self-important fidgets. My mother was a cruel mimic of these characteristics. *She* disliked them because they stopped my father's allowance soon before I was born, and because they were Liberals and she had been brought up by Mr Drummond, her banker father, 'a little Conservat-ive'. Arthur had also grounds for distaste. He had been, as the 4th Earl's youngest son, the old man's constant companion in his old age at Haddo. Then Arthur's invalid eldest brother succeeds, and within ten years of the former Prime Minister's death Arthur finds that his brother's *youngest son* inherits all that much loved place. As a youngest son himself his bitterness was great, and even rubbed off on *his* son and successor, always known as 'Jack', 2nd and last Lord Stanmore. Jack made it clear to me that he was not enthralled by the 'Haddo' Gordons, and left me unclear whether I was included as such, until I pointed out that I, too, had always reserved my position in the family.

We cannot leave the fidgety couple on board their steamer at Colombo, however. Next stops were Australia and New Zealand, then Fiji, Honolulu and San Francisco. Ishbel had two embarrassingly daft brothers (whom she loved), Archie Marjoribanks, ranching in Texas, and Coutts in North Dakota, of all ridiculous places. Two open-handed remittance men dependent on father's instalments. At last, in the autumn of 1887, the Aberdeens arrived home. 'Home' was not only Haddo House and Grosvenor Square. Early in their marriage they had leased a house at Mill Hill called Littleberries, built, it was thought, by Charles ii for Nell Gwynn. Later they took on Lord Tweedmouth's lease of Dollis Hill, a smaller house but large enough for Mr Gladstone as Prime Minister to be a constant week-end occupier, escaping from Downing Street thereby long before Lord Lee of Fareham gave Chequers for the same purpose. A house of the Regency period, Dollis Hill perched on its green knoll in the middle of a 500-acre farm on the very shore of London, and must have represented a convenient drain for money at a time when Lord Tweedmouth's finances were down in the mouth, if no worse. Included in the takeover was much elegant Georgian furniture.

By 1890 the Aberdeens were off on their travels again, this time primarily to Canada, but also to prepare for the Chicago World's Fair of 1893, for which they determined to erect a stand to exhibit Irish lace and other rural industries. With practical help from Andrew Carnegie, Marshall Field, 'the biggest dry goods man in America', and his partner Gordon Selfridge, an Irish village was later a great feature of the Exposition, and deemed a huge success. Meanwhile, having started that ball rolling with the help of these immensely shrewd business brains and without using any of Johnny's capital, they set out for British Columbia, where, unbelievably, they had bought sight unseen a 480-acre farm on the shores of Lake Okanagan. They had taken on trust the advice of Mr G. G. Mackay, an engineer from Scotland who had built Highland roads for Lord Tweedmouth, and who was now doing nicely as a property developer in and around Vancouver. The purchase price was $10,000 and Mr Mackay convinced them that in a few years it would be worth four times that amount. They were to grow fruit and hops, and to benefit themselves and the distressed local folk by putting up a jam factory. Mr Mackay did not offer them a bargain in or around Vancouver, where he really knew his business.

More unbelievably still, they put in Ishbel's dim brother Coutts Marjoribanks as manager; he having failed utterly to make a go of his

North Dakota ranching with pure-bred Aberdeen Angus cattle originally given to him by his anxious mother. The charming wooden house, with verandah round two sides, and the farm, were named Guisachan after the Tweedmouth property in Inverness-shire where Mr Mackay had turned plough tracks into carriage drives. We are only just on our way, on this incompetent, visionary, benevolent road to financial disaster. They had sold 27 Grosvenor Square, superfluous now that Dollis Hill was near enough to serve as a London address, at a profit. Having rebuilt the handsome Georgian London house for £48,000, with a fussy Victorian façade and a galleried ballroom over the mews at the rear, they sold it to an Australian for £65,000. That was his offer; they did not demand more. Whether the concurrent transaction of the sale of the Westminster lease yielded additional profit is not recorded. The surprise is that the enterprise made any profit at all. They decided to put £50,000 of the Grosvenor Square money into the purchase of the 13,000-acre Coldstream Ranch in the same area as Guisachan Farm. Mr Vernon, the vendor, would not sell in lots and held to his price. Lord Tweedmouth's response to Johnny and Ishbel's absurd enthusiasm was to call the venture 'the new Golconda', somewhat unfair to the Nizam of Hyderabad's principal source of diamonds.

A sad letter of March 1893 from his man of business in Edinburgh tells Lord Aberdeen that in 1891 personal expenditure exceeded income by £13,740; in 1892 by £19,930. To the second sum the investment in British Columbia – the new Golconda – had contributed about £4,000. 'These figures', wrote Mr Jamieson, 'are full of menace.' He goes on to propose remedies. What was the use? Tradesmen's accounts alone in one period of fifteen months amounted to £9,391.

The idea on the Coldstream Ranch was to plant orchards on a big scale – how eagerly they read up the likeliest varieties of apples and pears, plums and cherries – and to sell off sections. 'If we choose to give up buying a London house this fit of speculation will be justifiable.' But these were expectations. The local population were stick-in-the-mud at the prospect of making jam, so the factory was built but never used; the price of fruit and hops plummeted, and over the years more capital, borrowed this time, had to be put in to make good the incompetence of Coutts, whose huge feet made him so clumsy that he was always knocking into furniture and dropping things, and the dishonesty of a later manager. However, what their daughter Lady Pentland described as their 'play-house' at Guisachan gave them refreshment later on when Johnny was Governor-General of Canada from 1893 to 1898, and they needed occasional escape from the formalities of Government House at Ottawa and the necessary forays to the great provincial cities. As early as 1895 Ishbel recorded: 'This year we shall have a big deficit of income, though the Coldstream manager is confident of success. Probably it will either make or ruin us.' In pursuit of success, land reserved for cattle was planted with fruit trees and irrigated. The profits never came. They hung on to it until 1920, when Lord Woolavington bought it and at once turned it round into profit. No more red for him; just the magic of Black and White.

The only saints and do-gooders who should go in for speculative businesses are those who start with the latter capacity, and work onward and upward to the former conditions. In 1951 the *Vancouver Sun* magazine wrote: 'No ranch contributed more to the early progress of the interior of British Columbia. For here was planted the first orchard, and irrigation first established to revolutionize the northern end of the Okanagan Valley.' The praise was given to two pioneers, but the article would not have been written if the whisky king's acumen had not been employed in Coldstream Ranch's later history.

Having sunk all this delightful money in British Columbia, Johnny and Ishbel returned home and, still in 1891, put in hand the building, near the southern courtyard of Haddo House, beyond Archibald Simpson's elegant clock tower and cupola of 1828, of a wooden community hall with upswept, wooden shingle roof. It is probable that Mr Charles Sleigh, the estate architect, was responsible for the design; working drawings prepared by an Aberdeen builder show varying designs, especially of the roof structure. It is denied by Canadian authorities that the design executed (and extant in 1984) is in the manner of a Canadian rural community hall. This must be accepted – my 'hunch' that this was so is not good enough – but there can be no doubt that the wooden construction and especially the roof of shingles are of North American inspiration.

Johnny's appointment to be for six years Governor-General of Canada in 1893 was a consolation prize since the pair had set their sights on Ireland again. But 'We Twa' were not offered the opportunity to return to Ireland when Gladstone's fourth and final administration was formed in 1892, so the immediate chance to pour treasure into Irish rural industries and health education was for the moment denied to them. Morley had blocked a reappointment: he kept it very quiet that politically he was then against a 'popular' viceroy, and he was a jealous man. Gladstone offered all kinds of plum appointments and in the end

'We Twa' accepted Canada. Before they went the new community hall was put to good use. A grand county ball was given, and for this a temporary staircase from the end of the newly built family wing, leading to a covered causeway across the rough gravel, gave guests sheltered access to the ball. No half measures were ever contemplated. Yet they were not swanky, and shunned the company of fashionable people. A later rout for tenants and servants offered modified facilities of like kind. They then departed for years of vigorous spending in Canada. To mention one small item, Johnny built a wooden chapel at his own expense attached to Government House, although Ottawa was generously stocked with churches of many denominations. The building of the hall at Haddo, the covered ways for the party, and this chapel, all go to show how this couple could not 'think small'. Her ample physical presence was a symptom of an expansive temperament; left to himself Johnny would have been just as dignified and saintly – unable to refuse a helping hand – and his inability to grasp financial realities would only have mattered less because his outlays might have been smaller on each project. Such an idle speculation is offered to allow the reader to infer what is my firm belief: that this was a true partnership of a very odd couple, and that neither the one nor the other can be judged the more blameless or blameworthy of improvidence, undiscriminating generosity, impulsive spending, or fuss and fidget. But in daily comings and goings, even some of an official character, there is no doubt that Ishbel was *Die Feldmarschallin*. Hence others' attitudes to her were more strongly for or against than they were to him.

Back in Canada, as Governor-General and his lady, there were ample opportunities for denuding Johnny's resources, apart from the Coldstream Ranch, and these are now passed over because they have been elsewhere so well chronicled. Let it be sufficient to say that beneficiaries of the Victorian Order of (district) Nurses which Ishbel, backed by Johnny, set up in 1897 were saying 'thank you' to me in 1957. After five years, in 1898, with no home leave and a family of four children too often at a distance (my father crossed the Atlantic twenty-six times during his schooldays), Johnny resigned the appointment. Apart from the children's interest, grave financial problems were looming. The two big estates of Haddo and Cromar, and the piling up of debts and overdrafts, did not yet call for desperate measures, but they must have been worrying. He was only just over fifty, and came from a long-lived family. Gainful occupation depended on political appointments in which he continually spent more than he earned. This was not just a peccadillo of 'We Twa'; even the most skinflint of proconsuls did the same. They were expected to, and their level of salary and allowances was set at a low level with the implicit under-standing that they had private means: they were chosen from the ranks of the comfortable. If they were capable of calculating that acceptance would be uncomfortable, they could refuse the appointment, as many did, risking thus being passed over by fragile politicians for other posts that might better suit them. Remember, too, that at this time House of Commons members received no pay as backbenchers.

In their domestic arrangements the Aberdeens were now without a London residence. After Mr Gladstone's reluctant retirement from Parliament in 1895 he had no more use for their house at Dollis Hill. Johnny gave up the lease in 1897 whilst they were in Canada. The auctioneers' listing of fine eighteenth-century furniture sold for low prices is a source of envy. Four years later 96 acres of it was opened by Johnny as a public park: Gladstone Park it remains to this day. The rest awaited the rashes of cheap development in the 1930s. Only one short, curved street – Aberdeen Road – commemorates the former tenant and eager young sponsor of the comforts of Gladstone. To make up for their abandonment of Dollis Hill they took over in 1899 58 Grosvenor Street with a short lease to run; just a London perch for the season and for Johnny's parliamentary appearances. There was plenty of room, too, for dances for the young and dinner parties for the more mature. Standards must not be surrendered.

The Cromar estates in West Aberdeenshire, acquired by the busy Earl William between 1729 and 1733, were not subjected by him to such tightly drawn entails as were inflicted upon the Haddo estates and the contiguous properties in Formartine and Buchan of East Aber-deenshire, and had never had a mansion house suitable for aristocratic occupation. The property consisted of good grouse moors to east and north, the celebrated Muir of Dinnet with its carpeting of bell heather to the south-west, running almost down to the river Dee, and the Howe of Cromar at its heart, good farming land but needful of constant draining. The rent roll was, at the time of George Osborne's death in 1870, £2,219 compared with nearly £40,000 on the East Aberdeenshire estates. Probably the factor, as land agents are called in Scotland, farmed the best land for the family. Both Arthur Gordon and George, 6th Earl, in their time stayed at the Aberdeen Arms Inn at the main village of Tarland. Both men on separate occasions entertained a few guests to dinner at this modest hotel. The only available house was

Tarland Lodge, little bigger than a farmhouse, and used also by the factor on his visits. The estate was a potential source of capital. In George's letter to his father, the 5th Earl, of 29 February 1864 – the last letter received by the father before he died – he wrote: 'If you really still think it an advantage to sell Cromar I do not wish to stand in the way, and if I find it sold when I come back I shall not grumble.' (He would not miss the shooting, as Huntly constantly invited him to range over the Glentanar beats for deer-stalking as well as for grouse.) 'Mr. Jamieson certainly did not recommend its being sold three years ago but if it could now be sold at such advantage do so. I am older and wiser.' He also recommended retaining the grouse moors: 'if all were let in 5 or 6 years it would bring in more money than selling [the farmland] without the shooting. Bankers and fellows give incredible sums for shootings now, I believe £5 an acre for the season is the lowest computation.' He then goes on to show how, even taking advantage of bankers and fellows, a separate area of grouse moor could be retained for their own use. George's comments from his Uncle Arthur's address in New Brunswick show how quickly Balmorality, to use A. G. Macdonell's ingenious word, had seized Deeside, and was already attracting bankers and fellows. He was probably right, but nothing was done until the 1880's with Johnny's first sales of outstanding land nearer the Dee. An unauthenticated story following those early transactions is that the Queen remarked severely to her lieutenant that she did not understand it was the custom of Highland lairds to sell their land. His deferential reply is not recorded. He might have tartly asked how she had come by Balmoral? In the first place by lease from the 4th Earl of Aberdeen, and soon after by purchase from the Duff owners of the huge property. It was, of course, different when the Sovereign was involved.

Johnny and Ishbel stopped at Tarland Lodge for the autumn seasons, and built detached cabins and a rumpus room for the young people. Johnny had for years hankered for a mansion house and at last, soon after the return from Canada in 1898, a site was found, backed by woodland of pine and spruce and larch, facing a picturesque panorama of the Deeside hills from Clachnaben above the Cairn o' Mounth road to Angus in the south-east, via Mount Keen at the head of Glentanar, Lochnagar, not dark and frowning at that distance but blue in elegant outline, to Byron's 'Morven of the snows', against whose flat-topped pyramidal shape clouds and sunshine raced across its rough grass cladding to form the western horizon. Financial worries notwithstanding, a comfortable and large mansion was agreed upon to the design of Sydney Mitchell, with terraces, grass and granite-chipping walks, and an Italian garden walled in for the private enjoyment of the owners, whose ground-floor suite of rooms gave access to it.

The House of Cromar had to be paid for, and attention given to the needs of four children quickly becoming adult. Where, then, should the busy couple next turn? The Canadian investment never showed signs of being other than 'the ruin of us', the successful sale of Grosvenor Square was all too easily absorbed by expansive living habits, the renovation of Haddo House and the building of the nursery wing made a fine, plain house finer, and less plain: a worthy setting for the family's picture collection. No one Earl of Aberdeen had been identifiably a great collector of paintings, but since the time of William, the 2nd Earl, there had been a conventional degree of purchase, and in the case of the 3rd Earl, sale, coming to its climax in the acquisitions, sometimes amounting to the contraband loot of war, by the 4th Earl. He used his naval and military brothers as agents during the Napoleonic period to bring over silver and silver gilt as well as paintings, and his legitimate purchases graced the walls of his London house in addition to Haddo. Johnny and Ishbel decided to secure a valuation of the Haddo paintings. For this purpose Ishbel – the surviving correspondence is all addressed to her – engaged the Scottish Gallery of George Street, Edinburgh (managers P. McOmish Dott and J. Lumgair Dott) to make a list of the paintings and a valuation for insurance.

Mr Dott and Mr Dott can have had no illusions that insurance was the sole motive for seeking a valuation. That is why, in the case of portraits of living members of the family, including one by James Sant RA of Johnny and another of Ishbel by the Canadian James Mac-donald, which still form part of the fixed architecture of the library they created, values ranging from £100 to £250 were suggested. The Dotts knew they were not for sale. By contrast a genuine Guido Reni of a servant boy was considered to be worth only £80, and Veronese's 'Wild Boy', a gruesome painting of a boy both pixie-like and vulpine, the face covered with hair 'valuable as a curiosity', was marked at £15. This uncomfortable picture was sold by my brother at Christie's in 1947 for £32. The high insurance value placed by the Dotts on the family paintings is understandable, even though the artists' names have almost disappeared today from the canon. More dubious is the valuation of a Salvator Rosa – 'genuine' – a still-life originally for the back of a harpsichord, at £30; and what is to be thought of £20 as the value of Annibale Carracci's 'Butcher's Shop', the two men serving meat being his cousins, the founders of the Bologna school? This arresting and beautiful picture was sold in the 1970s for a very comfortable six-figure sum to help raise the endowment in the transfer of the house to the national Trust for Scotland.

The brief clip of correspondence from the managers of the Scottish Gallery still extant, all hand-written, concludes with the following:

2. Oct. 1901

My Lady,
    You do not wish to part with any of the Lawrence portraits or the three heads by Titian?

I am your obedient servant
P. McOmish Dott.

The painting by Titian referred to is now in the National Gallery in London, known as 'An Allegory of Prudence' or, more familiarly, as 'the Aberdeen Titian'. It is a triple portrait of three men, young, mature and old. Many identities have been supposed; Cecil Gould's *Sixteenth-Century Italian Schools* states that 'the old man on the left resembles Titian himself in old age . . . the central head represents his son, Orazio, and the youth on the right a young cousin, Marco Vecellio'. It was acquired by the 4th Earl of Aberdeen in London at the time of the Lucien Bonaparte sale in 1816. It was lent by him to the British Institution in 1828, and by his grandson Johnny to an Edinburgh Exhibition in 1883, the year of my father's birth. An insurance list giving a policy number and a date, crossed out, of 'November 18 . .' values this at £300. This list was examined by the Dotts, which is indicated by their marginal note against one or two of the items 'Not here'. Their own valuation of the Titian was £2,000, towering above any other picture in the house, the next in value in their estimation being Lawrence's 'Viscount Melville' at £800, 'J. P. Kemble', the actor, by the same artist at £350, and then a steep decline to Domenichino's 'David with the head of Goliath' (still there) at £150, and Pannini's superb 'Interior of the Pantheon at Rome' at £180. The 4th Earl evidently made a killing in purchases of the Bologna school, represented in his purchases by Carracci, Domenichino and Guido Reni.

Temptation was not resisted. The Titian was sold and was not the only victim of necessity. It is not recorded to whom it was sold, nor for how much, but almost certainly for less than the insurance valuation. What is certain is that it was acquired shortly before his death in 1918 by Alfred de Rothschild. He bequeathed it to Almina, Countess of Carnarvon, who sold it at Christie's in May for twenty-eight guineas. Johnny, profoundly bad at guarding his resources though he may have been, had probably made twentyfold that amount. The circumstances were exceptional. The last German offensive was well under way in April 1918. The famous Messines Ridge had been captured by the Germans at the cost of much blood; Haig's order of the day of 13 April made clear that capture of the Channel ports was the German objective. On 7 May Major-General Sir Frederick Maurice added to the gloom by his famous letter to *The Times* charging ministers with a series of lies about the military position. Above all, Bonar Law's budget proposals of 22 April increased income tax from five shillings in the pound to six and lowered the threshold of supertax from £3,000 to £2,500. It was hardly a moment for free spending, therefore, on 31 May, even at Christie's, even for an important painting by Titian. The surprise is that Lady Carnarvon let it go, but she was not only rich but wholly occupied by hospital work. After several changes of ownership it was presented to the National Gallery in 1966 by David Koetser. Lady Carnarvon was a notorious personage in her time. Supposed to be the love-child of a Rothschild, she founded the famous nursing home at 7 Portland Place, London, which is cruelly caricatured in the final pages of Evelyn Waugh's *Vile Bodies*. I wonder what the Aberdeens and Mr Waugh would have made of each other? Not much, I suspect. This was not the only picture sold during Johnny's ownership of Haddo House. The Dotts' annotation on the earlier list of pictures not prepared by them – 'not here' – implies that Johnny or his father the 5th Earl had already disposed of some works. There is a strong presumption of this but no firm evidence. Johnny's son Haddo, his successor as 2nd Marquess of Aberdeen, certainly sold some paintings, but no record of their sales has been traced, and his nephew, my brother David, 4th Marquess, also sold a Veronese Adoration and the Pannini of the Pantheon. The three generations all sold with a view to preserving for the family's posterity the house and its estate. Is it a mixture of pride and sentimentality that makes men behave in this seemingly irrational fashion? Selling the family heirlooms to be able to go on enjoying a return of one per cent on a landed estate? Whatever their motives, Johnny should be no more blamed than the others just because he sold a painting by Titian, whose values seem to be freer than most from cyclical changes of taste and fashion. Whether he sold it for its true market value in the early 1900s is another question. Probably not, and even as a young bachelor he undoubtedly started the trend in the Aberdeen family of being markedly unsuccessful in turning their inheritance to good account. To Johnny and Ishbel it was there to be used for the encouragement of good causes, not to be hoarded. As to increasing their fortune, they had no idea, certainly not on the scale of Andrew Carnegie or Marshall Field and their contemporaries and neighbours in Scotland, Lords Cowdray and Glentanar.

No sooner was the House of Cromar taking shape than Johnny was again appointed Lord-Lieutenant of Ireland after the Liberal landslide of 1905–6. They arrived in Dublin in state on 3 February 1906. So keen were they in the cause of Home Rule for all Ireland that, even after Sinn Fein attitudes had become clear, they managed to give a St Patrick's Night Ball to which members of the Gaelic League came and danced alongside officers of the Royal Irish Rifles in sets of the Connacht jig to the pipes of the 4th Leinster Regiment. It cannot be said they did not try, and on this occasion Nelly O'Brien, sister of Stephen Gwynn and a keen Gaelic Leaguer, sent an appreciative letter next day.

Of the long years in Dublin, the double term as Lord-Lieutenant and Viceroy (and Vicereine), I will write nothing. The whole history is well recorded in a host of books. Johnny and Ishbel's great projects for rural industries, health education and the like cost much energy and, without doubt, absorbed too much money. The theft of the Dublin Crown Jewels, a sensation of 1907 and for years after, had nothing whatever to do with them, except that certain fingers pointed, and tongues wagged, that Lord Haddo must have taken them because, after all, he had a black beard. It is with uncomfortable relish that I must record that the four men principally responsible for the safekeeping of the jewels, who, if not guilty of theft and *lèse-majesté*, were certainly guilty of neglect of duty and improper behaviour, all came to sticky ends.

The 7th Earl of Aberdeen retired from the Irish Viceregality in 1915 and in January 1916 was created Marquess of Aberdeen and Temair. Between that date and the end of the Great War of 1914–18 there were extensive and expensive travels in the United States and Canada to raise money for the Women's National Health Association of Ireland. This was Ishbel's baby, but Johnny came too. They had hoped to raise a required £20,000 in a few months; it took two years and involved meeting all sorts of quare fellows – and the female of the sort – but they never troubled who or what people were like, or whether they came from the wrong side of the tracks, so long as the cause they had in their hearts was the beneficiary. Ely House, Dublin, the headquarters of the

WNHA, where the Aberdeens had rooms on their occasional visits, thrummed with satisfaction.

The homecoming in 1918 to the House of Cromar soon exposed two major problems. Taxation, rates and upkeep of the Cromar estates at that time exceeded rental income by £2,000 a year. Johnny could not meet the deficit, nor could Ishbel by sending jewellery into Aberdeen for real sparklers to be replaced by paste. No other member of the family had the resources to buy the property from him and lease it to them for life. In the end Johnny wrote to Sir Alexander MacRobert. He had been a Tarland village boy who made an industrial fortune in India, and returned to his old home to live at Douneside, on the side of the village opposite to the House of Cromar. His delightful wife was dying of cancer, and the two pairs were on friendly terms. Johnny's proposition was to propel the house and the estate to Sir Alexander on the death of himself and Ishbel for a nominal consideration if Sir Alexander and his heirs would meet the yearly deficit on the estate until that time. Sir Alexander accepted this proposal; there were, however, difficulties in getting the lawyers on both sides to carry out the wishes of the principals. Meanwhile Lady MacRobert died, Sir Alexander married again, and the new ladyship insisted that the agreement should be extended to include the entire furnishings of the house, and fixtures such as Ishbel's Marjoribanks portraits of herself and her family set in the panelling of the dining-room walls. Everybody gave in to this extension of the agreement. Later, the expenditure deficit rose year by year, partly because of the Aberdeens' inability to moderate their expansive style of living, and, to keep Johnny from the depressions he found it difficult to quell, Ishbel offered to give up the house at his death, should that occur before her own.

That is the Gordons' side of the story; the MacRobert Trust, whose papers respecting this deal can be inspected in the Edinburgh Register House, have a somewhat different view. I have a third view, which may seem that of a prig unless it is placed in the context of my own pretty shaky, small-scale financial history. It does not seem to me just that persons of substance, whether the money is of their own making or is inherited, should overspend their resources when they get beyond the normal age of earning their keep, and then expect others to mop up the mess of a rising overdraft and a diminishing degree of solvency. In the case of my grandparents my attitude is, of course, deeply influenced by the loss of this lovely place to the Aberdeen family on the one hand, and my affection for them on the other.

At the same time that Johnny was grappling with the MacRoberts and sealing the fate of Cromar, he was engaged in 1919–20 in preparing for massive sales of the main estates in East Aberdeenshire, and starting the long process of making over the remaining Haddo Estate to his heir. The Earl of Haddo – Doddie – and his wife Florence lived in the House of Schivas, near Haddo and on the opposite bank of the river Ythan from the village of Methlick. Having earlier escaped the clutches of the 3rd Earl of Aberdeen, it was bought by his grandson the 4th Earl in 1844. Additions to the original sixteenth-century tower house have in no way spoilt its charms. Johnny now arranged that Doddie should take on Haddo House as well as its estate. First special authority had to be secured from the Court of Session to sell the huge outlying parts of the estate, amounting to some 45,000 acres, and to transfer the remaining 14,000 acres to the son and heir, without disentailment. The sales of 1919 realized £445,000, of which, after all deductions had been made – payment of expenses and discharge of wadsets* – there was available to the vendor by 30 June 1920 £4,918 1s. 6d! Schivas was amongst the property sold and, after an interval in other hands, it was bought in 1931 by Lord Catto. The entail on the total Haddo estates was finally broken by order of the Court of Session in 1924. As a minor, third in line as heir of entail of the childless uncle Haddo, my agreement to this release was given on my behalf by my father. He sensibly took the view that there was no happiness in trying to make his eleven-year-old son understand all this, so I was not told. He set aside for me the printed order of the Court, which I still have in its tattered manila envelope.

Johnny retained an interest in part of the land, which was not disentailed, and conveyed the proceeds of its sale, worth about £200,000, to his accountants, Messrs. Lindsay, Jamieson and Haldane. According to the Finance Acts of those times, this was designed to achieve a considerable saving in death duties, so long as the entails were not broken for three years. The desired immediate end was successfully achieved, and I propose now to round off this unhappy descent of a nobleman from the condition of being a proper millionaire at the age of twenty-five in 1872. After Johnny's affairs were finally wound up in 1935 the accountant Herbert Haldane reckoned that, after making all deductions for widow's and younger children's portions, and after payment of all debts and duties, 'the amount of the late marquess's personal estate . . . cannot exceed £204'. Johnny's London

*Mortgages or other loans raised on land or property.

solicitor Robert Hunter had cited an Act of Parliament of 1925 in furtherance of his wish that the will should not be proved. Mr Haldane wrote in September 1935 to Doddie, the 2nd Marquess, who had laboured persistently and more successfully than his Edinburgh lawyers in convincing the Estate Duty Office that certain entailed funds were not dutiable: 'I fully understand Mr Hunter's motive in not wanting to prove the late Lord Aberdeen's will.' The point here is that without probate a testator's affairs, and his dispositions, are not published. I may be breaking some law by making these revelations for the first time now, so let us swiftly return to the aftermath of war, to the year 1920, the era of providing homes fit for heroes.

By the time these traumatic transactions were completed 'We Twa', after unremitting work and travel since their marriage, settled down at the comfortable and overheated House of Cromar in 1920 in their version of retirement. Certainly they were quiet for much of the year, save for Ishbel's perpetual work and travels for the International Council of Women, of which she had been president since 1893. The summer and autumn season consisted of a continuous house party of a changing sequence of guests from rapacious old harridans to greedy grandchildren, and in addition many charming and accomplished men and women of all ages. A grand chef called Germain, of the same family as their respected house steward in Canada and elsewhere, was brought in for the season to fortify the competent cooking of the permanent, and permanently jolly, cook Mrs Craig. Germain, we learnt, had his breakfast brought to him in bed by a kitchenmaid – one wonders what else? – but we guests came down to the dining room, never sooner than nine o'clock, often later, to consume porridge and cream, eaten standing up, then to fall upon a row of those silver entrée dishes containing fillet of sole bathed in cream, or perhaps kedgeree, then kidneys, scrambled, fried or boiled eggs, bacon, sausages, fried bread. These were followed by toast or, best of all, big baps dusted with flour and with their centre thumb hole, brought in fresh by early train to Aboyne from an Aberdeen baker, and along the eight miles of road in time for our breakfasts. Ham and fruit were available on a side table. All this I first experienced in 1923 at the age of ten, then again in 1924, 1926, 1929, 1930. How we ate!

Johnny and Ishbel never appeared at breakfast. They presided over large luncheons and dinners, eaten late generally, because their domestic arrangements centred on the time the post went out, and guests' rumbling tummies were subordinated to the requirement of their huge mailings. We all anxiously waited on sofas and chairs in what can only be described as a lounge hall, protected from the front door by two glass doors of a vestibule, from which a door led to the men's cloakroom. Ishbel, with her powerful frame and substantial forearms, had the knack of carving a joint or a bird (several birds usually) sitting down at the end of the table. At the other end sat Johnny, telling anecdotes to the ladies on either hand, his beard wagging, and occasionally nodding off to sleep with a glass of brandy and hot water in his hand, and his chair tilted dangerously forward. He always recovered in time without help from the petrified guests. They employed no butler or footmen, the serving all being in the hands of three parlourmaids, the senior of whom, Beatrice, often had to stand to Johnny's left for minutes whilst he told a story to his neighbour on his right, she holding a huge silver tray full of coffee things. Her poor thin arms must have ached, and the silly women on either side were incapable of saying: 'Won't you have some coffee, Lord Aberdeen?'

Apart from Germain, the only indoor manservant was the piper, who paraded the terrace at eight o'clock every morning, and went round the table at the end of dinner making an unholy row. In the daytime he acted as handyman humping laundry baskets, getting in logs and the like. I suspect the Gordon Barracks at Aberdeen helped to supply, and possibly contributed to the pay, of these men. A majority of the guests, the Europeans and especially the Americans, assumed during the evening piping ceremony an expression of prayer. We young caught each others' eyes and sustained throughout ill-suppressed giggles. We were not scornful of the piper (but we were heedless of his feelings); we were laughing at the sycophantic, hand-clasping attitudes of the other guests. In 1929 Eleanor Elder and Hugh Mackay brought their famous travelling Arts League of Service Theatre to Tarland, and they were all put up in the house. One of them took over my room and I was banished to a basement room in servants' quarters just below terrace level, *en suite* with the room of Piper Geddes. He properly took advantage of this proximity to complain about the giggling, asking that we please control it. 'You see,' he said, 'sometimes it makes me want to swipe your ears with my elbow, and sometimes I want to join in and laugh too. It is not possible to laugh when playing the bagpipes.' I did my poor best to persuade without much success, but we at least never got swiped round the earhole.

It is now time to reintroduce Charles, 11th Marquess of Huntly, who had married his American wife Isabella in 1922. An annual event over which Marquess Charles presided, with Johnny beside him, was the Aboyne Highland Games. How I hated these occasions! The weather was always cold and blustery, I had to spend too long dressed in my Sunday-best kilt things, which were handed down, probably from an earlier generation, and which never properly fitted; my exposed knees mauve from the cold. Everybody was deferential or haughty – nothing natural – but at least, unlike the Royal Braemar Gathering, there were sideshows on the field where the grubby professional athletes ran or wrestled, where I could spend happy times, generally escorted by Mr Alexander Kidd, an elderly Aberdeen organist normally a guest not at Cromar but at Haddo House, whence we sometimes drove in ancient motors to this beastly ceremony. Mr Kidd was my saviour, a wonderful man with the young – he even tried to teach me fly-fishing – and enabled me to sample the palmist's tent and the fishtailed woman and the 'boneless wonder', an acrobatic contortionist whose act culminated in throwing either leg over the opposite shoulder to form himself into a human knot. Charles Huntly, meanwhile, would be in his official tent talking to cronies and sipping whisky to keep out the cold. Either a precarious hold on Aboyne Castle, comfortless and draughty, or rooms at the Huntly Arms Hotel, sent him and his wife gratefully as guests as often as possible to neighbouring houses. On one occasion at a dinner party at Cromar at which they were present, one of those embarrassing silences fell upon the large company whilst Marchioness Isabella was clearly heard, shrilling to Johnny, who was by now rather deaf: 'I didn't wanna marry Huntly; I was pushed into it.' This remark, heard by her husband at the opposite end of the table, fits in well with the sayings of this remarkable, stupid and fearless woman. A few fully authenticated statements run thus: 'I married three times: the first for love [Chicago Campbell], the second for money [Chicago Macdonald], the third for a title.' I was also present at Stratfield Saye, just old enough to stay away without parental chaperonage, when the occupants, Charles and Maud Douro at that time, asked the Huntlys to luncheon. Afterwards there were to be photographs, but only snaps by family and friends. Isabella said she must make herself look pretty, fumbled in her bag for lipstick and found none. She glanced at Huntly, who sheepishly shook his head in a negative, then at her son Arthur Bradley Campbell, always known as ABC, who shook likewise. 'How many times', she rasped in that piercing voice, 'have I got to tell you two boys ALWAYS to carry my spare lipstick in your waistcoat pocket?' Maudie Douro, whose brother Tom Glentanar now owned Huntly's former property in Aberdeenshire, was able to oblige the lady with the red-assisted hair.

Finally, there is no need to doubt that on one occasion when encountering George vi's Queen Elizabeth she commented: 'You're looking a little fat, Ma'am.' Then a meaningful nudge and a wink. 'Anything doing?' 'No, Lady Huntly, no.' 'Are you sure, Ma'am?' Onlookers then suspected Isabella was going to pat the royal stomach, but here the story ends.

Charles Huntly had a house in Grosvenor Square, still with its Georgian aspect and delicately plastered ceilings. It was on a corner site where the American Embassy now has its northern end – the Aberdeens' house had been a few doors down that flank – but in the Huntlys' house the plaster was cracking and the furniture missing essential castors and bits of veneer. With all her money she was prepared only to maintain herself and her handsomely aristocratic husband in a raffish kind of comfort. It was said she would let him go bankrupt over and again rather than pay his debts and tidy his houses with her substantial funds. My sister and her husband once stayed, en route to Scotland by road, at Orton Longueville Hall, his inherited English property near Peterborough, which already belonged to Isabella. It was the same sad story. The curtains of their room did not meet in the middle, the washbasin on the cracked marble washstand was grimy, and a hot water can with towel over was tepid. It was a sad reflection on a woman who is alleged to have burst into the apartment of friends in New York after she had accepted Huntly's proposal of marriage and screeched out: 'Say, girls, whaddya know? I'm going to be a real marquee.' Plump as she was she was not so voluminous as that and, in fact, looked quite svelte beside Ishbel.

The harvest of 1926 in Aberdeenshire was a nearly complete failure – I can remember the wind-and-rain-flattened oats quite green on the long September drive to the Braemar gathering – and this was difficult for hard-pressed landowners as well as for tenant farmers and crofters. Early in 1927 Johnny wrote to Lord Cowdray, the amiable millionaire who had bought Dunecht House for an Aberdeenshire residence, and the Forest of Birse, marching with Glentanar, for the shooting. Dunecht had been built by an expansive nineteenth-century Earl of Crawford, who put in it a galleried library with a great vaulted roof. Johnny asked if Lord Cowdray would guarantee his overdraft up to £3,000. Certainly not, replied the millionaire, nothing less than £5,000 would he guarantee. I do hope there was no call on this generous offer, especially since the 1st and 2nd Lords Cowdray died within six and a half years of each other at about this time. Johnny then fell ill, from worry and fatigue as much as anything else, and whilst he was in this weakened condition there arrived a letter from his son Haddo saying that he and his wife Florence were thinking of selling the whole of the Haddo estate. This news hardly lifted the gloom that had settled on the House of Cromar.

The Haddos' case was that when the factor Johnny had appointed in about 1900 retired in 1926 it was quickly found that he had been putting his fingers in the till by one means or another for all that time. That revelation, and the poor harvest, seemed too much to bear, especially as the Haddos' life was led principally in London, and the great house opened only for short periods except for the long summer and autumn, when they entertained house parties of a different character from the more easygoing cosmopolitan delights of Cromar. To us young the house seemed always to be full of old women, some widowed, some (improbably) ladyships, some gushing, all awful. There were of course exceptions amongst the guests, but how we longed to get away from the bourgeois, north-country régime of Florence Haddo, born Miss Clixby of Owmby Cliff, Lincs! My mother's mimicry of her was viciously accurate. What nasty snobs we were, not even humbled by our comparative lack of money and fine things.

In 1927 there were no visits to Haddo and Cromar, not at least for me, who had just endured my first term at Harrow School, and who had to be content with a holiday with the two younger boys and our nurse at loathsome Westgate-on-Sea, from which my escape was to Dreamland, the fun fair with switchback at Margate, and on bicycle to the inland delights of St Nicholas-at-Wade, Minster, and the tight-knit streets of Sandwich. All alone I went, to avoid the dreadful beach with smelly seaweed and sand in your socks, and the freezing bathing in West Bay at high tide, the water churned up and holding in suspension our demolished sand-castles. I was always in trouble for these lonely expeditions; always condemned for wanting to be different. I still feel a tiny chill of persecution.

It was in fact Florence Haddo who came to the rescue of the Haddo estate in 1927 by persuading her husband to sell pictures and probably a few other valuables. Then in 1930 the south pavilion of William Adam's Palladian mansion and the 1880 nursery wing built beyond it by Johnny and Ishbel were gutted by fire. Wisely they took the insurance money for the sunny Victorian wing and did not rebuild, and gave the interior of the eighteenth-century wing the character of an up-lofted garden suburb dwelling, which it still has, and reinstated the superb kitchen on the ground floor.

Meanwhile at Cromar life went on. Johnny and Ishbel's golden wedding had been celebrated in London on 7 November 1927 at a grand luncheon and reception at 27 Grosvenor Square, then belonging to Mrs Robert Fleming, grandmother of the writers Peter and Ian Fleming (who was responsible for the original Bond stories), and widow of the merchant banker and jute merchant. Johnny's best man Arthur Balfour was present, and was treated with unbecoming irreverence by this Harrow schoolboy, still small enough to be in 'Eton' jacket and collar. The Aberdeens were given a brand new Armstrong Siddeley motor of imposing size, for ever more driven by the peppery chauffeur Gordon, who continually crashed the gears and nonchalantly gazed out of the side window afterwards as though communing with a cow in its pasture. For many years Ishbel had needed only four hours' sleep at night, generally from 4 to 8 a.m. Johnny had to follow suit, and so did their faithful secretary, Mrs Mackenzie, known universally as Georgie, a large, placid-looking woman who descended from her top-floor eyrie, smelling of typewriter things and womanly gentility, when Johnny sounded his cuckoo call. Once my mother, sitting up late so as to be able to scold her young when they returned from a party, caught him emerging from their private quarters with a skullcap on his head, a rug over one shoulder, and gaiters undone at the top, the bottom fastenings causing him to trail them across the carpet like snowshoes wrong way on. Georgie retrieved whatever he wanted and he mumbled his way back to his study. He was exhausted, Ishbel was not. Georgie's wages were often badly behind, yet when she died in the 1950s, living in an Aberdeen bed-sitting-room, pleading poverty and drinking gin, she left £12,000. So she had her revenge. Ishbel was expert at the catnap. In the big Armstrong, on the platform at meetings, anywhere, she would nod off. On public occasions she always woke up in time to make her speech, and appeared to have comprehended speeches that had preceded hers, when she looked fast asleep. He dropped off too, but he was ten years the older, and getting deafer every year. He died in 1934 in his eighty-seventh year, a week after his last outing in the cold March winds to the funeral of his old friend and neighbour Lord Sempill at Craigevar Castle. Their daughter wrote after the funeral: 'Mother continued to look dignified when we came back to Cromar, though crushed by grief. She was up all night, as usual, doing her letters.'

A whirlwind then reaped where they had unwisely unsewn the seam of two hundred years' ownership by the Haddo Gordons of those smiling lands, so different from the dour Buchan and Formartine landscape. Sir Alexander MacRobert and his first wife were both dead before 1934. There reigned instead the second Lady MacRobert, who lost no time in claiming house, contents and estate according to the terms of the 1919–20 settlement and its extensions. Out went Ishbel within six months of Johnny's death, leaving behind many treasured possessions including the paintings on silk of herself and her family let into the dining-room wall. Also claimed was a great satinwood secretaire eight feet high, late eighteenth-century Irish work, with floral swags painted, not in the more laborious marquetry usual for that sort of piece. Johnny had given it to her when they were in Ireland, so it had sentimental as well as aesthetic worth. Let me again quote from Marjorie Pentland's *A Bonnie Fechter*: 'On Saturday 1 September 1934 the Cromar teatable in its sunny turret welcomed visitors for the last time. In her diary Ishbel wrote: "The Queen, with Lady Victoria Forester in attendance, came this afternoon." ' Others in the teaparty included my sister Jessamine, who remembers having to rush round the house finding a cigarette for the Queen to smoke. She found her box of State Express Turkish, surreptitiously bought. There was no smoking at the House of Cromar. Queen Mary lit her cigarette, sending out occasional puffs sitting bolt upright. Jessamine did not look upon this as real smoking at all. The journal continues: 'Tonight Lady Victoria telephoned that the Queen wished to purchase my bookcase by valuation and give it to me – wonderful! Lady MacRobert has consented to sell; valuation Monday.' It now stands in the morning-room at Haddo House, its glass-fronted upper shelves full of porcelain and fans. Even so, much beautiful furniture of the best English Sheraton and Hepplewhite sort, originally at Dollis Hill, had to be left behind.

One of Ishbel's last acts at Cromar was to bundle up all the papers relating to George Osborne and the posthumous proceedings, which Johnny had kept in his study at Cromar, and send them to her sister-in-law Lady Harriet Lindsay as being, now, the only living representative of that generation, asking her to sort them out and return them to Haddo House for safekeeping by the new Marquess. In returning them to her nephew, 'Doddie', my great-aunt Harriet wrote: '[Ishbel] authorized me to destroy what need not be kept. A great many ought to have been destroyed 50 years ago such as begging letters from imposters.' In this work she was helped by her elder spinster daughter Mary, as unattractive and forceful a schoolmarm as could be found anywhere in reality or fiction, but I do not think the two women between them threw away anything, except possible references – begging letters? – to or from Jane Ogilvie and her son Charles. The begging letters that have survived are pathetic in their patent fraud, from odd Americans, all men.

In her widowhood Ishbel unburdened herself a good deal to this grandson – we enjoyed talking politics together – and told me things not even Marjorie nor my father knew. One day she said: 'I suppose we made many mistakes; but I like to think we did more good than harm.' Amen to that. But those who are the victims as well as the beneficiaries of these inherited honours and glories and acres may well on occasion feel a bitterness. I do sometimes myself, even though I never expected anything, being the second son of a second son. My father and I were both self-made men, to use an outmoded expression. I am I; what on earth has it got to do with me? How should I miss what could never be mine, and am I not the richer for having known this odd couple, and for having had no fear of them, nor scorn, unlike so many of their associates, relations and descendant?

Charles, 11th Marquess of Huntly, died in February 1937, surviving his contemporary by almost three years. In his case his will had grant of probate in August of that year. Exclusive of any settlements from which he derived no benefit, he was worth £1,208 5s. 1d. He had started life poorer than Johnny and left it nearly six times the richer man.

Bibliography

Aberdeen and Temair, Ishbel, Marchioness of, *Musings of a Scottish Granny*, London, 1936

Aberdeen, Lord and Lady, *We Twa*, London, 1925
    More Cracks with We Twa, London, 1929

Aberdeen, Lord (7th Earl and 1st Marquess), *Tell Me Another*, London, 1925

Bolitho, Hector, and Peel, Derek, *The Drummonds of Charing Cross*, London, 1967

Buchan, Peter, *Gleanings of Scarce Old Ballads, etc.*, Peterhead, 1825

Bulloch, J. M., *The Gay Gordons*, London, 1908

Bulloch, J. M., *House of Gordon*, 3 vols, Aberdeen, 1893–97

Burnet, Gilbert, *Bishop Burnet's History of his own Times*, 2 vols, Edinburgh, 1724

Burton, John Hill, *The Scot Abroad*, Edinburgh and London, 1900

Chamberlain, Muriel E., *Lord Aberdeen: A Political Biography*, London, 1983

Crawfurd, George, *The Lives and Characters of the Officers of the Crown and State in Scotland*, Edinburgh, 1726

Ekwall, Eilert (ed.), *Concise Oxford Dictionary of English Place Names*, Oxford, 1936

Elliot, Edward Bishop (ed.), *A Memoir of Lord Haddo*, 2nd ed., London, 1867

Fisher, H. A. L., *History of Europe*, 3 vols, London, 1935

Fraser, Sir David (ed.), *The Christian Watt Papers*, Edinburgh, 1983

Gordon, Adam Lindsay, *Poems*, Melbourne, 1892
    The Last Letters 1868–1870 (ed. Hugh Anderson), Melbourne, 1970

Gordon of Auchintoul, Alexander, *A Life of Peter the Great*, Aberdeen, 1755

Gordon, C. A., *Concise History of the House of Gordon*, Aberdeen, 1890

Gordon of Cairnfield, Edward, MSS Genealogies of the Gordon Families, Aberdeen University Library

Gordon, General Patrick, *Passages from the Diary of General Patrick Gordon, 1635–1699* (ed. and trans. Joseph Robertson), Aberdeen, 1859

Gordon of Ruthven, *Britain's Distemper, 1639–1649* (ed. J. Dunn), Aberdeen, 1844

Gordon, William, *History of the Family of Gordon*, 2 vols, Edinburgh, 1726–27

Gould, Cecil, *Sixteenth-Century Italian Schools*, London, 1975

Grant, Dr Ian D., MSS Landlords and Land Management in North-Eastern Scotland, Scottish Records Office

Hake, A. Egmont, *The Story of Chinese Gordon*, vol. 1, Edinburgh, 1978

Humphris, Edith M., and Sladen, Douglas, *Adam Lindsay Gordon and his Friends in England and Australia*, London, 1912

BIBLIOGRAPHY

Huntly, Charles, 11th Marquess of, *Milestones*, 2nd ed., London, 1926
  Auld Acquaintances, London, 1929
Iremonger, Lucille, *Lord Aberdeen*, London, 1978
Macdonell, A. G., *England, Their England*, London, 1933
Mann, Golo, *Wallenstein, His Life Narrated* (trans. Charles Kessler), London, 1976
Martin, Kingsley, *French Liberal Thought in the Eighteenth Century*, London, 1929
Morley, John, *Life of Gladstone*, London, 1903
Moysie, David, *Memoirs of the Affairs of Scotland 1577–1603* (ed. J. Denniston),
  Edinburgh, 1830
Namier, Louis, and Brooke, John, *History of Parliament 1754–1790*, 3 vols, London, 1964
Palmer, Roundell (1st Earl of Selborne), *Memorials Personal and Political*, 2 vols,
  privately printed, 1892
Pentland, Lady Marjorie, *A Bonnie Fechter*, London, 1952
Scott, Sir Walter, *Minstrelsy of the Scottish Border*, Edinburgh and London, 1839
Scottish Records Office: Haddo House Papers, Gordon Castle Papers, Papers of Sir
  John Clerk of Pencuik
Wishart, Reverend George, *The Memoirs of James, Marquis of Montrose* (trans. Rev.
  Alexander D. Murdoch and H. F. Morland Simpson), App. XIII: *Deeds of Montrose*,
  Aberdeen, 1893
Smout, T. C., *A History of the Scottish People, 1560–1830*, London, 1969
Solomons, Israel, *Lord George Gordon's Conversion to Judaism*, London, 1913
Spalding, John, *History of the Troubles etc. in Scotland in the Reign of Charles I*, Aberdeen,
  1829
Trevelyan, G. M., *History of England*, 3 vols, London, 1926
Walker, John William, *Wakefield: Its History and Its People*, Wakefield, 1934
Walpole, Horace, *Horace Walpole's Correspondence* (ed. W. S. Lewis), Yale edition,
  London, 1937–
Wedgwood, C. V., *The Thirty Years' War*, London, 1938

Index

Note: The Earls of Aberdeen, the lairds of Gight, and the Dukes of Gordon are listed in order of succession.

211

grandfather of author, 7;
Ld. High Commissioner, Church of Scotland, 183, 186;
Ld.-Lt. of Aberdeenshire, 186;
Ld.-Lt. & Viceroy of Ireland, 186, 198;
MacRobert financial arrangements, 199, 207;
Marquess of Aberdeen, 198;
marriage, 181;
presented to Q. Victoria, 126;
retirement, 201–2, 205–6;
sale of land, 185, 194, 200–201;
sale of paintings, 195–8;
travels, 188–9, 198
Aberdeen, Marquesses of:
George, 2nd Marquess ('Doddie', earlier Lord Haddo), 8–9, 197, 198, 200–201, 205, 207;
David, 4th Marquess (author's brother), 197
Archibald, 5th Marquess (author) *see individual entries for relatives, schools, etc.*
Aberdeen Arms Inn, 193
Aberdein, Alexander, 72
Abergeldie, Gordons of, 18
Aboyne, Earls of, 69, 99, 184–6
Aboyne, Lord, 38–9
Aboyne Highland Games, 203
Adam, William, 65–6
Addington, Justice, 89
Alexander, Rev. W. B., 129, 135–6, 141–5, 153, 165, 167, 171–3, 180
Alexis, Tsar of Russia, 47–8
Allan, George, 131–2
American Seaman Friends' Society, 176–7
Anna, Empress of Russia, 57
Anne of Denmark, Queen of Scotland, 20
Anne, Queen, 55, 61, 62
Apraxin, Gen.-Admiral, 56
Argyll, Earl of, 41, 43, 59, 61
Argyll House, 122, 126, 127, 128, 132
Arts League of Service Theatre, 202
Atholl, James, Duke of, 68
Auchleuchries, *see* Gordon, Patrick, of A.
Azov, siege of, 51, 52

Baird, Charlotte (later Lady Haddo), 75, 77
Baillie-Hamilton families, 151
Baillie-Hamilton, William Alexander, 142–3
Baker, Mrs Walter, 175–6
Balfour, Arthur, 181, 206
Balmoral, 3, 45, 103–4, 184, 194
Barnaby Rudge, 93
Bartholchapel, Kirk, 173
Batoni, Pompeo, 74, 98
Baxter, Henry Forster, 164
Baxter, John, 65–6
Beaton, Cardinal, 19
Beechey (artist), 13, 101
Belgians, Queen of the, 122
Berg, Moses op den, 93
Bexley, Kent (birthplaces of author), 8–9
Bingham, Hiram, 121, 139, 152, 173
Binning, Sir William, 38
Black, Isobel ('Bell', later wife of Gen. Wm. G. of Fyvie), 13, 98, 100–102, 105
Blair's College, 101, 120
Blanckenberg, Andrew Charles John, 169–70
Bockhoven, Col. von, 47–9
Boddam, village of, 123, 128–9, 133

Bolitho, Hector, 7
Boswell, James, 82
Bothwell, Earl of, 19
Bowen, Rev. Thomas, 92
Bradley's school at Southgate, 125, 133–4
Breadalbane, Marquess & Marchioness of, 122
Bridges, Jane, 109–10, 114
Bruce family, 2
Bruce, King Robert the, 3
Buchan Ness, 123, 144
Buchan properties, 193
Buchan, Peter, 28
Buchan's Ballads, 40, 117
Bulloch, J. M., 14, 27, 29–30, 82
Bunbury, Sir Charles & Lady Sarah, 95–6
Bush Ballads & Galloping Rhymes, 114, 118–9
Butler, Col. Walter, 35–7
Byron, Catherine Gordon, 12–13, 17, 27–30, 75
Byron, Lord George Gordon, 6, 12–13, 17–18, 28–30, 43–4, 46, 194
Byron, Captain John ('Mad Jack'), 17, 28–9, 92

Cairnbulg Castle & estate, 72–3, 78
Cagliostro, Count, 92
Call, Blanche Ellen, 172–3
Campbell, Arthur Bradley, 203
Cant, Rev. Andrew, 41–2
Carlisle, Charles Howard, Earl of, 47–8
Carnarvon, Almina, Countess of, 197
Carnegie, Andrew, 189, 198
Caroline, Queen, 66
Carracci, Annibale, 196
Catto, Lord, 200
Chamberlain, Dr Muriel, 13
Charles I, King, 25, 31
Charles II, King, 47–8
Charles IX, King of France, 19
Cheyne, Elspeth (*née* Gordon), 21–2
Chicago World's Fair, 189
Chrichton of Frendraught, 38–9
Christie, Jane (later Duchess of Gordon), 99
Churston family, 9
clearances, Highland, 6, 16, 83
Clark, Sir John, of Penicuik, 65–6
Cluny, Cosmo G. of, 81–2
Cluny, John G. of, 81–2, 84–5
Cluny, Col. John G., of Braid and, 82–3
Cobb, Mr, 142
Coldstream Ranch, 190–91
Colney Hatch asylum, 125
The Complete Peerage, 68
Cosmo and Cosima, as first given names, 81–2
Coutts family, 64
Craig, Mrs, 201
Cowdray, Lord, 198, 204–5
Crawford (author), 60
Cromar estates, 127, 181, 184, 186, 192–3, 199
Cromar, House of, 194–5, 198–9, 201–3, 205–7
Crombie, Alexander, 77, 79
Cunliffe-Brooks, Sir William, 186
Cushnie, John & Margaret, 23

'Davidson or Gordon', Alexander, 27
Davidson, Marie (*née* Gordon, 10th laird of Gight), 26
defenestration of Prague, 32
Dering, Penelope, 76, 77
Devereux, Captain, 35–6

213